The County Books Series
GENERAL EDITOR : BRIAN VESEY-FITZGERALD

DERBYSHIRE

THE COUNTY BOOKS SERIES

A Series comprising 57 Volumes. It covers every county in England and there will be five books on Scotland, two on Ireland, two on the Hebrides, and one each on Orkney, Shetland, Wales, the Isle of Man and the Channel Islands

THE FOLLOWING TWENTY-SEVEN VOLUMES HAVE NOW BEEN PUBLISHED

PLEASE WRITE TO THE PUBLISHERS
FOR FULL DESCRIPTIVE PROSPECTUS

DERBYSHIRE

by

CRICHTON PORTEOUS

Illustrated and with a Map

London
Robert Hale Limited
18 Bedford Square WC1

First published 1950

PRINTED AND BOUND IN GREAT BRITAIN BY
WILLIAM CLOWES AND SONS LTD, LONDON AND BECCLES

CONTENTS

v

CONTENTS

ILLUSTRATIONS

vii

ILLUSTRATIONS

ACKNOWLEDGMENTS

The illustrations above, numbered 1, 3, 5, 8, 9, 12, 15, 19, 20, 23, 25, 26, 34, 38, 39, 40, 41, are reproduced from photographs by Mr Reece Winstone, A.R.P.S.; 11, by courtesy of Mr Doncaster, the present owner of Cartledge Hall; 14, 27, 29, 32, 37, 43, 46, 47, by Mr F. J. Chapple; 16, by Mr T. Edmondson; 17, by Mr R. Rawlinson; 42, by "The Farmer and Stock Breeder". The remaining 20 are reproduced from photographs supplied by Mr Charles Harris, A.R.P.S.

SPIRIT OF PLACE

I AM not a Derbyshire man, but I have lived in or been closely associated with the county for more than a quarter of a century. Life has taken me into many other counties, but on coming back always I have an enlivening feeling; as a writer I am at once encouraged. I seem to get closer into touch with life here than anywhere else. Many others, no doubt, are affected in the same way. What is the peculiar mood of this county, or the "spirit of place", as D. H. Lawrence called it, which causes these responses?

Before going further it is necessary for my own case to explain that when I write "Derbyshire" I mean chiefly that part of the county that I know best, the north-west, the Peak, and, more particularly still, a ten-miles radius from the Capital of the Peak, Chapel-en-le-Frith. That is the highest and wildest area, so that part of the influence that I experience there must be common. "I will lift up mine eyes unto the hills from whence cometh my help," said the Bible writer. This is the inspiration from soaring lines, and the illusion of extended, or increased, powers which comes of being on heights. From there one seems to be able to see farther; one looks down on other life in the manner of a god; and the slightly more rarefied air gives an increase in physical well-being, a greater buoyancy. But not in Lakeland, not in Wales, not in the Lowlands or Highlands of Scotland do I get the same inspiration and that feeling of intimateness with all life. Obviously, therefore, it cannot be solely the wildness of the hills that gives this inspiration or I should feel it more intensely among the far wilder Highlands.

Being born in a place predisposes one to "home love". This is the effect of association. My having lived so long in Derbyshire may have brought me to some extent under the same influence, but there is an argument against that. My father died when I was twelve months old, so that an uncle often had charge of me at holiday times and weekends. It happened that he took a house at Bugsworth in Derbyshire and later moved to Plumbley in Cheshire. Both houses were in country places where I wandered nearly as freely as a hare. The life at Plumbley went on for many years longer than at Bugsworth, yet never made any equal impression. Always now the Derbyshire memories come first, and seem the happier; I got much more intimately into that countryside than into the other. Perhaps this was due to some predisposition to hill country through my ancestry, but this explanation does not satisfy me, for the reason already given, that other hills have not affected me as do these.

So far negative, an attempt to discount ordinary influences. Let us now be positive and total the influences which exist in Derbyshire.

First, the hills do have their effect. Their lines lifted against clouds and, more seldom, against blue skies call to aspiration, to endeavour. The climate induces a certain hardness, a self-reliance, which is the essence of endeavour. The mists that so often lie among the hills shut one in with wetness, alone, tramping with soggy feet; then one must be a man, self-contained, or go down to where there are other men and merge one's integrity. The winds that draw up the valleys and banter the hillsides are careless of the man who goes among them, so that he must fight and endure or his life there will be a misery. Only it is not a matter of doing these things finely; that is the way of the Guardsman of history going into battle with banners and music. To live among these hills one must be more like the men of line regiments who crouched and swore and somehow grinned in Somme mud and came out with not much glory but very mucky. These Derbyshire hills are of the sort that demand a quiet endurance, a kind of greyness of life, and to find a Derbyshire man with a kilt and sporran and the Cock-of-the-North air of a Highlander would be strange. There is a normality here which is akin with the core of life; well, which is life as most of us know it. Not romance; everydayness.

Sunshine is in no way typical of this area and the inhabitants make it a grim joke. Derbyshire weather, they say, is "nine months winter and three months bad weather". So that in a normal season, when in most counties the hay harvest is forgotten, farmers here and good men too will be getting in their crop in August, and perhaps in September. Some inspiration comes from this, the sight of a job being persisted in despite so many adverse conditions. A successful Lancashire Fylde farmer to whom I praised Derbyshire asked at once: "But what can you grow there? There's too much land out-of-doors!" Surely the fact that men keep on and farm successfully, raising stock mostly but also crops, in most unlikely places, contributes some attraction to the county. In Devon, for instance, where vegetation grows so luxuriantly that it is a wonder that some of the valleys do not choke, I have never had from the land any sense of man's high endeavour. Endeavour there is on the sea, which has produced the best Devonians.

3

So we come to what I believe is the deepest secret of Derbyshire's inspiration. Not only do conditions draw out fine qualities of men now: through the ages these conditions have operated. Here men continually have fought and won or failed, and the evidence of this fighting remains more prolifically than anywhere else that I know.

Where is there a county with more remains of those pre-Roman peoples about whom so little is known? And these remains are not railed off; very few are protected except by being on private land, land over which few persons would hesitate to trespass, because there are no crops to spoil, there being no depth of earth. Which explains also why these remains have never been ploughed up. Land has always been plentiful. If something was in one spot, why trouble to remove it? Try some other spot. And so these evidences of the past remain to tell of the unknown men who lived and struggled and then died. Everywhere one feels linked with the past. One sees the end of so much dreaming, planning, working, one cannot but feel humble; and then, above all, comes pride that men should have striven so, and should still strive, and one feels that one's place is in the strife too. What if all does come to nought, it is fine to have fought, to have left a trace, even though at the last it may seem to be so little. That is the feeling that I get.

How good it is to go up steep Mam Tor (Mother Hill?) by the sheep track, with the hard wind coming up from the dark mist on a day when that is all, with the vague darker bulks of the encompassing hills, that is to be seen of Castleton and Hope Valley. Here are the great earthworks, concentric rings, how many hundreds of years old? Still there, save where the Tor is slowly sliding to destruction, victim of weathering.

4

What manner of people built these earthworks? Hardy they must have been, for nowhere in Derbyshire does the wind drive more roughly or snow hiss more viciously. They were not a skulking people but a proud, for there is defiance in the set of the lines they built; and the height and length of the lines show that they were not puny-minded. I have had here the same feeling as the first time at the Forth Bridge: that I was looking at an undertaking only possible to men of courage and forward-looking minds, and I felt humble before it.

From the top of Mam Tor on clearer days one gets the finest view of the new road that has been made at such great cost of money, time, and effort, round the foot of the shale slide that has given the tor the name "Shivering Mountain". There the road is, snake-like, almost doubled on itself, another piece of man's enterprise; and from Mam Tor top can be seen also the last reach of that other road of the Winniates. Coming up between the lofty towers and walls of limestone which throw always a slight shadow there, one's thoughts swing inevitably to the earlier men who chose this as the most obvious way, though very steep, to Mam Tor fort and the long shallow plateau of Rushup. Close by the pass is Odin Mine, worked we know not how long, and that other cavern of the strange blue-veined rock that the Romans are believed to have prized but knew not as Blue John. All this is land of history, not the history of births and deaths of kings and of the notorious, but the history of ordinary folk who were the private soldiers, the road builders, and the miners of other days. It is impossible not to feel the linking up of present life with the past here.

Except for the new road only evidences of the men of the times that we think of as very far past have yet been mentioned, and it is natural that there should be many more signs of men of closer times. Take the quarries hollowed out of so many hills. Quarries in such unexpected places that we are puzzled for what purpose stone could have been wanted there. Yet men dug and hewed with some purpose, were eager, hopeful, got, we suppose, what they wanted, and then left and slowly the turf crept over the scarred rock and took it under its easeful cloak once more.

Along this Rushup plateau men are quarrying again. Near Eldon Hole, which the men who garrisoned Mam Tor no doubt knew, the side of the hill is being cut away in great benches by pneumatic drills. The crushing plant trembles the corrugated iron tower in which it is housed, and seems a monstrous thing, dominating with its roar a surrounding half-mile of country. Only here industry is in true perspective, for the men working on the benches look midgets against the long swelling outline of the higher hill; the sound of the shots that burst and hurl sharp rock fragments over the squat buildings that are like air-raid shelters is lost in the wide sky almost as easily as a cuckoo call. In our cities industry impresses as it never can do here, and climbing the nearly obliterated track by the present workings on to the top of Eldon Hill and finding the turfed-over holes and gashes made by earlier men, one realises that in due course time will win over what is now being done. And yet there is something exhilarating in seeing man's effort going on, continuing that endless story of effort that has been put forth so often, and has paused and started again, and paused and restarted till now.

A mile across Eldon Hill and the roar and popping of the quarry becomes only memory, and here is a round pond holding dark still water, which the breeze roughens a little at the eastern end as though it were sleek black fur being rubbed the wrong way by an invisible hand. Some man thought and planned, and then carted and put in carefully the stones with which the shallow hollow is lined. And here his handiwork lies with not even a sheep near, yet is the pond another gage thrown down, as it were, against nature in the fight that began with life and must go on till life ends. There is something fine, I repeat, in these evidences that lie everywhere of man's never-ending battling, which has always, so far as we may judge, been but a forlorn hope though never undertaken as a forlorn hope; always man fighting with the ideal of ultimate victory.

This is high writing. I smile, adding word to word, having let myself be carried away. Yet what has been written I will let stay, hoping that by its exaggeration some of the feeling that I experience may be passed on.

Even the walls that run everywhere are inspiring. The gritstone walls, bound so cleverly on top by the thinner stones stacked against one another, all leaning one way; and the limestone walls, rougher in design —no thin slats to finish these—yet smoother, rain-pitted, nearly clean of the lichens that like gritstone. For many of these walls now we cannot see much purpose, yet for every one some man had a reason and built well. A hedge can be quickly set. It can be trimmed and laid, and be made into a very good hedge, but if it is to last as long as a drystone wall, this work will have to be carried on by different hands, by several generations. A man may plant well, but thereafter the success or failure of the hedge depends on countless chances; but the man who builds a wall builds once, and everything thenceforward is against his wall standing. Only if it be well built will it last without patching

7

beyond his lifetime and the lifetimes of his children. Therefore, I respect these walls and through them the men who built them.

The walls typify the spirit of this place, but there are also the wells, scooped out of solid rock; bridges built with a cunning that has kept them till now as trustworthy as in Roman days; dams put across streams and still there to catch the power of water, though it is no longer needed. Everywhere ruins of industries: lead mines, quarried from prehistoric times to within present memory; pits where men crept diagonally into the hillsides down mile-long tunnels till 1918, when new transport made the low-grade coal not worth hauling; mills where brewing, wool-combing, and the making of lace went on till combines killed little industries—all these lie in the valleys and about the hills, abandoned, grown over by fine grasses, heather, ling, and brambles, but seldom completely hidden. So it is that there is a past and a present here in Derbyshire together as nowhere else that I know of quite the same, quite so concentrated, as it were, for this county is the centre of Britain. All peoples who have ruled our land have sought health, or leisure, or wealth here. Peak Forest was a hunting ground of early royalty; today there are the great houses, or the remains of the great houses, of more landed families than in any area of the same size. Yet, with all this temptation to boasting, Derbyshire remains more typical of ordinary working life than of the fashionable and the advertised. The frown of the moors, the austerity of climate, have in the end always triumphed over any boastful spirit, so that the county remains simply . . . Derbyshire.

*   *   *

And now that I have set all this down and have read it soberly, I find that there is nothing that might not have been written in some degree of many other counties. It is so difficult to analyse one's feelings about any place; one's response to anywhere is somehow inherent and really beyond reasoned explanation. Anyway, I have put down the best explanation that I have been able to formulate so far. And I am glad to have written it for Derbyshire. Whether the explanation I have given is correct or not, I end with the conviction with which I began: that there is a spirit of place peculiar to Derbyshire, and that those who are attuned to that spirit will always get some greater inspiration, some greater joy out of Derbyshire than from anywhere else.

CHAPTER I

OVER THE BORDER

A BOOK must have order. Some county books start from the north and take the reader southward, or from east to west. Some go to the towns, in the order of the alphabet perhaps, and work around them. But in such a county as Derbyshire I would rather explore more haphazardly, so that I am going to shape this book differently. Where I went I want to take you; thus, if all goes well, you may come on beautiful views unexpectedly, find castles and old houses round corners where you look for rocky chasms, and mills and quarries where you expect loveliness. For Derbyshire is a county of the unexpected, a lot in a small area, a county of strange companionships. But let us set off, and exploring by the route that I took, it may be that even those who know their Derbyshire much better than I do may find freshness in a new approach.

What a place to begin is Buxworth! Certainly it is only just within the border, and was the ultimate northern limit of the ancient kingdom of Mercia, but after that, what? To me it has the attraction of the older, well-remembered name of which I cannot understand why anyone should be ashamed. It is good Anglo-Saxon: "bug", a boundary, "worth", a village. They were not ashamed of its being Bugsworth when I first went. From the station we climbed leftward and then turned leftward again up Dolly Lane, a name to which nobody can object. To me, straight from the enclosing streets of Manchester, Dolly Lane was at

once attractive and set the mark of romance on Derbyshire for ever. From the little shop at its corner the
lane rises narrowly between wall-topped banks and
after a short distance bends as a lane should, so that
immediately I wondered what was round the corner.
I found that the lane went up more steeply, winding
still, and now there was shade of oaks and mountain
ash from the right, and on the left a woodland of
lichened trunks and shaggy undergrowth that looked
an ideal place for happy hunting.

So the lane climbed on and then passed a white-
washed cottage, stone-built and low, with a gleaming
milk churn upturned against the wall to drain, till
suddenly the lane left its groove and its trees and came
out on a clean hill-shoulder, and below, leftward, was
a spread of valley, and on the right the long slow rise
of higher hill and a curiosity-arousing skyline. Here,
too, on the right was the stone shaft of a disused pit, a
blunt square chimney. I do not remember that these
interested me particularly that first time, but later I
explored the place as far as I could and wondered about
the men who had worked there and why they no longer
did so. Were they all dead? Had something dreadful
happened? I never inquired and now know that to
have done so would have spoiled the half-fearful
pleasure of those explorations.

For a quarter-mile the lane went on across the hill-
shoulder and then beside another cottage, grey and
larger, the lane went headlong between deeper walled
banks with the tops of another woodland peeping over,
this time on the right. Now the way was so steep that
many rains had washed the stones up till it was like a
stream bed, and I wondered what kind of a home the
uncle I was with had got. Still the lane wound, and
there were brambles and bracken on the banks. I

wanted to climb and look over the walls, till unexpectedly we came into a farmyard: a barn on one side, shippon and stables on the other; two pigs asleep in our path, fowls dusting in the barn and picking among the stones, and three squatting ducks that got up hurriedly and waddled off with a *squark! squark!*

I had not known that Uncle Jonas had taken a farm and this yard and the farmhouse below the shippons were surprising. I expected him to go in, but instead he took a sharp right turn and I realised that the place though farmyard was still lane, for now it became only lane again and fell farther and travelled along the side of a wide valley. But at the lane's lowest point Uncle Jonas turned to an iron gate and I saw beyond it an up-slope of drive. On the right was a dell with sycamores and oak trees and a stream, and at the top of the drive a house of gritstone with a tremendous slant of roof that would almost have done to toboggan down because it reached nearly to the ground. We went through a white wicket and along a flagged causeway and I saw the valley all at once, with scattered farms and their grey smoke-feathers and a railway line in the bottom up which a toy-like express was toiling, leaving a long pure white scarf of steam; and beyond was the other hill, reared to wild moorland with a dark wood of firs like a square patch on its back. Down the valley were more hills and in the distance on a sweeping ridge was the cluster of a stone village. The expanse and variety made me overlook the foreground, but eventually I could notice the garden on a level terrace with a flagged path down the centre to another white gate at the bottom of four stone steps, with damson trees at either side. Below was a croft, sloping down and hollowed a little, ending at a ten-feet high drystone wall up which ran a flight of stone steps. I won-

dered what for. The house fronted west and on the
north side the garden was protected by an eight-feet
high wall with Victoria plum and pear trees against it.
Through this fruit-wall, at the end of the flagged
causeway that ran right across the house front, was a
door. The thickness of the wall made the door-place
like a very short tunnel which led on to the open hillside and gave another view down the valley to the
distant village.

Everything here delighted me. The main room was
a big kitchen. It was low with a great range set in the
front wall, and beside it on the left was a deep alcove
and window, like a look-out. How many hours I spent
here when rain was lashing the flags and wind was
bantering over the house I do not know. But how
secure one felt within those two-feet walls! I liked to
watch the long grey rain-curtains swinging down
between us and the opposite hill; and sometimes the
sun would peer down and there would be short seg-
ments of rainbow wandering lost, as it were, in the
deep valley. Then the rain would clear and I would
run out on the washed flags and see the opposite hill
turned to bluey-grey and the square wood on its forehead a perfect blue. Even as young as I was then I
recognised this as beautiful and tried to draw the
scene with crayons, and the truest I could get to the
colour of the woodland was cobalt blue. A blue wood:
it seemed magical, and I determined to go there sometime.

But before wanderings across the farther hills came
more immediate exploring. The dell beside the house
obviously had to be looked into. There the chief
attraction was the stream, pure as the best glass, but
always in a hurry. Day and night it plunged into a
stone-lined well where ferns perpetually nodded in

play with splashing drops. I could climb in and peer along a narrow tunnel down which the stream ran, though what it did down there I never saw; but after travelling hidden for a hundred yards under the lane the stream poured from a round cavern in a wall built against a high bank and then behaved as all normal streams should, making the quickest way to the River Goyt in the valley.

Even Uncle could not help playing with this stream. He showed me where it could be spread nicely between the feet of two sycamores and some elderberry bushes. The ducks would like a place in which to swim, he said, instead of having to be content with squatting and dabbling all day. So we began to collect boulders and stones grubbed from the dell's steep sides, and dug a heap of gravel from the bed of the stream where the dam was to be. Then one hot Saturday when the stream was nodding, as it were, we suddenly attacked and with clods and gravel stopped its flow some way above where we wished to work. How we slaved after that, rolling boulders, packing stones, till we had two thick walls about a foot apart. But now the stream had overcome our temporary stop and came questing curiously against the stonework. We worked more feverishly, shovelling more gravel from where the pond was to be into the space between our walls. We worked ankle deep, knee deep, nearly thigh deep and then leapt out and threw the gravel from the bank on to our dam, prodding and stamping it till it was solid. Then at last with the day beginning to dusk we leaned by the sycamores and watched the stream go round in slow, muddy wondering. Dark came and we had to climb to the oil-lit house before the water reached the dam level, but we felt even more proud than weary. And in the night there was thunder and a cloudburst, and in the morning the stream was plunging triumphantly into its well and there was no dam.

We had to wait for six weeks before we could try again, but in the meantime we salved some of the old boulders, and brought more and heavier boulders from longer distances. The stream was so confident over its first triumph, I suppose, that it felt it could ignore the great mounds we prepared. Anyway, it ran on with untroubled clearness while we on the banks planned a more drastic attack. One day we got two iron rods and drove them in till they stopped on rock, and still the stream did not seem to mind, rippling round them and gossiping pleasantly, just a little more than usual. Then we waited for a full day and attacked with clods, abruptly as before. We built as before but with the first wall backed against the iron rods and we rammed the gravel till it seemed like rock.

"I don't think it'll wash that away," said Uncle, standing back, "unless there's another cloudburst," he added more humbly.

There were showers in the night, and in the morning through the bedroom windows came a rushing sound such as we had not heard before. We leaned out in the bright morning and listened wonderingly till the explanation came to us all simultaneously. "The dam!" I rushed out in pyjamas and there was the stream making a beautiful glassy curve and crashing whitely on the stones below. The sound it made pouring into the tunnel a few yards farther on we were accustomed to, but this was glorious. The pond had drawn the ducks before us and they were cruising as happy as children with a new toy.

Inevitably such a stream had to be explored. Above the thorn hedge, Uncle's boundary, that guarded the upper end of the dell, the stream crept rather mysteriously round many holly bushes. Then, where it widened into a shallow pool with sedges, there were the stepping stones of a field-path that came off the hill on one side apparently from nowhere (there being no path to be seen more than twenty yards from the stones) and going on only to disappear again up the other side. Above the pool the stream came gushing from beneath the bridge of a drystone wall which marked the end of a secluded valley where the stream came spilling and swirling down steps of rock, sometimes almost hidden between bosses of green and golden moss, tufts of brown-flowered sedges, and beds of wild mint that in season gave scent lavishly. In the pools below the tiny falls brown trout swam. How often did I lie with heels up and hand going numb in the ice-fresh water trying to "tickle" one! When tired of that I would scramble up the valley sides where were rabbits in abundance, each colony with its terrace of sand where cheeky individuals would sit till the last moment and then pop away with a derisive show of white. At first I thought that the proper punishment was to block all the holes with stones so that the offenders should never get out again; but there was always some hole that I missed out of which a rabbit would poke as soon as I went off. Bows and arrows and catapults were tried, but I never managed a kill.

At the top of the valley was another wall, seven feet high, and beyond was another valley, but it was a long time before I explored this. It was less intimate, wider, more exposed, and on its southern edge stood a grey farmhouse and buildings which had to be passed stealthily. Very often there were cows in this valley too. But when eventually I ventured up I found that after half a mile it became scarcely a valley at all, its sides fading into moorland where the stream ran un-

16

" Relic of forgotten men ", Two Dales, Matlock
Old lead mine, Wardlow

obtrusively in a deep gutter of peat. Around here was chiefly Yorkshire fog and wire grass with flickering patches of cotton grass and more occasional heather, generally where rock outcropped. Following the lessening course of the stream I came eventually to an almost perfect circle of water the colour of black oak, a pool that appeared to be tilted off horizontal. This was an illusion due to the moor slope, but before I understood it gave the pool the fascination of magic.

Beyond the pool I never ventured alone till school-days were past, but on noteworthy days I went farther with Uncle Jonas, who seemed to like the moorland. Generally these expeditions were made when weather had stopped work in garden or croft, so that all my memories are misty or rain-soaked. It was a wide featureless place where gritstone sheep jumping up from peat holes were as startling as wild animals. The higher we tramped the darker the day would grow till we were breasting through cloud. And then the moor ended abruptly in a rock edge and if we were fortunate there would come a break in the cloud and we would see a new valley with its tiny houses and swaying strip of road. Occasionally as we stood in the skirt-hem of flying cloud sunshine would pour out below so that the valley was like another country, a promised land. Among the rocks of the edge were shallow caves and there it was a pleasure to crouch out of the wind and crunch an apple and dream. I dreamed of enemy troops marching unsuspectingly along that road, and of rolling boulders on them and swooping down to inflict utter rout, a dozen from the hill defeating a hundred below in ten minutes at most. And then, after this imagined victory, how heroic I could feel facing again on the moor, plugging with slopping feet into the flowing dark of mist. At the end of the long hard tramp

2*   17

Dolly Lane, Buxworth
Clough near the Snake Inn, Kinder Scout

was the snug house waiting. Happy days, and who would not go back if it were possible!

This hill is that which on the Ordnance Survey is marked Chinley Churn (1,484 feet). The road in the new valley was that which runs from Chinley to Peep-o'-Day (charming name!) and Hayfield. I find that the moor is neither so wide nor so wild as it was, and the rock edge that seemed so romantic is rather prosaic, having been made largely by quarrying, though the quarry has been abandoned. But I have given all this as I remember, because it is so typical. The solid stone house, with its dell and sheltering sycamores, the stone walls, the moorland and mist, and the rock edge sheering plateau from valley—all those you will find duplicated many, many times in North Derbyshire. And those are the memories that have conditioned all my experience of the county. When Derbyshire is mentioned, I think first of its moorlands and snug gritstone homes, and of waving folds of mist flowing across the hillsides.

But there are other memories. You recall the stone stairway running diagonally up the ten-feet wall at the croft foot? Where did it lead? In a sense it led nowhere, only over the wall, yet in fact the steps led me on into all those contacts with Derbyshire people that have been so stimulating and happy. Behind the wall was the continuation of the lane by which Uncle Jonas had brought me and beside the lane, built into the wall as in a grotto, and actually under the level of the croft, was a stone trough, four feet long, two feet across and two feet deep, with water as cool and clean as any I have known. A rusted half-pipe of iron fed it from the back, causing a perpetual reversed fountain of silvery bubbles under the surface; and the overflow at the right-hand end into a mossy slot made a com-

18

forting, chuckling undertone to the splashing from above. In the crevices of the grotto were tiny ferns that lent their cool greenness to the water which on even the wildest day could never be disturbed by wind, though a spate would sometimes be too much for the overflow and then over the trough's front edge the water would swill in a fluctuating glissade.

I found this well fascinating. Strangers stopped to drink or dabble hot hands; local people took the few steps aside presumably because the well drew them, for there was never anything new to see. Over the top of the steps hung the branches of a mountain ash and I soon found that by lying quietly along the wall I could watch without being seen. Everybody peered into the well; nobody looked up. If there were two or three together they talked without fear of any eavesdropper, and the words came up as clearly as if they had been specially spoken for me. Not that at my age I heard much of any particular interest, but it was fascinating to lie so close yet unsuspected.

To the well also came cattle from the farm just up the hill. They stayed about and pulled the lane-side grass, and one day there came wandering with them a girl of my own age with fair hair and a white pinafore. She began to scoop water and slop it towards a black-polled cow that seemed to have something on its mind and never moved. Tiring of this, she looked about for stones and began to drop them in.

"Don't do that," I blurted.

She looked up, didn't seem a bit surprised. She picked another stone and deliberately threw it in.

"I'll tell," I said.

"'Tisna yours," she answered flatly.

"It is."

"'Tisna."

"It is."

"It's ours—for the cows," she stated.

The end was that I scrambled down and we both dropped stones in and watched the little clouds of brownish silt that burst upward and then settled like dust. When that finished I wandered with her up to the farm. Already I felt in love, because I was not used to being with girls and she accepted me so naturally. She took me in, and her mother, busy and outspoken, knew where I came from and let me go about as though I were one of her own. So, naturally, soon I knew the farmer and saw my first Derbyshire shippons. This was long before the Milk Marketing Board and there was, so far as I am aware, no order about shippons, so that they were low and dark, the door being the only window, as an Irishman might say. But how cosy the shippons were when there was wind and mist. The walls were two feet through; above, the baulks were stuffed eight feet thick with hay; and the two hurricane lamps, usually lit very early, gave with their creamy flames considerable heat, and what was more important made the cavernous place *look* warm. The floor was cobbles and there being no straw off the hills it was the farmer's custom at the beginning of winter when the beasts were brought in to cover all the beds with a layer of sods, grass up. These sods soon settled into a mat, dry and absorbent. They acted also as a deodorant, I believe, and those sods under the beasts' rear feet that got sodden and trodden through were regularly replaced. It was a natural method of bedding down evolved through experience, but now officialdom says that it was un-hygienic. The ceiling of such a shippon has had to be lifted by three feet, windows have been put in, the cobbles have been concreted over, and the order is, no

clods, use straw. But still there is no straw. If there is
any sawdust to be got the cattle get a skittering, or
maybe a few dry sedges, but generally they lie in a
high, airy place on bare concrete, hygienic enough
perhaps but cold, though warmth is what they need
most at this high altitude.

Even the old farmhouses have not been altered like
the shippons. They are still low and so warm that
when the fire is big at once one begins to yawn as I
did when sometimes I was left in the care of the
parents of my new-found friend, my Aunt and Uncle
having gone out and not coming back till late. The
walls of the kitchen—we always stayed there, I cannot
remember any other room—the walls were cream-
washed and the light of the oil-lamp made them prim-
rose and the waverings of the fire sometimes made
them seem to move, so that it was almost as though I
was being rocked to sleep to the creaking of crickets,
which is one of the sleepiest sounds I know. I would
droop over on the horsehair settee and what a trouble
it was to waken when Uncle came! And how dark and
blusterous the night seemed, but quickly the air
revived me, and that too is one of the fine pleasures of
the Derbyshire highlands.

My small friend knew a much older girl from a
farm which stood in a ring of sycamores about three
hundred yards on the other side of my uncle's house.
Thus I got to know her, then her brother, who is still
living. I will not say much about him, because I have
not seen him lately and I should have to discuss it
with him, but he will not mind my saying that at that
time he seemed to me to be a kind of Samson. He
delighted in doing hard things. He invited Uncle
Jonas to a tug-of-war and towed him and me round
the farm lawn which made a green platform projecting

over the valley. Then he called the farm youth, who was fairly husky, and towed the three of us across the lawn. Perhaps he will not mind if I tell also about one of his favourite jokes. He would invite town friends to go "a little walk round" over the hills. They would go unsuspectingly and he would lead them to the Cat and Fiddle, the second highest inn in England (1,690 feet), and then across the moors by devious ways of his own, encouraging them when they grew tired by telling them, "Oh, this is nothing. This is only a short walk." Very few went a second time. Uncle Jonas didn't! I was too young for this trick, but perhaps it is a pity, because this man knew the countryside, the wilder parts, as no one else did. Thirty miles of the roughest moorland, preferably in rain or wind, made a nice afternoon's enjoyment for him, and probably he would have been spreading muck all morning. When I grew old enough to have gone with him Uncle Jonas had removed and I was interested in another part of Derbyshire. I have brought in this friend of so long ago just to emphasise another point: that the only way really to get to know a place or a county and its people is to live there. I have heard some persons say that Derbyshire people are dull. That is merely a confession that they have never got to know them. All over the county in cottages and farmhouses strange and sterling characters live, if only one can get to know them. Well, no doubt that is the same in all counties, but in Bugsworth I got a fair sample of North Derbyshire, its country, its weather, and its people.

The village had its own small craft, that of riddle making, and this is still continued, When I first went there the canal extension from Whaley Bridge was still quite busy and the wharf at Lower Bugsworth was worth a visit to see the unloading and the transfer of goods to the light railway, which also was still running. It brought from Peak Dale loads of limestone with which the boats returned to Manchester or Macclesfield or perhaps even farther, but of this Peakland Railway I will write more later on.

From Bugsworth, before Uncle Jonas left, I grew old enough to walk along the River Goyt to New Mills and along the canal to Whaley Bridge, and on one occasion walked as far as Taxal (which was then Cheshire but is now Derbyshire), where I saw the yew tree in the churchyard. There is a much more impressive yew at Darley; nevertheless the Taxal tree should be seen, and the church stands very pleasantly above the pretty Goyt, so that it would be unfair not to have mentioned it.

CHAPTER II

ECONOMY AND EASY WALKING

At fourteen I had already grown fond of walking and never minded being alone. These are two very desirable qualities if one would get to know Derbyshire.

Uncle Jonas had now left Bugsworth, but the memory of it remained and I longed to go back. I was put into the cotton trade, beginning at eight shillings a week, five shillings having to be given in at my Chorlton-cum-Hardy home for my keep. With the remainder I was supposed to buy what clothes I needed, so that the railway fare out to Derbyshire was generally beyond me. Nevertheless, I managed to get out occasionally to Marple, the nearest point. Any who are very hard up, as I was, might try the same place. I got many good walks from there.

The first obvious walk was by the Etherow (shamefully spoiled river!) to the Roman Lake. Why it is called Roman nobody seems to know, but with its little island and surrounding wooded hillsides it is very pleasant there on a summer day. I could not afford a boat then, but later had many an enjoyable row there. It is big enough. Going past the lake my usual route was along the main road towards New Mills, then left and up the lane of Strines which after going under the L.M.S. railway line begins as a leafy tunnel and after a climb reaches open moorland. Here is the hamlet of Tarden, a gathering of half a dozen gritstone houses. Somehow I got to know a farmer who though obviously poor was very hospitable, and in

September 1918 a memorable camp of seven of us was held on his upper land. The site gave a wide view of the wooded Etherow Valley, but towards evening a shrewd wind began to seek us. The fire on which we had cooked tea had been doused because of the black-out order, but it became so cold that eventually after a wordy council we stumbled along the hillside to a shallow clough that gave shelter to some rowans and hawthorn bushes. Fumblingly we gathered bits and boughs and finally put a match to them. Our first two attempts flickered out, but then the wind leapt upon the flames as though glad to find a plaything at last, and in a moment or two we had a glorious bonfire much bigger than we had planned. We had decided that if the local police came we would all run different ways, and none towards the tent, and so escape in the dark. After the first flush we soon had a fine glow of embers round which we sat with the wind touring roughly through the tops of the thorn trees and out over the moor. There is a touch of wildness in the memory that I find good still; and then the night went calmer and we saw stars revealed. With us was one who knew the constellations and at midnight we climbed to the summit and there, as near to them as could be, we looked up at the immensity of the Great Bear, at Cassiopeia's sparkling throne, and picked out Vega and the dog-star. A Derbyshire moor top, night and stars—it is a combination that I can still enjoy!

From Tarden the lane rightward was sometimes taken into New Mills, but more often I turned left and with long views towards Werneth Low went back to Marple by Mellor. This was not a long walk, but I was still young, and in any case I often prefer to let short walks take a long time; that is the way to see most, in Derbyshire and anywhere.

A more favourite way from Marple was to start up the Mellor road and then by the field-path on the left climb to Mellor Church. I know of none that stands more finely. Those who go to worship there on rough rainy days pass the test. Beyond the church the path climbs to the crest of Broadhurst Edge and soon there was the valley of the River Kinder with its mill at Birch Vale and the single-track line to Hayfield. The great plateau of Kinder Scout can be seen bulking high over where Hayfield lies, and I used to stand by the lane-side wall and look across respectfully, for the plateau dominates all that district, but it was too far to go there yet.

Bearing left from the summit of Broadhurst Edge, I sometimes went towards Aspenshaw Hall. This lane is steep and nearly always there was water oozing down. Well I remember going with a friend one Boxing Day when we found the lane entirely glazed with ice. My friend put his foot out to test it and at once began to slip. I was astonished to see him suddenly break into a rapid, exceedingly dangerous-looking race. Down he galloped with curious staccato strides. I expected to see him toboggan helplessly at any instant, but incredibly he kept upright and at a turn sixty or more yards down managed to run off on to the grass verge. When I got to him, by keeping cannily on the side, he was panting and almost incredulous at his escape.

"I wouldn't do it again for a fortune," he declared, staring up the iced slope.

Where the road turns rightward in the valley my way went left along the field-path to Rowarth, the "hidden village". There it stood under the broad green slope of Cown Edge. There was the little mill with the unusual iron waterwheel which I never saw revolve (it has now gone), and the group of cottages beside the short main street which began and ended at nowhere. Between the wars, made known by a popular guide-book issued by the *Manchester Evening Chronicle*, Rowarth was often visited by hundreds of ramblers on summer weekends, but in the week the village was as quiet as any village in the remotest Scottish Highlands. Now even broadcasts have taken place from there and the inhabitants have learned all about catering and will willingly provide a meal, but when I first went I was satisfied with a glass of milk and then took the grassy path that started up the hill from the end of the street near the school. Soon the village looked small and the slopes became wilder. You may come on a rocky lane that leads to Charlesworth, but I preferred to keep to the moor and the bleak plateau and come suddenly on to the top of Coombes Rocks and look down on the great semi-circular bite, or bowl, that lies tilted into Longdendale. Sometimes the bowl below seemed to gather the wind in its arms and hurl it at the cliffs. With my delight in wildness, I liked to arrive on the edge at dusk with a rain-mist blowing up. The rocks looked black. With mist hiding the cliff foot one seemed immensely high. It was a joy to go along by the cliff edge fighting the wind, its roar in one's ears, its buffets hitting the rocks. It was a joy to go down with long strides almost into Charlesworth. Then the way was left more soberly through the darkness along the side of Longden-dale and so down into Marple and up the Brow to the station.

At the bottom of Marple Brow there remained for many years after heavy horses had almost ceased to be used for goods hauling an enamelled plate of a great Shire with head down towing vigorously a well-loaded lorry. The plate asked drivers to loosen the bearing rein before going uphill. So many town persons coming on trips to Mellor or to the Lake stopped to look at this plate that I used to think it the best sited advertisement the R.S.P.C.A. could have had. It was a landmark by which visitors were given directions as though it might have been a pub, "The Climbing Horse".

There are many other pleasant walks to be made from Marple. It is a good place in which to live if you work in Manchester and like hills. Hayfield is within easy walking, but if you wish to go over Kinder it is better to go by bus or train to Hayfield and save energy for the plateau.

Chapter III

THE KINDER HIGHLANDS

ANYBODY interested in Derbyshire must go over Kinder Scout sometime. It may be approached by public paths from Hayfield, Glossop, or Edale. Between the wars the railways began to issue special tour tickets which made it possible to book to Hayfield and back from Glossop or Edale, or any way round that was preferred. The railway companies had not become so considerate when I first decided to tackle Kinder. Economy forced me to tramp from Marple through Mellor and down the road overlooking Birch Vale into Hayfield.

It is a village that has not changed much in the last twenty odd years. Its square-towered church and stone houses look small under the great bulk of Kinder, for which the people have a practical respect. When there has been a cloudburst I have seen the main street a river, water rushing in at the back doors of houses and shops and coming out over the front steps in foaming cascades. With the hills on three sides being steep, spates come so quickly that many persons get taken unawares and some are caught and drowned in the worst floods. One Whit-Monday the river rose so rapidly and powerfully that it washed away a bridge near Bank Vale Paper Mill and carried the offices, a corrugated iron building, nearly a hundred yards and wedged them under the road bridge. Two heavy safes were carried on by the river like boulders.

But that morning when I first visited Hayfield there

29

was no flood, only a slight mist. It was a weekday, or doubtless there would have been many other visitors, for the village even then had become very popular, but I found it quiet and remote-seeming. Built in the bottom at the meeting of the roads from New Mills, Glossop, and Chapel-en-le-Frith, Hayfield is typical of many North Derbyshire villages. When travel was by coach or horseback, it must have been an important stopping place from Glossop to Buxton and beyond. It has its own cotton and paper mills. But I was not interested in them and took the way past the church and behind the Royal Hotel, searching for some romantic-looking start for the famous path which I had for so long wanted to try. And there was no romance, only a gennel between two prosaic house gables, and the gennel led into a croft where fowls had pecked the earth bald. There was a nag with ribs that made me think of a toast-rack. The path was stony and climbed steeply. Then I was through an iron gate in a high wall and there were the moors and freedom with the sandy path ahead for a mile or so. A pipit flitted from a bunch of thin grass and when three grouse went off with a startling *whirr!* I laughed and shouted.

At first the view was all wild. Then it opened on the right and I saw Kinder Reservoir far below with its trees. Derbyshire's one lack in natural scenery is lakes and I am glad of the reservoirs that add to its beauty. At that moment the sun shone through the mist and the water seemed almost to float, a piece of silver tissue held in place by the gossamer threads which were the little streams coming from Kinder Edge. What a vast way it seemed over the lake to those sombre rocks above the sweeping rock-littered slopes. I sat in the sun and absorbed the beauty and grandeur of the finest sight that up to then I had seen; and I do not know now what place I would put before it.

I stayed there nearly an hour. Whenever I go to that view-point now inevitably I think of the Mermaid's Pool and Mrs Humphry Ward's *The History of David Grieve*, but I had not read it then. Although it is a book that in these days of tabloid news takes some reading, no lover of Kinder will begrudge the time, for it contains the brooding spirit of the Edge and the country over which the Edge looks. A sunny day such as I had is a blessing not often enjoyed, and mist and winds are more familiar there than sunshine. Before she began her book Mrs Ward stayed several times at Upper House, Kinder, to get a thorough knowledge of the district, so that she knew the prevalent moods.

But on my day the sun shone for a time. At last I went on. For some way the path continued along the hillside with wide views rightward; then it fell and I was at the bottom of William Clough. Down the clough drops a stream, on this day small and clear and companionable, but sometimes a peat-browned rushing flood. Some of the falls are five or six feet deep and the path gives corresponding scrambles. At places the sides of the clough were steep, almost bare, peat. The view was very restricted until nearly at the top, where the clough gradually ran out into the peaty hillside and the last hundred yards was a scramble up a bleak peat slope. By this time the sun had gone behind misty cloud and showed only as a blur, but it was still pleasant and quite quickly I emerged into a new world. In front was spread a great area of the plateau, bare of any growth higher than a foot or so, a great waste of peat sweeping up to the right another five hundred feet to Kinder Edge which dominated all the rest.

31

How refreshing was this emergence from the enclosing sides of the clough. Since then I have gone up the clough in stifling heat and emerged to be met by such a wind that it became a breath-taking fight to make way against it; and quite often that first slope of peat is like bog and many who start out bravely up the clough turn back here. These are the Bank Holiday visitors, men in bowlers with wives with handbags and umbrellas. Often they are in parties, red-faced men hauling stout women up the five-feet climbs.

Particularly on August Bank Holiday a strange sight is to be seen from this first peat saddle: a continuous string of people, some going down, more coming up the clough, and along the hillside beyond as far as eye can see. Black suits, gay dresses; men and women in shorts, in plus-fours, in riding breeches, anything that is imagined to be suitable for climbing; even men hauling go-chairs or carrying children. Looking towards the Snake Inn over the plateau one sees a string too, though a little thinner, the narrowness and difficulty of William Clough always causing congestion. But over the plateau there are little clots on either side where parties have stopped to picnic, and if it is a reasonable day, on the saddle itself there will be quite a gathering of persons resting after the climb, persons who perhaps expected to see Edale or Glossop immediately below on the other side and who are now appalled by the moor and debating whether to go on; and persons from the Snake enjoying their first sight of Kinder Reservoir and the sweep of valley and its backing hills.

On such a day I like to rest here too and watch and listen. Lovers holding one another by the hand, or even arm in arm, go on seeing nothing except each other, so that it is a wonder why they troubled to climb

Froggatt Bridge and the Derwent
The Derwent on the way to Chatsworth

so far. Young women, pink from the clough, sit on newspapers while their young men clean the clay from their high-heeled shoes, unaware that over the plateau the peat is worse. Farther over the moor I have seen young men carrying their women from one moor-grass clump to another, so that for these men crossing the plateau must have been real Sandow work. I suspect that some persons newly-wed have had their first clashes of temper here, for I have been amused in mid-moor to hear young men being angrily told off for ever having suggested such a trip, the men having obviously had no knowledge of what the crossing would be like. Indeed, this path over Kinder on a fine summer Bank Holiday is something to remember, and over the happy, dreaming, or weary, or angry passers-by brood the estate watchers, a little apart on the slope over-looking the clough and the saddle guarding the tempt-ing way up to the Edge and all across the moor, lest anyone from design or innocence should trespass and upset the grouse. It is the one thing that is unpleasant, this watchful herding of holiday-makers, where in a space so wide all must keep to a path a few paces across. I have thought: what an incitement to any who believe in the public ownership of all land. Are these keepers not in danger of being set upon? But the people pass by and the keepers stand apart and nothing unlawful happens. It is very English.

But on that first visit I had the clough and the path to myself and not one person was to be seen on the plateau. Having reached the saddle and seen so much, I wanted more, and after very little hesitation left the path for the tempting slope to the Edge. That is the way to walk, never with any set plan. Start out and then travel where the attraction of the moment beckons. That to me is real freedom. So I went up the bare

3

steep slope quickly, keeping low and off the skyline. Soon I was among the blackened grit boulders that litter the summit. My boot nails scarred them whitely as I sprang from one to the next. The cliff fell sheer for fifty or sixty feet; on the left were rocks and the rough ridge hiding me from the moor. Unless I had already been seen, which seemed unlikely, it would take a good man to find me there.

Far below, the reservoir was grey now but still beautiful. Just occasionally a sunny patch swept down the littered slope under the cliffs and glided over the valley, lighting momentarily its many colours, revealing an unsuspected cottage or farmhouse and then leaving it in obscurity again as though by magic. Towards Stockport the hills appeared in endless chaos to the misty horizon. I dawdled. Eventually I came to the Downfall—a narrow gap leading from the plateau, full of great rocks amid which the tiny Kinder stream tinkled and lingered gently. Then there was a sort of cavern under the stream into which it dripped and gushed down tiny crannies, to combine into a fascinating glissade which disappeared over the smooth ledge in front of me. From a point a bit to one side I watched the water falling like a long streamer of silver gauze which the light breeze swayed easily and sometimes blew away into fine spray. It was a picture of peaceful play between wind and water and I sat where I could watch and ate Cheshire cheese sandwiches and plum cake, which Thoreau said was the best food to take on a walking tour. Far below, the water ran together into a tiny stream, which ever joined by other little runnels eventually reached an arm of the reservoir. Occasionally a jackdaw flew across the scene and I could see a sheep here and there among the rocks. Once or twice I saw a lone grouse flying, but everything else was silence and restfulness, though I knew that in the great caverns and rounded potholes behind me when heavy rain was over the plateau the furious water swirled and fought to hurl itself over the cliff. Sometimes the wind in its fury would hurl even the whole of that volume of water leftwards and rightwards and upward. Part of this as I sat there I could imagine from the water-wear on the rocks, but in later years I found this battle between the wind and the Downfall worth a walk. I was living near Chapel-en-le-Frith then and would go to Hayfield, but would branch off the Kinder path by the pump-house below the reservoir and follow the path round the southern planting that leads to the way from Jacob's Ladder. This path goes parallel with Kinder Edge and under right conditions the flinging and white tossing battle of the Downfall is spectacular.

But on that first day the Downfall was a tiny thing and the breeze played with it very gently. After lunch I wrote a little; then, finding that I had been there two hours, I packed my rucksack and crossed the stream and climbed the opposite slope, still keeping below the true skyline. At the top of the slope was a crown of boulders to which a sheep track led and as I followed it a man in heavy boots and leggings and holding a stick rose only a dozen yards in front of me. It was a simple capture. My chagrin was less when I learned that he had been stalking me from the moment I got to the top of William Clough and left the path, but subsequently had completely lost me for two hours and had just decided that I must have dodged him when I walked into his ambush.

"That's something, anyway," I said. "While I was enjoying my lunch you were crawling around."

He only smiled and said that it was his job. And he

asked for my name and address, which I gave truthfully, never under such circumstances feeling guilty. I asked what happened next. Even about that he was accommodating, and when I said I would like to go to Edale, he set off across the moor in as straight a line as possible. It was the first time that I had been out on that tumble of spongy peat hummocks and oozing, boggy channels. As we scrambled down and out of the "groughs" and walked carefully across the softer patches the keeper told me that every fine day he had to keep vigil all day, particularly, of course, when the grouse were nesting. I thought what a lonely job. His face was more like parchment than ruddy. He did not think, he said, that more than one in twenty trespassers escaped if he got within a reasonable distance. However young and swift they might be, when he saw what direction they were taking, usually he could head them off, none knowing as well as he the best cuts across, and the few routes off, the moor. Many persons when caught would slang him, and that only made it worse for themselves. I took care to be civil, but in fact I found him so interesting that when he stopped under Edale Head and pointed to the path below I was sorry and stood a little longer to hear more about the moor. It was only here that I learned that when first he saw me he had not actually been on watch but had been on his way to the William Clough path for his home in Hayfield, so that his seeing of me had been quite accidental.

"And now you have to go back all the way we've come. Why didn't you say?" I asked. "I could just as well have gone to the Hayfield path and to the Snake that way."

He only smiled again and said that it was all right. He was a most reasonable keeper and I did not expect to hear about the matter again, nor did I, though I cannot promise that everybody will get the same treatment! Indeed, now I am much against trespassing on Kinder Scout, for I have learned of the arguments and long negotiations that took place with the landowners (when a fighting fund of £1,000 was raised in case the dispute should have to go to court) and of the 1897 agreement by which permission was given for the public to use for ever the staked path from William Clough by Ashop Clough to the Snake road. I believe that we, the public, should stand by our side of the agreement, though this does not mean that I think that agreement enough. Kinder Scout is an ideal place to which there should be public access at all times. It is the wildest country so far south in Britain, the wildest country that we have within the reach of such a large population. Very soon it will become a national park. But no such thoughts came on that day when I swung down Jacob's Ladder into the valley of Edale. At its upper end the valley was bare and lonely like many a Highland glen, but then it opened very nicely into a wider pastoral place of scattered farms, with the beginnings of the River Noe winding there as it were specially for the brown trout that fly-fishermen like to stalk. Only I had no time for fishing. I had let the best of the day pass and wherever else I ended I could not afford to end on that side of Kinder. So I took the less wild though still interesting path which climbs from Edale over Ashop Moor to join the main Edale–Glossop road in Woodlands Valley. This is the only road off which motorists can see Kinder top, and at weekends now that we are once more at peace they make busy use of it. Their stopping place is the Snake Inn, 1,070 feet above sea-level. It must have been a very important place when horse-coaches laboriously and dangerously crossed the moor; now it is a comfortable road-house.

That day I had no time to stop nor the inclination, for I had no wish to keep to the road all of the seven miles to Glossop. Three miles past the Inn I found the path on the right through Doctor's Gate. There was a rough cairn marking the beginning of the path clearly, and though by now the night was almost black I thought that I might follow the way by the feel under my boot soles. It was a wild track, this that the Romans chose. I looked up and around at the many heights showing dimly against the blurred sky. In the deep gully was a midnight black of shadow, and though my whole wish was to get on swiftly the fear of a twisted ankle made me go cannily with only the purl of an unseen stream to tell me that I was going right. Without compass or even a light to see my map, it was a foolish little venture perhaps, but it was a fine way to get a real appreciation of the wildness of Doctor's Gate. Coming down the defile, the sight quite suddenly of the lights of Glossop in the valley far below was a heartening one and I strode down whistling, if a little weary. Glossop seemed a friendly place after the lonely dark, though it is not a place that I have come to like very much, but for that there are reasons.

Anyone who cares to take this day's tramp will pass through scenery as typical of the Derbyshire highlands as any that I can tell about.

CHAPTER IV

THE PALACE OF THE PEAK

To THIS time my experiences of Derbyshire had all been of those parts within easy daily travel of Manchester. I did not know what variety the county offered, but I now got the opportunity of seeing some of that part better known to Sheffield people.

We went on holiday to Froggatt. We went by train to Grindleford. The journey on from Chinley was full of interest, first through Cowburn (Co'burn) Tunnel (2 miles 182 yards) under Rushup Edge, and then along Edale Valley and beside the pretty River Noe to Hope. From Bamford to Hathersage we were beside the Derwent. The houses of Grindleford scattered up the slopes below Totley Moor were striking, but it was a pity to see so many of them built of materials that glared out from the green and grey of the country. Since that time very many more houses have been put up and Grindleford is one of the most popular of Sheffield's "dormitories".

I was to sleep in a tent at Froggatt, the cottage to which we were going being only large enough to provide one bed. My tent was an "A" seconded from the French army through a cheap stores. Although it turned out to be waterproof enough and sufficiently sturdy to stand some rough gales, it was certainly heavy. After climbing the steep road from the station we were told that the best way to Froggatt was by field-path on the left through the woods. It was August and hot. The path in places was a series of stepping

39

stones, very necessary after heavy and sustained rains, but this day the stones were only so many stumbling blocks, the tent with its thick poles lying over my shoulder, forcing me to keep my head down in such a way that it was difficult to see many paces on. Nevertheless I was conscious of the beauty of the way. Through thick beech woods (now gone) we climbed past a clearing with wire-netting where there were a few late coops of pheasant chicks, then through a pleasant area of birches and mountain-ash trees where mossy boulders hid among heath and bracken; and so to a narrow wall-held track that led along the hillside with views of the river in the valley, and a very different view on the left of Froggatt Edge.

Here in a small, irregularly shaped pasture we saw on the fine short sward a button mushroom. Promising ourselves some early mushrooming, we went on and came to the tiny hamlet and the stone cottage with the small patch of orchard above it that was to hold the tent. We had actually considerable difficulty in finding anywhere even approximately level and eventually the tent was put right up against a gritstone wall, but as the weather later turned very rough the wall became a good windbreak, and the healthy air and abundant exercise enabled me to sleep through anything with a piece of bedrock more or less as my pillow.

I do not know how old Froggatt is, but it was unspoilt then. It lay just below the main Calver–Sheffield road and children played anywhere without fear. If a climb was wanted there was the Edge behind; or if one's mood was more for sauntering it was an easy and pleasant matter to go downhill to the comely bridge and there were river-side paths back to Grindleford or on to Stoney Middleton or Calver. The district was entirely new to us and the long rocky edge of clean-looking rock was the first attraction. There was the slope of tumbled boulders and bracken and then the cliffs. Climbers tell me that there are no climbs worth the name at Froggatt, but for a boy there were cracks and ledges and cave-like holes that provided short scrambles that seemed dangerous enough, and that gave just the same sense of thankfulness and satisfaction to a boy as the experts get after climbing famous crags.

Along the top of the Edge ran a track from which extensive views of the valley with the Derwent in the bottom could be had. Now I believe the track is closed to the public, though at that time it was semi-public on the understanding that there should be no wandering from it over the moor. But there was small lure, for the moor was the usual almost level plateau, quite tame after Kinder. The track went the length of Froggatt Edge and Curbar Edge; then, after a short gap and an old "pack-horse" cross, it continued along Baslow Edge, and there was the big, curious boulder known as the Eagle Stone alone on the moor. We were told that no young man from Baslow was ever considered fit to get married before he had climbed to the top. There was an orthodox, fairly simple way up this stone which anyone could try, but the stone was also a plaything for more serious climbers who set each other problems of getting up in the most difficult ways. Beyond the Eagle Stone the track went on to a pedestal of gritstone with "Wellington 1866" cut in it, standing finely on the very edge with a surprise view down on to Chatsworth House, which looked like a great oblong box with its sloping woodlands behind and the beautiful Derwent in front.

What a good centre I found Froggatt! Having seen

Chatsworth from above it was essential to see it closer. We went on the byroad under the Edge to Calver, where we walked by the river and found the old mill not too unsightly. On the left of the main road to Baslow stood Cliff College, built by Mr Hulme of Manchester, a rallying place of "conversion" Methodism. It had its own chapel, where during our holiday we went one Sunday morning and I recall still the fine singing of the many students. On "Cliff College Sunday" Methodists from all over Derbyshire and neighbouring counties gather and often there is great enthusiasm and the services give much inspiration. It was a good idea to build the college in such a pleasant place.

Baslow village a little farther on was neat and attractive. Often it is very quiet because of the five and a half miles from the nearest station at Grindleford, but on fine summer weekends motor-coaches and motor-cars swarm here, passengers stopping for meals and drink on their way to, or from, Chatsworth Park, the main gate from the Sheffield side being only a short distance away.

Chatsworth is visited at some time by nearly everybody who comes into Derbyshire. Undoubtedly to its setting has been due much of its fame. Dr J. Charles Cox says "there is no other park throughout the whole of England that can compare with it in variety of scenery". As I have never been able to explore the rest of England's parks I cannot confirm this, but within the ten-miles circumference of Chatsworth Park are contained excellent pieces of practically every type of country in Derbyshire; which is the same as saying of every type of country in England, excepting only coast scenery. I find Chatsworth too much like a museum, and the park close to the House too park-like, too carefully groomed and tended. On one of the few days then when the House and gardens were opened to visitors, on toll for charity, I remember being taken down the long corridors and being told where to look and warned not to touch; and in the gardens it was the same, with the addition of notices stating that the taking of photographs was not allowed, so that I felt obliged to get to the back of the party and take a view. The photograph came out well, but unfortunately it was not the best part of the garden. Now House and gardens are regularly open and there are few restrictions. The old Hunting Tower, on the well-wooded hill to the north-east of the House, looks like a castle, though I am told that it was built simply as a look-out for the ladies of Chatsworth. There was fox-hunting in the district then and the ladies would watch the riders from there. Now all local foxes are shot. Queen Mary's Bower, which is between the model village of Edensor and the bridge leading to the House, is a square of grass enclosed by a low well-built wall and a moat. Over the moat, entrance to the Bower is by thirty steps to a stone gateway at the head of which there is a stone shield with an iron plate bearing the arms of Mary Queen of Scots, who often whiled away weary time here when she was Queen Elizabeth's prisoner, in the custody of the Earl of Shrewsbury. This Bower is older than the great house and is the place I like best at Chatsworth. I like to idle under the shade of the great sycamore there and think of the prisoner with her retinue of ladies, and if some of the fawn deer come feeding quietly by, so much the better. It is a place also where one can imagine Robin Hood with laughing Maid Marian, which means, of course, that the Bower is a place to put one in a romantic mood, which the great house very definitely is not.

Many local people still tell of a passage supposed to have connected the Bower with the House. They explain that it cannot now be used because when the great pipes were laid through the park to carry water from the Derwent Reservoirs to Derby the workmen had to break through the passage and that it was then made up.

Within living memory there was no toll to go through Chatsworth House and a visit was even more popular than now. On a Good Friday morning as many as two thousand persons were known to pass through before noon.

But I will write no more of Chatsworth House, for I can put down nothing that cannot be found in any one of a score, or maybe a hundred, other books. In a collection of old volumes on Derbyshire gathered over twenty years I have been impressed by the dominance that the Cavendish family must have held in the seventeen- and eighteen-hundreds, for nearly every book of those times is dedicated to one or other of the Dukes of Devonshire, and after that obviously had to contain some glowing description of the present famous house or of the earlier one. "Art sits triumphant, and bids fair for a corrivalship with Nature. Chatsworth, like a sun in an hazy air, adds lustre to those dusky mountains." After that I was rather amused to find in an 1883 edition of Baddeley's guide *The Peak*, picked up second-hand several years ago, the only uncut pages were those describing Chatsworth House! If readers in 1883 had had enough, what about those of today?

But there is much of interest about the park still to be picked up from local people. One of the great days remembered is a visit of Queen Victoria. She arrived in the evening and entered the park at the Blue

Gate (the lodge nearest to Rowsley, close by the one-arch bridge) and fireworks were set off on either side of the private road all the way to the house. The men who lit them had orders to do so just as the horses of the royal carriage came level with them, there having been several rehearsals beforehand to get the animals thoroughly used to the sudden gushes and showers of flame and colour. Everything went off splendidly. This was the occasion, too, when the Crimea cannons on the hill round the Hunting Tower were fired for the last time.

An even greater day—the greatest within memory—was the funeral of Lord Frederick Cavendish, who was killed by Fenians in Phœnix Park, Dublin, on May 6th, 1882, while trying with his umbrella to defend Burke. On the morning of the funeral watchers were put at every gate and stile into Chatsworth Park with instructions to count every person who came in. They are said to have totalled a million! So many special trains were run to Rowsley that it was impossible to unload them at the platform and they were lined up in the sidings, the passengers being allowed to the roadway through a wide gap specially made in the hedge and fence. One of the persons from whom I got this story (in his eightieth year when he told me) was a gamekeeper and had been enrolled as a special constable for the occasion and was stationed at Edensor Church, where the interment took place. Among the mourners was Lord Gladstone, then very old. He had a carriage with a low step at the back so that he could get in easily. The gamekeeper-constable was just shutting the door for him to drive away when a man out of the crowd rushed forward shouting, "I *will* see the old man before he goes", and tried to climb into the carriage. My friend got him by the collar, but he swung his right fist round and the keeper fell back with the genesis of a very painful black eye. When he struggled up he saw his assailant on his back four deep in the crowd where he had been thrown by a tall plain-clothes guard who had come down from London. "No politeness today; just hit 'em hard," he advised my friend, which suggests the general temper of the day. It was more than a funeral; it was a demonstration of British feeling against the assassinators, and no one felt sure that the Fenians might not also choose the occasion for some other devilment. The headstone over Lord Frederick is very simple, with only the date of his death. Other Cavendish graves in Edensor churchyard are generally simple too, and they lie in a pleasant corner as peaceful as any to be found any-where, and it is strange now to think of thousands of excited sightseers surging everywhere when Lord Frederick was buried.

My friend the ex-keeper had many tales of royal visitors to Chatsworth, including King Edward the Seventh and King George the Fifth when he was still Duke of York. King Edward usually rode a pony from stand to stand and was very autocratic. He shot well, but always liked a friend in the butt and was some-times more interested in talking than shooting, which seemed to the keeper very reprehensible. In a record year twenty-five thousand pheasants were shot on Chatsworth. During the breeding season all the keepers had been called together and told that the feeding expenses were too high and must be kept down, but when the total game count was made it was found that the number of birds shot almost exactly equalled the number of hen eggs used for feeding, which was considered very reasonable.

There were many deer on the estate and the keepers

thinned them occasionally, using buckshot. The venison tasted like mutton, said my friend. Fawns were sometimes sold for five shillings apiece.

The most remarkable shooting experience that my friend could tell me of happened on the moor above Chatsworth when an eighteen-stone man shot a grouse being driven towards the butt. The dead bird continued to come forward with such velocity and struck the man so hard in the centre of the forehead that it knocked him flat on his back. For some time afterwards he went about with a stiff neck and two noteworthy black eyes!

Everybody knows of the weeping willow tree of metal in Chatsworth garden and how taps can be turned on to drench anyone beneath. At one time it was a regular joke to catch visitors in this way, till one day a certain lady in a very expensive fur coat was soaked. She instructed her solicitors to write to the then duke. He did not deign to fight the claim, giving instructions for it to be paid at once, but he also gave orders that the water was never to be turned on again unless a person specifically asked for it.

One of the prides of Chatsworth that no longer remains is the Great Conservatory that covered an acre and was 67 feet high. In it was a rubber tree, and palm trees that eventually grew so tall that they began to push the glass out and had to be lopped. Hidden from general view were 200 canaries in cages, and their singing was a surprise and delight to visitors. But when the 1914 war began the upkeep of this vast place became too great. This is not surprising, for it took eight miles of piping and five boilers using 400 tons of coal annually to keep it to the required temperature, and in addition to the horticultural staff, there had to be men almost continually renewing glass

47

panes and painting. Painting it must somewhat have resembled doing the Forth Bridge, where as soon as they have finished at one end they begin at the other again. The Great Conservatory was built on a frame of iron with the main supports grooved so that seats, known as "butterflies", could be hauled up to enable painters to get to any part. On sunny days it was sometimes very pleasant high on the glass and many a man took a snooze there between whiles, so that the painting did not always get done as quickly as might be. Finally the place was sold to a scrap-iron merchant of Matlock, Timothy White, and as the quickest way of destroying it it was decided that it should be blown up, but six attempts had to be made before it crashed in 1923.

The originator and designer of the Great Conservatory is claimed to have been Joseph Paxton, whose name is associated closely with the Crystal Palace, originally put in Hyde Park, London. Paxton had unique influence at Chatsworth with the sixth Duke, whose story has been written by Violet R. Markham, granddaughter of Paxton. Her book, *Paxton and the Bachelor Duke*, should certainly be read for its interesting stories of the Chatsworth of a hundred or so years ago. Her grandfather must have had tremendous energy, and seems to have made the most of his opportunities. His granddaughter says there is no truth in the story that the actual designer of the Crystal Palace was a Chatsworth estate worker, John Marples, yet I have to support Mr J. B. Firth's report which she questions that many old Chatsworth people all say that Marples was the man. He is described as having been a genius but very shy, which Paxton certainly was not.

One other Chatsworth tale and then I must move on. In Queen Victoria's time the Duke generally

Pre-Norman Cross, Eyam. The big sundial tells the time round the world

stayed in Derbyshire only for the shooting season, living the rest of the year in Devonshire House up in London. When he went, the gold and silver plate had to go from Chatsworth too. It was packed with the utmost care and loaded on a wagon drawn by four horses. Besides the horsemen, four men went with it as guards and considered themselves very lucky, for with them they took always a nine-gallon barrel of home-brewed Chatsworth ale and the journey took three weeks. The wagon was driven thus slowly so that the plate should not be jolted, and every place where the wagon was to stop at night was warned beforehand. At each place the local police provided additional men to sit up with the Duke's guards and there was much treating, for the Chatsworth ale had a reputation and anyone for the privilege of a drink from the barrel would stand two or three drinks of the local liquor. Thus by the time the Duke's men reached London they had generally taken the equivalent of three or four nine-gallon barrels, but as the plate always got to its destination safely I suppose that everybody was satisfied. Chatsworth people say that the plate is more valuable than any owned by our Royal Family and that Queen Victoria did not hesitate to borrow it when she had her more important guests. But I like to think of it best travelling the country roads behind the four gallant Shire-horses, surely as strange a wagon-load as ever went along our Derbyshire roads.

Much of this information I have, of course, picked up since that first visit from Froggatt to Chatsworth, but it seemed best to bring it all in here.

It was very hot and close that first day in the valley by the Derwent. Traffic was busy on the road that runs through the park to Rowsley. We were glad to keep

4*   49

Cartledge Hall, Holmesfield, where most of Robert Murray Gilchrist's tales were written

on the thick turf on the roadside and then to take the
walking route up through Edensor village. We were
even too lacking in energy to climb the stone staircase
to the church and explore the sloping burying-ground
beyond. The church stands well and is worth visiting;
and the burying-ground is what a favourite old writer
of mine, Dr Gordon Stables, would have called "calma-
tive", a place in which to idle and muse. Edensor
village, for all its quaintness and prettiness when the
roses and other blooms are out, must always remain
rather quaintly unreal and "dead". It is *too* quiet, *too*
peaceful. I should not like to live there. We had a long
toil out of it, the great trees keeping the air from us.
Now I always advise my friends to take this road from
Bakewell end, climbing by Bullcross. On top we were
glad to find a little more air. The steep path twisting
down the birch wood to Bakewell Station was pleasant,
with the tall steeple of the church beckoning us. At
the station the town bus was just about to start, so we
scrambled on and clung to the edges of the wooden
seats while the vehicle swerved and throbbed violently
downhill. We were surprised at how quickly we got
to the town, not because of our speed, but because of
the shortness of the distance. It must be a profitable
service.

By the Wye the air was fresher, just as the water
was clearer and sweeter than that of Derwent. It has
been said that Dwr gwent means "fair water", but if
so it is misnamed, for pleasant though the Derwent is
in many of its stretches it is very seldom clear. This is
not because it gets the horrid effluent such as ruins the
River Goyt, but because it flows through gritstone
country. Generally the water has a brownish look due
to the silt it carries. Now the Wye, all of its length
over limestone, has a clean, sparkling look. When the

sun is on it you may notice a delicate harebell blue,
the same colour as snow when seen in the right light.
Anyone who has been in Buxton baths will remember
the beautiful depth of colour. Just below Rowsley
Bridge where the Wye joins the Derwent it is strange
to see the very different waters flowing side by side
and then reluctantly, as it were, agreeing to mingle.
But at Bakewell the Wye is worry-free with no thought
of Derwent. In summer there is no nicer place to rest
than on one of the seats under the lime trees, or on
the grass, perhaps (if you are not too particular about
what other persons say, which it is foolish to be), sitting on the edge with feet in the gentle current. Just
below the bridge is an ait. It is covered with bushes
and makes an ideal breeding place for mallards and
other duck and water-hens, so that you should have
plenty to watch. If you are lucky you may see a hatch
of ducklings ignore their mother and bobbing on the
ripples like black bubbles somehow swim up to the
bridge and keeping by the stonework of a side arch
struggle their way through. Then down they will glide
in the smooth centre-current of the main arch as happy
as schoolboys on a slide.

Children come here to throw broken bread on the
water. If the ducks are hungry there is some rare
dashing about and splashing to get to the bread first,
and then a strange thing may happen: the bread will
disappear before any of the ducks get there and they
will stop and turn back as though it were quite usual.
Which it is, for the fish here are wise and have learned
to gather for feeding too, and doubtless know more
about the ducks than the ducks know about them.

There are few rivers better than this Wye in which
to see trout. A short distance upstream from Bakewell,
where the road from Ashford goes under trees beside

the water for a little way, it is difficult to get visitors along, there are often so many fish to be seen from the footpath, while just beyond the kerb all the traffic between Matlock and Buxton rushes by. It is just another instance, so typical of Derbyshire, where peace and the rush of civilisation lie as close as lovers on honeymoon night. At Bakewell bridge the fish are only a little more distant from the hurry, and not a hundred yards farther down is the weir and the flume that drives the sawmill wheel, or did, for I confess that I have never heard it turning. But we will come back to Bakewell and the Wye later, for I am fond of both, only now I have still to get back to Froggatt. That first day we walked straight back by the main road through Baslow, for we had spent our time at Chatsworth. But today you may take the bus for a part of the way, and even if you walk, the lime-dust of those days is gone. The dust that there was then on many Derbyshire roads is something to remember, another of the things of the "good old days" that I do not wish back. When the same dust was turned to mud it had the consistency of dough and did its best to suck everybody's boots off.

CHAPTER V

THE PLAGUE VILLAGE

ONE could not stay at Froggatt and not visit Eyam (pronounced Eem). We went across the Derwent and through fields to Stoney Middleton. These fields were starred with flowers and made me aware how much richer was the growth here than in the bleaker parts of the county that I had explored before. Later I found that all this central part of the county was well known for its abundance of flowers, including some rarities. The Rev W. H. Painter, author of *The Flora of Derbyshire* (1889), claimed that 1,001 species could be found in the county, but it is unlikely that there is that number now. The late Henry S. Salt records, for instance, that the Lady's Slipper, once abundant on the Heights of Abraham, has become extinct due to selfish collecting of specimens or to thoughtless plucking, and there are many others that have gone. But the flowers that drew my imagination were only of the common sorts, buttercups and ox-eye daisies, many of the parsleys dainty as lace, clovers and vetches, yellow and pink and blue, and by the stream a robust display of butter docks, their plump blossoms just freshly out and their leaves unworn.

From the pleasant field-path to the gloom of Stoney Middleton in the bottom of its dale of tall limestone rocks was a big change. I should not like to live here, though the houses have a curious picturesqueness, many of them standing high above the road with long flights of stone steps to them. Once the village was prosperous because of the local lead mines, but we were told that only a few men continued to be employed there, and that most of the people depended on the boot factories. Well, there was the look of a factory village about the place, and we did not stop.

Middleton Dale was impressive because of its high cliffs. I looked out for the Scots Pedlar's Cave where the remains of a body were found in the days when men wore buckled shoes. His buckles were all that was left by which he could be identified, so long having passed between his disappearance and the discovery. Then there was Lover's Leap to look for, which suggested death again, for it looked impossible that anyone could jump over and not perish. Yet tradition says that in 1760 a girl named Baddeley, disappointed in love, jumped off the rocks but landed with only a few bruises and was able to walk home unaided. Some say that her clothing caught in a bush just before she hit the bottom and broke her fall, others that her crinoline acted in the manner of a parachute. I find this the more attractive idea and wonder if the hat she left on the cliff top in the correct way can have had any resemblance to the maroon beret of our airborne troops. Perhaps some of them might like to adopt the fair crinolined Miss Baddeley as mascot. But when I first stared up at the rock off which she leapt in despair I felt only the pathos of the tale and would not myself have liked to risk the jump. Thus we came to the turn to Eyam on the right through a short gorge where ivy grew up the rocks. Eyam, despite its sad tale, was quite a cheery place to get to after the defile. The village stands high over Middleton Dale, yet is sheltered by higher Eyam Edge beyond. I remember it warm and quiet that sunny day; it seemed too healthy to have had the worst plague of any place in Britain.

Eyam has been known as the Athens of the Peak, and even so sensible a person as R. Murray Gilchrist says Eyam is noteworthy first because of its literary associations. He then tells how there lived here "the bluestocking Anna Seward, who in later years won for herself the title of 'Swan of Lichfield'". When she died this "Swan" left all her papers to Sir Walter Scott, thinking no doubt that he would be able to hatch them into wonderful books. But her poems were real "ugly ducklings", for Scott wrote to a friend that "most of her poetry is absolutely execrable", which is pretty strong from one who was usually fairly generous. In addition to Anna Seward, who only lived in Eyam till she was six anyway, Murray Gilchrist tells that William and Mary Howitt were also associated with Eyam, but frankly, I am not very impressed. I think Eyam much more interesting as "the Plague Village" than as either "the Athens" or "the Queen" of the Peak, for though so much has been written about the plague there, it is one of the few events in country history that the imagination can never quite complete.

Going about the village and seeing the cottage on the street at the west end of the Church from where the plague is said to have started, carried there in a box of suitings from London, looking at Mrs Mompesson's tomb, she the wife of the brave and true Rector who with the Rev Thomas Stanley, a nonconformist, did so much to encourage the people in their great trial, or looking at the little group of Riley graves by the field-path back to Stoney Middleton, try to realise that for more than twelve months the people somehow endured the threat of terrible death which they neither understood nor knew how to alleviate. They were more used to rough living and hardships than we are, but

55

they had less understanding of causes and effects and would therefore be much more open to superstitious fears of the wrath of gods and devils, so that I believe that what they went through must have been a greater test to them than it would have been to modern villagers. Yet the people remained here throughout that terrible twelve months and after isolation had been agreed on, there appear to have been few, if any, attempts at escape. We do not know for how long in that twelve months isolation was the policy, but one surmises that it must have been decided on in the October of 1665 when twenty-three persons died. William Wood, the first edition of whose book *The History of Eyam* was published in 1843, says:

"A kind of circle was drawn round the village, marked by particular and well-known stones and hills; beyond which it was solemnly agreed that no one of the villagers should proceed, whether in-fected or not. This circle extended about half-a-mile around the village; and to two or three places or points on this boundary provisions were brought. A well, or rivulet, northward of Eyam, called to this day 'Mompesson's Well', or 'Mompesson's Brook', was one of the places where articles were deposited. These articles were brought very early in the morning, by persons from the adjoining villages, who, when they had delivered them beside the well, fled with the precipitation of panic. Individuals appointed by Mompesson and Stanley fetched the articles left; and when they took money it was placed in the well or certain stone troughs, to be purified, thus preventing contagion by passing from hand to hand. The persons who collected the money were careful to wash the money well before they took it away. When money was sent it was only for some extra or particular articles: the provisions and many other necessaries were supplied, it is supposed, by the Earl of Devonshire."

During the plague smoking was made compulsory for all the children, being regarded as a safeguard against infection.

Mr J. B. Firth, in his very good *Highways and Byways in Derbyshire*, says that the rigid isolation of Eyam was perhaps not so voluntary as some writers try to make out, and in support he says that the whole countryside became frantic with terror, so that "as far off as Sheffield strangers who were suspected of coming from Eyam or near it were driven away with sticks and showers of stones". Nevertheless, in such a district it was impossible for every way of escape to be watched and I feel that had some of the villagers tried they could have got away in mist or in darkness, or even in daylight, and some record or tradition of it would have come to us.

Wood mentions two persons who passed the circle round the village and neither tale, as he tells it, suggests that the guard set by neighbouring villagers was quite as heartless as Mr Firth says. One was a woman who lived at Orchard Bank, Eyam, and who had some very pressing business at Tideswell Market, so she set out there on foot. The road-watch asked her where she came from, and not knowing where Orchard Bank was, he then asked, "And where is that?" The woman replied: "Why, verily, it is in the land of the living." And the man then let her pass. When she got to the market she was recognised and at once people shouted against her and eventually she was driven back to Eyam with stones and sods, but had she not gone openly into the crowded market I fancy that she might easily have got right away.

The other person who passed the cordon was a man who delivered cartloads of wood for a living. One day the most direct way to where he was going lay through Eyam, and though protests were made, he obstinately drove right through the village. The day was wild and wet and the man caught a cold, but his neighbours, knowing where he had been, immediately suspected that he had the plague.

"They threatened to shoot him if he attempted to cross his threshold," says William Wood. "The consternation of the inhabitants of Bubnell and neighbouring places excited the notice of the Earl of Devonshire who had the particulars of the case laid before him. The noble Earl, being anxious that no unnecessary alarm should be created, reasoned with the persons who waited on him from Bubnell on the impropriety of rashly judging because the man was ill it was necessarily the plague. He told them to go back and he would send his doctor at a certain hour the next day to investigate the nature of the man's illness. The interview was appointed to take place across the river Derwent. At the appointed time the doctor took his station on the eastern, and the invalid on the western side of the river. The affrighted neighbours looked on from a distance while the doctor interrogated the sick man at great length. The doctor at last pronounced him free from the disorder; prescribed him some medicine; and the man, who was much better, soon recovered."

This tale, which appears to be corroborated in part at least by the doctor's prescription which William

58

Wood claims to have seen in the possession of Mr W. Howard of Barlow, a descendant of the carter, does not suggest either that it was impossible to get out of Eyam had the attempt been made after the circle was agreed round it. Therefore I think that the isolation in which the villagers continued was more voluntary than Mr Firth would have us believe. However, one speculation is as likely to be as right or wrong as any other nowadays, but there is certainly interesting matter to muse about as you go round Eyam's roads and paths and fields.

The worst month in Eyam was August 1666 when 77 persons died; and then in the October the plague ended, 259 persons from 76 families having died. A great burning of all bedding, clothing, and furniture began, scarcely enough being saved for living purposes, and that being fumigated in the best ways that the people knew. The whole story has been written up by at least one novelist (*The Brave Men of Eyam* by E. N. Hoare) and may have been treated by others that I do not know about. William and Mary Howitt have told the story in verse, but I fancy that the best record is still that of William Wood, unfortunately now long out of print. Mr Clarence Daniel, of Main Street, Eyam, a young shoe repairer and local preacher deeply interested in geology and local matters, published in 1932 a little book, *The History of Eyam*, which is useful and easy to carry in a pocket.

Actual documents from the plague time are very few. There are three letters written by the Rev William Mompesson, one dated August 31st, 1666, to his children George and Elizabeth, who were sent to relatives in Yorkshire very soon after the plague began and before isolation was decided on, telling them of their mother's death; another is to his patron

Sir George Saville; and the third to his friend Mr John Beilby, in Yorkshire. There is a bit about the plague in *De Spiritualibus Pecci: Notes (or Notices) concerning the work of God, and some of those who have been workers together with God in the Hundred of the High Peak in Derbyshire*, written by William Bagshawe, known as the "Apostle of the Peak". And finally there is the Eyam parochial register of burials. All else is tradition and hearsay.

The tragedy is commemorated annually on Plague Sunday, the last Sunday in August, when an open-air service is held in the little dell known as Cucklett Church where, during the plague, Mompesson preached rather than have his parishioners gather in the church with greater risk of infecting one another. Although the August was the worst month of the plague, that is not why this Sunday has been set aside. Before the plague a Wakes, or Feast, had been held every year on the first Sunday after August 18th, St Helen's Day. A Wakes is always a time of reunion when relatives and friends gather together, and when the plague was over, that was the natural day to set aside. Sometime in the eighteenth century, however, probably following several late harvests, the people of Eyam decided to change the Wakes to the last Sunday in August when all hay should be in and time could be better spared. Accordingly the day of the plague commemoration was changed, too, and so many persons now attend that loud-speakers have to be used.

From Eyam back to Froggatt: rather than take the same way through Middleton Dale as we did, it is worth while to go up Sir William Hill. Above Bradshaw Hall near the crest of Sir William is High-cliffe Nook where R. Murray Gilchrist came to live when he was twenty-one and able to escape from the

cutlery apprenticeship in Sheffield, which he hated.
Here he started his long career of literature and wrote
some of his best tales, including those in his fine *A
Peakland Faggot*. He was very methodical, making it
a rule to write something every day. He was a cheerful
realist, and I like to think of him tall and broad,
striding about these hills and talking with the people
whom he loved. The Milton of his tales was Eyam,
and Bakewell he made his Calton St Anne. As a friend
wrote:

> He knew the name of every flower that springs,
> And loved the hills, the dales, the edges grim;
> The moors, the birds, the fields and fairy rings,
> All were a pleasure and delight to him.

Murray Gilchrist left Highcliffe Nook in 1892 to go
to Holmesfield. All down Sir William Hill to the
Grindleford road there is a splendid view of the
Derwent in its beautiful vale and of the rock edges
and dark moors beyond. Across the valley above
Calver is the little village of Curbar which experienced
the plague in 1632, several families being wiped out,
but it was not nearly as bad as at Eyam. Eyam is the
last place in England where there is any record of the
plague. It is curious that it should have been so deadly
in so normally healthy a district. Chesterfield, which
lies eastward beyond the moors over Curbar, had the
plague in 1586–7.

In 1757 five men were digging a grave near the
Saxon cross in Eyam churchyard when three of them
suddenly became ill, their trouble closely resembling
the plague of 1665. All three died and there was for
a time a terrible fear in the village that the plague had
come back, but nothing further happened.

Eyam Cross is one of the best of its period that remains. It has five neat scrolls cut in relief on the shaft with a trefoiled leaf in the middle of them. Some experts think that the slender foliage may be Roman work, but if not, then it was copied from Roman designs.

CHAPTER VI

WHERE LITTLE JOHN WANDERED

FROM Froggatt we found no more pleasant walk than to Hathersage. We went first along the road from Grindleford Bridge. The river runs swiftly here, and there were tall trees with welcome shade making the wide gorge seem wild and lonely, but with that loneliness of remote country which it is worth going far to find.

Hathersage was stone built, scattered up the hillside above the river. When Edward Rhodes arrived about 1800 he says there were exactly a hundred houses, but it had grown from those days. Everybody who visits Hathersage goes naturally to the Church, which stands at the higher end of the village. Dr Charles Cox considered that it has "the fairest situation of any church of this beautiful and varied county", but there are so many beautifully situated churches that I prefer to leave him to defend his own opinion. It is an attractive church and, says Dr Cox, "is in the main a good example of country work of the fourteenth century. ... It was restored—not badly for the date—in 1851–2", so that I take it that he had a particular liking for Hathersage Church generally, which is something that the parishioners may be proud of, for Dr Cox is the first authority on all Derbyshire churches and not over lavish with praise. Inside there are some interesting tombs to members of the once great family of Eyre, including one who fought with Prince Harry at the battle of Agincourt, and another, much more interesting to me in those days, on which there are engraved in brass the figures of ten sons and four daughters, whose father, Robert Eyre of Hope, died on March 21st, 1459. There seems to have been a fifteenth figure once and it is said that this was another daughter, but illegitimate, so although those who set up the memorial thought her worthy of her place, some later person was scandalised and had her cut out.

More interesting than anything inside the church to anyone with the long, happy thoughts of youth was the grave outside found suitably beneath two yew trees, a piece of gritstone at each end with ten feet of grassed earth between them. This was the reputed grave of Robin Hood's greatest friend and chief lieutenant, Little John. Hathersage may, in fact, be called the centre of the Derbyshire Robin Hood country, but though one who keeps a somewhat romantic temperament who would like to claim for the county a big share in the life of Robin Hood and his merry men, I have to confess that later search has not brought nearly as much evidence of the outlaws in the county as I should have welcomed. But when I stood by the grave in Hathersage churchyard that first time I felt on sacred ground, and I see no reason why any other youth who has read and thought of Robin Hood should not share the feelings there that I had. For there is no hero more true to the spirit of old England than Robin Hood, and no country in which he can be more suitably imagined than round Hathersage. Therefore I range myself with those who believe that at least Little John may have been buried there, and will give all the evidence I can to support that theory, and retort to all critics: "Well, if you know any better evidence against his having been buried there, I am ready to listen."

Obviously there is nothing now to be got from the

Little John's grave in Hathersage Churchyard

oldest memories round Hathersage about Little John, so that all the evidence on his behalf must be from records. Some claim that Little John was born at Hathersage, but the most that is generally claimed is that he was born somewhere in Derbyshire, and that, of course, might as well have been in Hathersage as any other village. In *The Derbyshire Gatherer* published in 1880, I find:

"Little John (as he was jestingly called from his being so much taller than his companions) or John the Nailer, the friend and companion of Robin Hood, was born somewhere in Derbyshire, in the early part of the thirteenth century, and was brought up to the business of nail making, which trade he followed for some time till his wonderful strength and prowess determined him to try his fortune elsewhere. Little is known of his career until the Battle of Evesham, in 1265, where he fought with the rebels under Simon de Montfort, Earl of Leicester, who was defeated. Many of his followers, including Robin Hood and Little John, were outlawed. . . .

"When Robin Hood died at the age of four score years, at his own request he was buried by Little John in Kirklees Park, Yorkshire (his native place). . . . After performing these last sad duties Little John felt his own end approaching, and sought his native place. It is reported on his beholding the vale of Hathersage he said his career would soon be ended, and on arriving at a cottage near the church he entered it, and soon after breathed his last. The cottage, a rough stone structure, built without lime, we believe, is now in existence. . . ."

Next let us look at *Rambles in the Country Surrounding the Forest of Sherwood.* This was written in the

5   65

eighteen-forties by Mr Spencer T. Hall, a native of Sherwood Forest, who carefully collected everything about Robin and his band. The house in which Little John is reputed to have died, he says, "is a rustic old place, with exceedingly thick walls. . . . In it lives Jenny Sherd, a respectable old widow. . . . I had a long conversation with Jenny Sherd, who was full of faith, not only of Little John having died in her cottage, and in his being buried in the churchyard, but that the very grave still pointed out . . . is the precise spot."

Perhaps before going on with Mr Hall's account I had better put in the story accepted by Rhodes when he visited Hathersage. He tells that a tall man from Offerton, probably nicknamed Little John because of his height and breadth, was the real person buried in the grave. When in October 1784 the grave was opened "that it might be rendered still more marvellous", says Rhodes, "when the bones were recommitted to the grave, the stones that originally marked the stature of the tall man of Offerton were removed farther apart". Probably Jenny Sherd knew all about the story, so we will go back to Mr Hall's report.

"I ventured", he says, "to suggest to her, that the present sexton did not feel sure the grave pointed out was Little John's, though he did believe him buried somewhere in the churchyard; and that people more learned had doubted his interment there at all. 'Ah,' said Jenny, 'it's very easy for one man to set his judgement up against a whole parish, who have all as good, and some of them a better chance of knowing than he—but some folks are so odd and perverse they'll hardly believe their own senses; and as to larned folks, why, mester, I'll tell

you—it isna larning that makes folks wise—it isna
education at a schule as always gies 'em sense.
Books often rack folks' brains out o' their heads—
but they may be sometimes studied a long while
afore they'll put ony in.' There was no arguing
against such close rustic reasoning," continues Mr
Hall, "so I asked the good woman to tell me all she
herself knew on the subject, which she proceeded
to do in the clearest and straightest manner possible
—no counsel could have stated the case more
cogently. She said that she was now seventy years
old (I should have hardly supposed her sixty), and
that she was born in this cottage. Her father,
William Bohem, who lived in it from his youth, died
at the age of ninety-two, and he would now (1841),
had he lived, have been one hundred and twelve
years old. He received from his predecessors in the
cottage, at the time he entered upon it, the assurance
that Little John had died there; and they had
received the information sixty years before from
those who had preceded them—and this was the
way in which the tradition had been preserved from
Little John's time, not only by the inhabitants of
that house, but by almost every old family in the
place. I suggested that it was a small house for a
big man like John the Nailor to be in; and in reply
she assured me that within her own memory the
interior consisted only of one large room, which
was open to the rig-tree. She said I might see by
the style of the cottage that it was many hundred
years old; and there was a statement in the tradition
that his body stretched nearly across the floor when
he was dead. Her father, although an artisan, was a
learned and intelligent man, having a good knowledge of the Latin and Greek languages, and being,

withall, very scrupulous about crediting idle tales, had full faith in the whole tradition, believing that an entire parish could never have consented to a falsehood on the subject; and especially as all well-informed people for many miles round gave their credence implicitly to the fact.

"Jenny well remembers Little John's grave being opened by order of Captain James Shuttleworth, and a great thigh-bone being brought directly from it into her cottage and measured, when it was found to be *thirty-two inches in length*; and though decayed a little at the ends, it was thick throughout in proportion to that length. Two shovels had been broken in digging the grave, and the bone had been broken near the middle by the third shovel striking it; but she says the parts exactly fitted each other, and is sure there was no artifice about it, notwithstanding what the present sexton (who, by-the-bye, never saw it) may say to the contrary. The name of the sexton who opened the grave was Philip Heaton, and the great bone was taken by Captain James Shuttleworth to the Hall; and his brother, Captain John, was so offended at him for having it exhumed, and he met with so many severe accidents—two of them in the churchyard—while it was in his possession, that at the end of a fortnight he had it reinterred in its old place. Some years after, however, being in garrison with his regiment in Montrose, in Scotland, he sent to her father proffering him a gun guinea if he would take it up again and send it to him in a box; but her father would not comply with any such request. However, about fifty years ago, a party of 'great folk' from Yorkshire had it re-exhumed and took it with them to Cannon Hall, near Barnsley. Up to that time Little John's cap was kept hanging by a chain in the church; but even that the Goths just mentioned took with them. Jenny remembers it all very well; and, with every other person in the village, has a particularly distinct recollection of the green cloth cap that hung in the church, and which everybody 'knew' to be Little John's."

Returning to *The Derbyshire Gatherer* we find something else which helps to clear to some extent Jenny Sherd's story about the apparent theft of the cap from Hathersage Church. There it is stated:

"When the British Archæological Association met at Sheffield, in August 1873, one of their excursions was to Wharncliffe Chase, where they were shown a bow which had been at Cannon Hall for 160 or 170 years, and which was supposed to be the original bow of Little John. . . . The bow, some arrows, and a quantity of chain armour were hanging at Hathersage Hall in the reign of Charles I. At the time of the Revolution the estate at Hathersage came into the possession of a family of the name of Spencer, one of whom succeeded to the estate of Cannon Hall. About that time the bow and armour were removed to the latter place, and the armour was in existence there till about seventy years ago, when it was stolen by some workmen who were making repairs to the building.

"The bow bore the name of Col. Naylor, with the date 1715, and he was supposed to be the last man who ever strung it. It required a power of 160 lbs. to draw the bow to its full; only 90 lbs. is the power which men of the present time use at archery meetings. The wood is now in so tender a condition that it is possible it would break if it were fully strung, but in 1715 the horn at both points was perfect, and Col. Naylor shot a deer with it."

The Oxford antiquarian Ashmole says that he saw this bow in the reign of James in Hathersage Church. E. Hargrove in his *Anecdotes of Archery*, published in York in 1792, says that when he visited Hathersage the initials J. L. (John Little ?) were still to be deciphered on the stones at either end of the grave.

Other reminders of Robin Hood and his men in green in the neighbourhood are in the name Robin Hood's Hill at Castleton, and Robin Hood's Stride near Youlgrave. The Stride is a tumble of rocks with an upstanding pillar at either end twenty-two yards apart, the taller eighteen feet high. There is a drawing of these rocks in the British Museum (Add. MSS. 6318), under which it says: "The tradition of the neighbourhood is that Robin Hood and Little John stood upon Eastwood rocks, about one and a half miles off, and shot at this stone [which ?]; Little John's arrow hit it, but Robin Hood's fell short in the valley below." I have never heard this tradition locally, but when with my mother and aunt during that first stay at Froggatt we asked a farmer about the stones he replied pleasantly and courteously that all he knew was that Little John was supposed to have stood with one foot on one pillar and the other foot on the other and in that position to have relieved himself, and that was how the stream began that now runs from between the pillars. The farmer added: "I dunna know 'ow he did it, though. He mun abin bigger than Goliath!"

The two pillars are known as the Weasel Pinnacle (which is the smaller) and the Inaccessible Pinnacle (which can nevertheless be climbed by at least two

routes, though one is a test for even expert rock men).
Presumably this would be the pillar that Little John
shot at. Well, with all this evidence at least it can be
said with certainty that no other place can make a
better claim than Hathersage to Little John, so I for
one shall continue to enjoy thinking of him as having
roved about the wooded Derwent gorge and over the
fair hills around, and I am glad that the Ancient Order
of Foresters looks after his grave and makes a pilgrimage there every year.

I have been asked what connection with the outlaw
chief is supposed to exist at the little village of Robin
Hood, on the moor above Baslow. So far as I know
there is none. The village seems simply to have taken
its name from the local inn, which has a painting of
Robin on its sign.

Apart from its church and its associations with
Little John, Hathersage is the centre for many other
interests. Those who enjoy Charlotte Brontë's *Jane
Eyre* will like to follow Jane's adventures round here
as far as they can, for Hathersage is the Morton of
the novel. Moor House, where St John Eyre Rivers
and his sisters lived, had as its original Moorseats, the
house on the hill behind the church. Whitecross, where
Jane was put down by the coachman after she had run
away from Thornfield Hall, is the cross-roads above
Longshawe and Grindleford Bridge by the Fox House
Inn, which is about an hour's walk from Moorseats.
Charlotte Brontë stayed at Hathersage with Miss
Nussey, sister of the vicar, in 1845, and wrote her
novel two years later. Those who are deeply interested
in *Jane Eyre* will find more about its connection with
Hathersage in J. B. Firth's *Highways and Byways in
Derbyshire*, Mr Firth having been a great admirer of
the novel.

North of Hathersage, about a mile from the church, is North Lees Hall, once a home of a branch of the Eyre family, which suffered such great persecution for remaining Roman Catholic in Elizabethan days. In a bit of woodland below the house are the ruins of what was once a chapel destroyed by a Protestant mob in the time of William of Orange.

On our way back from Hathersage we crossed to Padley, near Grindleford railway station, to see the ruins of that other better-known chapel, then used for cattle, from which the Padley martyrs were seized. Dr Cox says that the Eyres once had here one of the largest mansions in the district, but there is not much of it left except this chapel. Anne Eyre, the heiress, married Sir Thomas Fitzherbert of Norbury, also a staunch Catholic, and their son John Fitzherbert was living at Padley when on Candlemas Day 1588 the raid came. John and two priests, Nicholas Garlick and Robert Ludlam, were taken away. John Fitzherbert died amid the filth in Derby gaol, of which W. Hutton wrote in his *History of Derby* that it was erected "in a river, exposed to damp and filth, as if they meant to drown the culprit before they hanged him. A worse situation could not have been chosen. . . . The wretched inhabitant was open to the public and they to him." But the two priests survived in this place somehow until July 25th, 1588, when with a third priest, Richard Simpson, they were hung, drawn, and quartered. The three heads and the quarters of the bodies were stuck on poles and exhibited in towns throughout Derbyshire as a warning to all other Romanists. This story has been written by Robert Hugh Benson, Roman Catholic priest and novelist, under the title, *Come Rack! Come Rope!*, which is a quotation from a speech made after torture by another martyr who was hanged at Tyburn. These are sad memories to be associated with Padley, for when the Eyre mansion was first built there it must have been as pleasant a place as could have been chosen, and it is good to be able to record that since my first visit the chapel has been restored. After eighteen months of negotiations the farm on which it stands was secured in January 1932 by Mgr Payne, Rector of St Mary's, Derby, and Vice-Capitular of the Nottingham diocese. Later the farm was resold, the chapel retained to be made a more fitting place for pilgrims. How long the building had been used as barn and shippon is not known, but its ecclesiastical character was only rediscovered about 1905; while some small repairs were being made the workmen uncovered parts of a timbered roof which could not have been meant simply for a farm outbuilding. From that time began the annual July pilgrimage. It is said that the bowl of a font from the chapel was used for many years as a water trough outside a cottage below the Maynard Arms at Grindleford, and that when the cottage was pulled down the bowl was transferred to a farm over the road, but was later taken away into Dovedale district. Few chapels can have had a more chequered history than Padley.

CHAPTER VII

THE EDWARD CARPENTER
COUNTRY

FROGGATT has within easy walking distance Bradway and Millthorpe, but unfortunately I did not on my first visit know of Edward Carpenter. He must at that time have been living in his Millthorpe Cottage, for it was not until 1923 that he moved to Surrey, where he died on June 28th, 1929. He called the house he went into at Guildford "Millthorpe", so that this little village must have remained an affectionate memory, and a number of persons who knew him well considered that his last years would have been happier had he remained in Derbyshire, because he missed the hills and old associations.

Carpenter, with Bernard Shaw and William Morris, was a founder of the Socialist movement and has left one of the unique books of the nineteenth century, but Derbyshire has never made the claim to him that she is entitled to.

It was Derbyshire scenery that inspired much of *Towards Democracy*.

Carpenter began writing it in April 1881 at Bradway. "I knocked together a sort of wooden sentinel-box, in the garden, and there, or in the fields and the woods, all that spring and summer, and on through the winter, by day and sometimes by night, in sunlight or in rain, by frost and snow and all sorts of grey and dull weather, I wrote," he has recorded. During the summer of 1883 he had a cottage built at Millthorpe

74

and there he moved in the October, taking his "sentinel-box" with him. He put it by the edge of the brook that ran "full of grace and music" at the foot of his garden, and there facing the sun and the south he continued to write, "rejoicing always to get the sentiment of the open free world" into his pages.

His life at Millthorpe followed a pleasant routine. He got up about seven, usually taking a dip in the brook, a sunbath, and a run round the garden; or a sponge-down in a sheltered corner of the lawn. Then, after tidying his room, a little work in the yard or garden, and breakfast, he settled to his writing. His afternoons he kept free for more work in the garden, or recreation, chiefly walking. Round Millthorpe he found the footpaths so numerous and ill-defined that he said when he had nothing else to do he went out and discovered a new footpath. In the evenings he read and generally played the piano for a little while and then before going to bed he invariably took a walk along the lane, usually alone. That is the life of one who was obviously a great lover of Derbyshire and he has left tribute in his poem, "Little Brook without a Name", which he has put next to the end of the definitive edition of *Towards Democracy*, giving it that place, I am sure, not without a wish that others too would keep it in memory.

Carpenter was once described by William Morris as "a dreary cove", but that opinion hardly tallies with this little bit from a letter that Carpenter sent to Charles F. Sixsmith: "We had great fun. I dressed as a Moor and George as a Jap. We called on my sister and Miss C. and rode in a trap with them to Froggatt Edge to the great delight and wonderment of everybody on the road. George was in excellent form and did some first-rate fooling."

75

Henry S. Salt was a friend of Carpenter's and has written: "I remember how on one occasion, when we had had a long walk round Kinder Scout by Edale and Ashop Head, we arrived in the evening at the Snake Inn, where we had planned to sleep, and finding it full, were compelled to trudge another eight miles down the valley to Ashopton. This, for a man of nearly seventy, was no light task; but he did it as if it did not trouble him in the least." Henry S. Salt also tells how, knowing Carpenter's impatience with the irregular, he asked him whether the crooked spire of Chesterfield, visible at many points in his neighbourhood, did not irritate him. "He confessed that it did; he had once written, in fact, to the authorities at Chesterfield and urged that the crooked should be made straight!"

To Millthorpe travelled visitors from all over the world. A silver-miner came from Sierra Nevada, on landing travelling at once to Millthorpe, and after a few words with Carpenter, off he went next day to his ship and home again. Here is a picture given by another American; it is probably what I should have seen had I gone over from Froggatt during that first holiday:

"The long grey stone house was singular in this that it stood with its back to the road, and the gate was at the end. As I went around to the front of the house, facing on a beautiful garden, I was met by the great man himself, and most affectionately welcomed. He was attired in a simple, soft suit, with knee-breeches, stockings and sandals. Around his waist was a silken sash. His complexion was rather dark, the skin smooth, the eyes light brown, brave, and kind. He took me by the hands; his manner was nervous, almost to a slight tremulousness. One felt in the presence of a shy, scholarly recluse, a

THE EDWARD CARPENTER COUNTRY

little bashful as it were, to be under the scrutiny of new eyes. His whole presence was spiritual and sweet, yet with a slight subtle suggestion of the rebel. This was no ordinary man living no ordinary life."*

Many of the visitors to Millthorpe were undoubtedly cranks. Just after there had been serious trouble at Walsall over the making of bombs it happened that a barrel arrived at Millthorpe and some of Carpenter's anarchist friends, says Henry S. Salt, "got a suspicion that the barrel contained live bombs which the 'comrades' had sent to that remote locality to get them out of the way. The cask was therefore handled with extreme care, and not opened till every precaution had been taken to guard against an explosion. It was found, however, to contain nothing more deadly than a hundredweight of Blenheim Oranges and Ribstone Pippins from Somersetshire."

No doubt Carpenter had thought of ending his days at Millthorpe and he had spoken to at least one friend about being buried coffinless in his orchard there. He fancied cremation, but realised that it would be more bother and would attract a lot of attention. He left Millthorpe chiefly because his housemate, George Merrill, wanted a change to town, and because he thought he would see more of his friends. Also, ever ready like Thoreau to slough away his possessions, he was just then approached by a wealthy friend who offered to buy the Millthorpe house and furniture and keep it intact as a memorial. So after forty-three years in Derbyshire the change was made and instead of being buried in his orchard Edward Carpenter lies in Guildford Cemetery, but the district round Totley will ever be the true "Edward Carpenter Country".

* J. William Lloyd, *Edward Carpenter: in appreciation.*

CHAPTER VIII

"AUNCIENT BUCKSTONES"

MANY years went by after Froggatt before I stayed in Derbyshire again, and then it was a holiday that turned out to be of great importance, for it led eventually to my setting up a home in the county. This time my mother took rooms at Chapel-en-le-Frith and there I joined her one March Saturday. I had only once before been to Chapel-en-le-Frith, on a snowy Easter when with a party of Boy Scouts I had been on a walking camp from Hope into Cheshire. I remembered the long tramp up the Winniates by Castleton, and our arrival in Chapel-en-le-Frith valley with snow coming down thickly, darkness deepening, and the fields all lying too sodden for tents. We spent the night on hay on a friendly farmer's "baulks", one end of it being open so that we could look down on the cattle. Their warmth must have helped to make the whole building warmer, and their occasional movements, or gentle lowing, and the chink of their neck-chains up and down the stanchions were comforting, in restful contrast with the heavy buffeting against the rough stone walls, and the swishing of rain and snow across the slates on the old rafters only just over our heads. In fact, I remembered the night as a particularly comfortable one, but the morning was grey and still wet, though the snow had stopped. We tried to light a fire by an overgrown hawthorn hedge, but even when it was lit we could scarcely cook because of the wind and our breakfast was a poor one. So eventually we tramped out of the village not in a very cheerful mood and I remembered the steep main street as a dismal, rather unfriendly place. It did not look much brighter when I walked down from the station to begin my holiday, for it was nearly dark, and there was a wet glisten on the pavements. It seemed very narrow and shut in, but fortunately the house where I was to stay, "The Eaves", was high out of the village. There was a terrace at the front and when I went there in the morning I found a fine view below, in which the village that had seemed so drab and narrow was a suitable and unobtrusive centrepiece, with its square-towered church upheld on a small hill so that it seemed to keep watch dutifully over the houses clustered among the trees round about.

The valley in which Chapel-en-le-Frith lies cannot compete for beauty with the Derwent Valley below Hathersage, or with the green seclusion of the lower part of Edale Valley, but it has a certain broad beauty and is best seen from one of the hills around, such as the terrace at "The Eaves", or from Eccles Pike. Although there are not very many trees when one is in the valley, seen from higher up it seems to be quite well wooded. Many of the growths that appear like trees then are only hedge bushes that have been let grow wild.

That first day I was attracted, as everybody who likes a climb must be at Chapel-en-le-Frith, by the long flat outline of Combs Edge, which it is said is Capetown's Table Mountain in miniature. It lies to the south, overlooking the whole valley, though when one is at the lower end of the village, Townend, as it is called, Cowburn and Rushup Edge become more dominant. But they lack the black edge of gritstone that cuts off the plateau of Combs Moss from the slopes that run into the valley.

There was a keen, strong wind when I went up that first time and it blew against me, so that the climb seemed stiffer than I had anticipated; but when I got on top it enhanced the bleakness and loneliness of the place, and I was rather glad of the conditions. For at some time back lost to history the extreme end of the Moss was used as a fort or camp, and with the wind roaring there and great clots of dark grey cloud rushing forward as if to overwhelm everything, it is more easy to imagine oneself back in elemental days such as those when the camp was made. The end of the Moss, about 1,600 feet above sea-level, goes to a point with cliffs or very steep sides nearly 450 feet deep protecting it, and where the moor of the plateau runs out to this point a double mound and ditch about 200 yards long was made, so that a triangular acre or so is enclosed that could be very easily defended. Looking over the deepest part of the cliffs, I saw another valley below, the valley of Combs, and I wondered whether when the camp was occupied all that low land was lost in hawthorn and holly and bramble scrub, and I supposed that wolves would have ranged there, and perhaps wild boars and even bears. And then I thought what a pleasant place it must be when the sun shone; and that was my first glimpse of the valley that was to become my home for fifteen years. Had anyone told me so then, I should have been as incredulous of it as any early inhabitant of the camp could have been had I tried to tell him that one day over the spot where he was a man-made bird would soar carrying a man who had been launched into the air at Hucklow, or that only a very little later and a bit farther over the Moss a bomb would crash and explode, having flown itself from somewhere over the North Sea. It is strange to associate these thoughts of the most ancient and

Modern limestone quarry near Buxton

.the most modern. Perhaps the people who made this camp were engaged in bitter war with other savage tribes; on Christmas Eve 1944, when the flying bomb hit the Moss at 2 a.m. and killed a sheep, we were still fighting bitter war, though our methods had changed considerably.

This camp above Castle Naze, previously called Castle Dykes, is classed among the oldest remains in Derbyshire. The double mound and ditch, or fosse, across the moor are cut through in the centre and this is supposed to have been done by Romans, who finding the camp already made used it as an observation post. These men would come from Buxton, only five miles away, where the Romans had a fairly important station. Now Castle Naze chiefly attracts rock-climbers. The crags are classed as good for the inexpert, but I remember one youth falling to death.

Combs Moss is so typical of many of the plateaux of North Derbyshire that here seems to be the reasonable place to say something about the geology of the district. Those who are deeply interested should get *The Scenery and Geology of the Peak of Derbyshire* by Elizabeth Dale, in which there is a geological map and descriptions of all the chief features. Coming to Chapel-en-le-Frith as a complete dunce about geology I thought that the higher, rougher hills of dark millstone grit were the older, and the lower, softer-outlined hills of limestone to be seen southward from Combs Moss were the newer. Of course this is wrong. The oldest rock of the county is the limestone, said to lie in parts 2,000 feet thick, though at Buxton the bottom has never been reached. When one thinks that this bed was laid down somewhat in the same way as coral, and consists of the remains of myriads of tiny sea organisms, a vague idea of the immensity of time that

6*

Winniates Pass

went to the making of such a thickness can be imagined. Then either the land grew out of the sea, or the sea went away, and the sea organisms died, and a vast swamp was formed into which rivers poured sand and rock particles from higher places, and out of all this was made the gritstone, which in Derbyshire is of many types, layer above layer lying with shales between. Looking across at Combs Moss from Eccles Pike, or from the valley, one can see these layers. The flat top consists of Chatsworth grit. There is an escarpment, showing plainly at either end, and then another level shelf or bench, this time of Kinder Scout grit; and lower again another shelf, this of shale grit. To one not particularly interested in noting the different types of grit, there is still interest in going along the old track which runs below Castle Naze to Dove Holes and noting how the change in the underlying rocks is faithfully shown in the stone walls. Where the change to limestone begins the walls have a magpie look, with the white quickly increasing as one goes on till the walls are all limestone. Those who go by the old L.N.W.R. line from Chapel South station to Buxton may note these same changes in the walls that guard the line. But the differences in the underlying rocks may be picked out also merely by watching changes in the country and vegetation. The line runs under the foot of the Moss to avoid the necessity of a much longer tunnel. The chief trees are oaks, beeches, and sycamores, and the moor edges grow heather, bilberries, and bracken. Between Dove Holes and Buxton the line runs through a shale area and the weathered rocks are gone and there are no outstanding features. There are scarcely any trees; no heather, no bracken, only coarse grass and sedges. Then on the mountain limestone round Buxton you may scarcely find an oak and the rounded hills grow only short fine grass. Here, too, is wild thyme and there are rock roses, and in the valley Crane's-bill and Herb Robert.

The rocks round Combs Moss are angular, and under the cliffs the slopes are littered with great jagged rock-pieces that have fallen owing to weathering. This is typical Chatsworth grit, much harder than Kinder grit, so that the rocks on Kinder Edge are much more rounded, due to the stone there containing a larger quantity of felspar which decomposes and crumbles more easily. On Kinder one finds rocks curiously hollowed round the bottom, having almost a mushroom appearance, and this is due to under-cutting by sand hurtled against them by the winds. There are no such rocks on Combs Moss.

Although I know so little about it, had I time I should like to specialise in the geology of Derbyshire, for there is so much diversity. I once began a university extension course in a Derbyshire village on the subject, but after going to three lectures and not having heard even one reference to the geology round about I gave up the six-miles walk which had been necessary to attend. It was sadly disappointing that a professor could give such dull lectures in a district where there was so much to be seen, even by casual observers, that would have illustrated his subject so well and have stimulated interest in the best way. So, that I may not become a bore myself on the subject, I will leave it with the suggestion to the universities responsible for extension courses in the different parts of the county that they should advise their lecturers to ally their subjects wherever possible with local references that their students can understand. If this had been done, I feel that I should know a great deal more than I do about a very fascinating Derbyshire study.

Nobody staying at Chapel-en-le-Frith would miss going to Buxton. I found the walk up Barmour Clough nice enough under the trees there, but later on, past Dove Holes, it was monotonous and it is better to go by bus rather than walk by this route.

Dove Holes is as exposed a village as can be found in Derbyshire and it is further disfigured by the tremendous dump of lime waste, like a miniature mountain (known locally as Mont Blanc), that over-shadows the cottages of the higher end of the village. I remember thinking as I walked past the dump the first time that it looked dangerous, and in April 1933 in the night the cottagers were awakened by a tremen-dous rumbling and then a crash. Nearly five hundred tons of the slag had avalanched over the road, almost to the height of the cottages, though fortunately not even a window was cracked. A woman in one of the bedrooms waved a light and saved the Buxton Royal Mail van from crashing into debris. Dynamite had to be used before the block could be cleared and the Manchester–Buxton traffic had to be diverted through Peak Dale. From time to time some of the ash is carted away for roadmaking, and it would be a good thing if a use could be found for it all.

At Dove Holes, near St Paul's Church, is an ancient stone circle, similar to that at Arbor Low but known as the Bull Ring. It is believed to have been made some two thousand years B.C., about the same time as the Arbor Low circle and Stonehenge, but it has been much spoilt by stone having been taken away to build a farmhouse near by, and for gate-posts and shippon doorposts. It is said that when excavations for more stone were made about 1840 two skeletons were dug up. They were shown to a local surgeon, who said they suggested to him men nearly seven feet tall. Arbor

Low lies about eleven miles away and some people believe that an old track once ran between the two circles.

At Victory Quarry, Dove Holes, men at work in 1901 suddenly broke into a previously unsuspected cave about 90 feet long, 4 feet broad, and 15 feet high, with bones and teeth all over the floor. These were found to be the remains of mastodons, sabre-toothed tigers, elephants, rhinoceroses, horses, deer, and hyenas. Never before in England had remains of such variety and completeness been found, and Sir William Boyd Dawkins, opening Buxton New Library and Museum on September 26th, 1928, said that they were "the very oldest collection of remains of animals from caves that have yet been met with in the whole world". From the fact that there were many more bones of young mastodons than of full-grown ones, and that hyena teeth-marks were on many bones, Sir William surmised that the remains had been washed out of a hyena den on the hill top and carried down a crack into the rock. Hyenas could easily kill mastodon calves, but did not often dare to attack adults.

Approaching Buxton from Dove Holes one gets a wide view of the town, though not the most picturesque one, but the many hills that stand all round are impressive. Buxton is a true hill town and has many claims to fame. It is the highest, the coldest, and the wettest market town in England! Even as long ago as 1572 a Derby physician, Dr Jones, writing on "The Benefit of the Auncient Bathes of Buckstones which cureth most grievous sicknesses", warned everybody to go there "well-clothed", for, he said, though "very wholesome and pure, the ayre is farre colder and more sharpe than many parts of the earth". In summer this "ayre" is very clean and sweet, but in winter it can be very "snell", as a Scot would say. It was bitter that day of my first visit and drew along the fine main street, Spring Gardens, as up a flue. Later on another uncle of mine lived in Buxton for ten years and told me how some of the older and poorer inhabitants dodged the rain and cold sometimes. Round the Crescent and between it and the baths there is a continuous colonnade where one can walk to and fro for quite a distance always under cover, and if this exercise is not enough to keep one's feet warm on a cold day, there is a grill under the glass canopy of the artificially warmed mineral baths. Through this grill rises escaping heat from the baths and I have often been amused, since learning about this, to see on winter days old men standing on this grill. There was in particular an ex-cabdriver who in his time had taken many noted and notorious persons round the sights of the neighbourhood who was often entertaining to talk with.

So much can be said of Buxton, and this seems to be the place for it, that I will put it down, though naturally I did not learn all on my first visit. Buxton is thought (from the many relics dug up hereabouts) to have been the site of settlements from days long previous to recorded history, and was certainly of considerable importance in Roman times, but it is curious that after the Romans went it remained very small until after 1863 when the opening of the railway from Manchester made the town at last comfortably accessible. Writing in 1928 Mr J. A. Goodacre (*Buxton Old and New*) said: "Within the lifetime of present residents it was a mere village, with less than 1,500 inhabitants. In the early years of the nineteenth century it had a population but little more than half that of Bakewell at that time. In 1821 it had 184 houses, and only 1,036 residents. Forty years later the figure had risen to 1,877; in 1881 they totalled 6,021; and in

1921 the census returns were 15,651." Mr Goodacre
also says that it is probable that when the Crescent was
built (in 1780) there were not more than 800 residents
in the village, which shows how great faith had the
builder, the fifth Duke of Devonshire. Dr Jones, two
hundred years earlier than that, had stated: "It
(Buxton) is situate in a goodly seate, passing healthy,
and in tyme would grow to bee very wealthy"; but I
fancy that he would have been disappointed over the
length of time that passed before his prophecy became
fact. Undoubtedly it was the bleakness of the surroundings and the hardship of travel by coach that kept
Buxton small for so long. Gazing across now from the
Slopes to the plentiful Corbar Woods it is difficult to
realise how bleak it looked before the same Duke of
Devonshire had the many thousands of trees planted
which we now enjoy. The woods literally brought
some of the softer beauty of Chatsworth and the
Derwent vale here, for most of the trees came from
famous nurseries at Darley, south of Chatsworth.

The Crescent is said to have been built with revenues
from Ecton copper mines near Alstonefield and is
made of stone quarried close by and faced with free-
stone from a mile and a half away up the Manchester
road. The architect was John Carr, a Yorkshireman,
who also designed Harewood House, Yorkshire. The
Crescent is built in the same style as the crescents at
Bath, which spa perhaps it was meant that Buxton
should rival. The fifth Duke also had an immense
stable put up with a covered ride round so that in bad
weather well-to-do visitors of the day could do what
the poorer folk now do round the Crescent and Baths,
exercise while keeping dry and comfortable. The ride
is said to have been very fashionable and popular.
Stables and ride were all covered by a great dome. It

is 164 feet across and covers a ground floor space of nearly 18,000 superficial feet, and is believed to be the largest unsupported span in the world. This dome now shelters the patients of the excellent Devonshire Hospital, for in 1858 the entire stables were handed over by the sixth Duke of Devonshire to Buxton Bath Charity and where there had been stalls for 110 horses beds were put for 300 patients. More than 200,000 persons since then have had treatment, including a lot of army casualties during the 1914–18 war.

Many persons must have wondered why the Great Stables were built in so much better a place than the Crescent, but it was planned that the Crescent should be on a far different site, some think near where the stables were afterwards built, and it would then have looked down on the River Wye which ran where the Crescent is now and had to be hidden in a culvert, about 200 yards long. To enable the Crescent to be put on the site originally intended it was necessary to buy a small field, the greater part of the land required already belonging to the Duke, but the owner of the field demanded not less than £2,000. A very generous offer of £1,200 was made, and refused. There was deadlock and so the present site was chosen. It is probable that the extra cost of building on the lower land far exceeded £800, because the land was boggy and piles had to be driven to support the great weight of masonry. It was also necessary to move a drinking fountain, and to cut down the woodland which previously extended beside the Wye from the present Pavilion Gardens to the foot of where the station approach is. This part of Buxton might, in fact, have been even more picturesque than it is but for the dispute over one small field, the position of which even is now not known.

Adjoining the Crescent are the baths, at the Spring Gardens end the artificially warmed mineral baths, and at the Pavilion Gardens end the naturally tepid mineral baths. Fortunately, not having suffered from rheumatism or any of the other unpleasant complaints that the waters are claimed to be good for, I cannot say anything from experience about their curative powers, but I know of no indoor baths more pleasant to swim in than the natural tepid swimming pool. I never expect to see more beautiful water than that which bubbles up continually from the holes in the white-tiled bottom. It is harebell blue and brilliantly pure, and of a gracious natural warmth. After bathing I have always experienced great difficulty in keeping awake, and then follows a fine feeling of well-being.

The swimming pool building was put up by one of the Dukes of Devonshire, but on December 31st, 1904, all the baths and the Pump Room and the mineral water rights were transferred to Buxton Urban District Council for £55,000, payable over 60 years at an annual rent charge of £2,426. Payment will be completed in 1964, but before the war anyone who wanted to go into the swimming pool and had the effrontery to plank down a shilling and say "Resident" at the pay-office was allowed in for that sum instead of half a crown, which should have been the charge to non-residents. I must confess to owing something to Buxton ratepayers myself on this score and am glad to record that I have always been treated well, the attendant hosing me down with cold water after the bathe and swathing me in an ample and nicely warmed towel to go to my private sitting-room just as though I was truly one of those who paid his wages. What the charges are now for a course of treatment at the baths I have not asked, but it is safe to say that they are very different from those of 1572 when Dr Jones gives the charges as follows:

An Archbishop £5;   A Duchess £2; and
A Duke £3 10s.;   A Yeoman 12 pence.

    Although nobody seems to feel certain about why the water is warm the most probable theory is that, deep beneath, the water is turned to steam by the intense heat of the earth's centre and rises through fissures till it condenses at a point from where it flows and appears as a spring. The water is charged with radio-activity, possibly due to its passing through radium deposits. Efforts have been made to find radium at Youlgrave and in other lead mines near, though without success, and it is perhaps more probable that the water gets its radio-activity from more or less ordinary rocks, most of which contain some minute traces of radium. St Ann's Well has never been known to vary in quantity of flow and has kept almost exactly at 82 degrees Fahrenheit for as long as thermometers have been used.

    One wonders if it was hotter in Roman days, for Lucan described the water as being "extraordinary hot". When the remains of a Roman bath were discovered near by, the tiles were said to be harder than the stone itself and the red plaster as hard as brick. Dr Charles Leigh, writing in 1700, put forward the strange opinion that the plaster must have been made of "a mixture of lime and powdered tiles cemented with blood and eggs".

    There used to be an old well chapel opposite, it is believed, to where the public pump now stands and in this patients would go to give thanks and hang crutches that they no longer needed, as is still done at Lourdes. This practice seemed to some men of Lord Cromwell's like idolatry and about 1583 Sir William Bassett took all the crutches and other relics and ordered the chapel to be locked and the wells and baths to be sealed. But ideas soon change and twenty years later the baths were open again and were visited by some of Queen Elizabeth's ladies and by her prisoner, Mary Queen of Scots, who found it "incredible how the bath has soothed my nerves and dried my body of the phlegmatic humours with which, by reasons of feeble health, it was abundantly filled". It is not known why this old well chapel was pulled down. The present St Anne's Church, built in 1625, appears to have remained scarcely altered.

One of the most striking modern sights in Buxton is that of the War Memorial on the Slopes overlooking the Crescent and the well. On the front there is an angel with wide wings, holding a laurel wreath forward as though in blessing. Floodlit on the dark hillside the figure stands out austerely and with serenity, and remains in memory.

The Pavilion Gardens were laid out, and the concert hall and covered promenade put up, by a private company, but all came into the possession of Buxton Corporation in 1927, and I have thought it a pity that the grounds at least are not freely opened like any other public park. Twenty-two acres of pleasant paths, open spaces and woodland, nearly in the centre of the town, are thus shut off from many who do not always want to pay to go in. Still, I suppose that is a matter for the ratepayers to decide, but rather than pay (unless it is for some special music) I prefer to go along Broad Walk and so eventually up to Grinlow Tower, much better known as Solomon's Temple. The present tower was built with money collected in the town, but one may still go there free. The only reason suggested for the name seems to be that about 1840 the land on which the tower stands was rented by a Solomon Mycock of the Cheshire Cheese Inn, but whether he had a habit of going there, or for what reason it should be called his "temple", is lost. In 1933 two Americans tried to buy the tower, intending to have it taken down and transported home. They made an offer of about £100 but did not get it. Why they wanted it nobody knows, either.

The tower is 1,200 feet above sea-level, the most commanding building in Buxton. Elizabeth Dale advised her readers to begin their studies there with a geological map and a compass, all typical features of the county except the coal measures being in sight.

Buxton is the centre of a great lime industry. Known in the trade as "high-calcium, Buxton or white lime", the lime quarried hereabouts is used all over the world. It has a very high calcium content and is rich, or "fat", and slakes exceptionally quickly. It is the only lime suitable to be used in the refining of beet sugar. To get the limestone the rock is first "bared", that is, the soil is taken off the quarry top so that it shall not get mixed with the stone. Then "primary blasting" with high explosive brings down the rock face, the bigger lumps being split by "secondary blasting" into sizes that can be broken by hand. As much as 100,000 tons has been brought down by one primary blast, but even such a weight is quickly gone, so flourishing is the trade.

Up to well within memory limestone and other local rock for building was blasted by gunpowder. Men did it as piece work, and at weekends they would go round farms all over the district buying straw. A short tunnel having been bored, or picked, in the rock, gunpowder was poured in and a long straight straw, also filled with powder, was arranged to act as fuse. After a stopping plug had been driven into the hole, fire travelled down the straw and gave the operator time to scramble away before the charge exploded. Now all charges are fired electrically.

In May 1933 King George VI, then Duke of York, pressed a plunger in a hut in a field just above Buxton Central Quarry and fired 3,700 lb. of ammonal, bringing down 32,000 tons of limestone. This blast was fired from 600 yards away, a record distance then. While on this visit the King also went to Hindlow Quarry and had presented to him a nineteen-year-old worker who had been at his famous Southwold Camp. The two chatted together and the King said how cold he found it in Derbyshire.

The King's distance record stood for five years only, until on July 12th, 1938, Lord Stamp of Shortlands, chairman of the L.M.S. Railway Company, pressed a button on his desk at Euston and fired a £900 charge of ten tons of gunpowder 150 miles away, blowing out a whole cliff face in Caldon Low Quarry, near Ashbourne. The limestone dislodged amounted in volume to about the bulk of the St Pancras Hotel in London, and weighed 100,000 tons. Lord Stamp heard the explosion through a loudspeaker.

Lime is made by driving carbon dioxide out of the limestone by heat. In the old days the stone was burnt in open-topped kilns like very wide stone funnels. They were brutes to control and a burning took five days. I can remember seeing men at this unpleasant work and emptying kilns at Peak Forest. Now an electrical process is used, and the kilns operate continually, but some of the old workers say that none of the lime is as good as the best produced by the earlier methods.

Buxton visitors who feel that the lime works spoil too much scenery should think that employment is there for thousands of local workers.

CHAPTER IX

COUNTRY "LIKE A DRUM"

CHAPEL-EN-LE-FRITH is a usual starting place for Castleton and on my first holiday I duly took the long, slow-rising road to Rushup Edge, which later I was to learn carried so many strange cavalcades when the Chinley–Dore railway line was being made. In less than a mile one comes to the old farmhouse known as Slack Hall, with a fine chestnut tree planted on Queen Victoria's Coronation in 1837 in the grass plot behind, and a fine large yard at the side. Just inside the gateway down to Ford Hall, in a little walled enclosure, is the Quakers' Burial Ground, almost hidden in trees. There are four green stones against the wall in one corner, two against the wall on another side (one with the date 1671), and a mound where a grave was opened in 1927, and that is all. Though so much traffic passes on the road, few persons visit here; it is a forgotten place of peace.

A few steps farther up the Castleton road one looks over into the vale where Ford Hall shelters with its quiet attendant cottages and buildings. In dry summer it is often hot tramping up the long slope to Rushup and then it is pleasant to sit on the wall and watch the slim fountain rising from among rhododendrons and other shrubs in front of the hall, and see it wavering and sparkling as the slight wandering airs touch it on the shoulder, as it were, and try to nudge it over. Few halls in Derbyshire lie more cosy than this with the moors so close behind. Just a short way west is as pleasant a little valley as can be found in these parts. It is known as Happy Valley, though it is best seen not from this side but from the Chapel-en-le-Frith side, by going down Bowden Lane and up Bowden Head, leaving the lane at the top to squeeze through a narrow stile. The path goes through a close woodland and all at once one comes to a surprise view of Happy Valley, peaceful and beautiful, the centre of it all the sparkle of its trout stream. The builder of Ford Hall knew a good place and must have been a lover of quiet country. The exact date of the original building is not known, but it is thought to have been begun in the reign of Henry the Third. Ford Hall was the home of the "Apostle of the Peak", William Bagshawe, who, after being ordained a minister of the Church, refused to accept the Act of Conformity in 1662, and became a leader of Nonconformity in Derbyshire. From Ford Hall he travelled all over the district preaching, teaching, and encouraging others.

If you are not interested in these memories, before going on past Slack Hall notice the lane to the right. This goes to Sparrowpit and a short distance up it there was a great fight which is still spoken of in Chapel. One of the men was Bendigo, the Nottingham bruiser, but I have been unable to learn whom he fought. What is chiefly remembered is the crowd in the early morning, Castleton Road and the lane being choked with horse-drawn vehicles of all kinds. The fight was held here to be out of the way of the police, but with all the traffic converging on such an unusual place, at such an unusual time, surely the police for miles round must have suspected something? Whether they were afraid to interfere, or did not feel that it was very serious, I do not know, but the fight was fought to an end, Bendigo winning.

At the top of the long rise from Chapel the Castleton Road runs for nearly two miles almost level along the side of Rushup Edge. This is a bleak place in winter and when snows come deeply the farmers in the shallow on the right have a hard time. Now there is an occasional bus, but what was it like before? At the end of the long straight, the road swings sharply left and drops steeply under the shale slide of Mam Tor.

I never come this Rushup way without thinking of a friend of mine. He is now nearly seventy, a small, slight man, but in his younger days he managed (and later owned) a grocery business in Chapel, and it was part of his work to walk from Chapel one afternoon of each week round Castleton, Hope, and Edale, not taking the straight road, but going off to get orders from many outlying farms, and he did it in snow, rain, fog, or any weather. Often it would be ten at night before he got back home, and his day would start next morning again at six. Some modern hikers are proud of covering thirty hill-miles on a Sunday, but men of this type walked up to that distance nearly every day and thought nothing much about it. All my friend took in the worst weather was an umbrella and two sheets of brown paper to wrap round his legs on his short cuts to some of the farms across wet moor grass and heather. Later, not because the walking was too much for him, my friend got a horse and trap to save time, but even then the journeys were not always easy. He tells of one winter's night when he had stopped at one of the inns in Castleton. There was another Chapel man there, also with a horse and trap. My friend looked out up towards the Winniates ("Winnats" on the map) and saw darkness and coming storm and decided to travel at once, but the other preferred to stay and have another drink. Snow was drifting thickly

Entrance to Peak Cavern, Castleton

when my friend started. The drive to Chapel, seven miles, took three hours, and he was the last man through. Somewhere below the hairpin bend under Mam Tor the later man was stopped by drift. He got down to lead his horse, but somehow in the dark and banter the horse got scared and plunged madly ahead. In a moment man and horse were separated. After futilely searching round the man struggled back to the inn. The horse got to Chapel sometime next morning, being found there in the street nearly exhausted.

A much more common peril on this road was strong wind and my friend often drove in fear of his trap being blown over. On one occasion he was being followed by another man in a similar trap when he heard an unusual noise in the roaring of the wind and turned to see the other trap and horse capsizing over the bank. Although they rolled for some way, fortunately neither driver nor horse was hurt seriously.

When I was walking this way in 1943 I got into talk with "Little Jack" the roadman, who, although he was born in Manchester and was brought up a moulder, had been on this length of exposed road for twelve years. When there was wind nowhere else there was wind there, he declared. He had known several light low-horse-powered cars hurled over. Another friend has seen a railway container, of the type used for moving furniture, blown off a lorry. It was smashed to pieces, but there was nothing in it.

The sliding side of Mam Tor has given roadmakers many a problem and will probably give them many more. I wonder if it gave the early people who built the fort on the summit any trouble, or if it was their digging that started the first run of scree? Now the scree is yearly taking a little more off the remains of the ancient earthworks, as though in revenge. They

Combs Reservoir, looking north

sited their fort well, did those early men, dominating as it does the vale of Castleton and Hope, but, as I have already said, they must have been a people careless of wild weather, for on the crown of Mam Tor the winds blow even more wildly than on the road.

As he lay dying Mr Arthur Rowland Wager, of Stockport, asked that after cremation his ashes might be thrown to the winds from Mam Tor summit. Mr Wager was a member of the Manchester Wheelers' Club and held a number of cycling prizes, one for a fifty-miles race arranged by the club. He was very fond of Derbyshire and was once challenged to cycle to the top of Mam Tor and managed it. His mother, father, wife, a cycling friend, and the Rev G. P. Combe of Stockport climbed Mam Tor on July 26th, 1932, in hissing rain. There was no ceremony except a short prayer and then his father, one of the others holding his coat so that he should not be blown away, opened the box he had carried and the ashes were spilled into the winds.

It is surprising that more lives have not been lost on the side of Mam Tor, for anyone may easily go over the edge. There was at Edale a camp of Boy Scouts, two of whom were wandering on Mam Tor when a gritstone ram approached. The lads being town bred thought it looked threatening and they ran wildly away and over the edge. When we found them, attracted by their shouts, they were seventy yards or so down, afraid to stir because of the movement of shale they at once started. We got them up with ropes, but it was a ticklish job. Rhodes in his *Peak Scenery* says that though he had been told that Mam Tor was one of the Seven Wonders of the Peak, "yet we observed nothing wonderful about it, for we could not persuade ourselves of the fact that it is incessantly

98

shivering away without any diminution of its bulk", but he adds that he heard very distinctly from his bedroom in Castleton the rush of stones down the Tor slope.

The old way into Castleton on this side was through the Winniates, the steep, deep winding gorge east of the present main road. On sunny days it is often very hot and enclosed, on dull days it is very gloomy and sad, sometimes wind draws through very bitterly and this may have given it the name "Wind Gates", but at all times it is an impressive place. By climbing one of the steep sides an interesting hour may be spent looking down on the cyclists and walkers plodding through, occasionally stopping to stare at the rock towers and cliffs; or throwing stones at anything, the rock bits strewn everywhere being always tempting. It is better not to try climbing the rocks, for they break easily. There is on my desk a cutting telling of a Stockport man who one Sunday in April 1937 fell 700 feet from the Lion rock, bouncing down to the roadway, where he was picked up but died on the way to hospital.

In 1926 I went to a demonstration in favour of the Access to Mountains Bill which was held midway in the gorge. About 400 persons attended, most in rambling kit, and we listened patiently in sunshine, and I thought how strange it would have been had one of the old turnpike coaches come plodding through. How the inside passengers would have goggled from the window and how the outside people would have craned, astonished at the motley of both sexes, indeed perhaps unable at first to tell which were women and which men. Would the coach have echoed with laughter; or would the passengers have settled back in disapproving silence? I fancy the driver would have enjoyed it all tolerantly, anyway, for the old coach-drivers must have been an understanding lot. The meeting was orderly, even serious, and it seemed an appropriate place for it; one more added to the innumerable interesting pictures on which the rocks have looked down.

It is so impressive a place that it is disappointing that there appears to be only one old story about it and that not very convincing, more sordid than romantic. A man and woman, who may have been on a runaway marriage, are said to have been attacked, robbed, and killed here by five local lead miners. The authorities of those days never traced any of the murderers, but eventually the last of them, after being ten weeks on his death-bed, confessed, and from him it was learned that one of his companions had fallen to death from a precipice, another had died under a rock which fell on him near the scene of the murder, a third had hanged himself, and the fourth had died in terrible pain after contemplating suicide. The story is told luridly in *Tales and Traditions of the High Peak* by William Wood, as "the most striking instance on record of Divine judgment".

Round about and under the Winniates is cavern country. I am not one of those described by Mr J. B. Baddeley, of Guide fame, as "the subterraneously inclined", but Peak Cavern and the Blue John and Speedwell mines are sufficiently different from each other to justify a visit. There is interesting reading about all three in Mr Ernest A. Baker's *Moors, Crags and Caves of the High Peak*, from which I quote:

"The Derbyshire caverns are surpassed in brilliance by the stalactite caves of Cheddar, by the many-hued masses of incrustation in Lamb's Lair, and the snowy terraces and rich emblazonries of Swildon's Hole and other caves in Somerset. They can show nothing so grimly impressive as Gaping Ghyll and Helln Pot, in Yorkshire. But in variety of configuration, and, accordingly, in the variety of sport they offer, our caves are equal to any. Though a dry cave, the Blue John is remarkable for its diversity of interest. . . . The Speedwell is another type of cavern altogether . . . its inundated levels open into natural canals and deserted water-channels that enfold romantic possibilities of discovery. Peak Cavern . . . combines a number of features that are not often found together, and the thoroughgoing explorer must be prepared to descend swallets, to climb fissures of unknown height and to paddle his skiff into most uncanny waterways."

Mr Baker describes the "charms" of cave-hunting.

"First, of course," he says, "must be put the beauty and sublimity that lie concealed in the subterranean darkness. There is a tremendous suggestion of latent power about the rifts and cavities in the solid structure of the earth. A stream on the surface of the ground is beautiful, or may be a grand object; but put the same stream in a deep cavern, or a stream that is not half so big and powerful, and the impression it makes on the senses of those who see and hear it is incomparably greater. A little waterfall enclosed by the resonant, bell-shaped walls of a cave awakens thunderous echoes that rival the noise of a great cataract; the far-heard muttering, the terrible crescendo as we draw nearer and nearer, and the deafening and soul-shaking voice of the imminent torrent plunging into dark abysms, is a sound never to be forgotten, a sound to haunt bad dreams. But not merely these gloomy streams, with their black swallet-holes, strange disappearances, and stormy descents, are enveloped in a mystery that fascinates while it awes; it is the same with all things underground. Every cave is a cave of illusions. Mere size and height measured in so many feet are as nothing compared with the vastness of the impression that it makes with its hidden distances, impenetrable shadows, and the vagueness of its fugitive outlines. Ordinary means of illumination reveal only the area immediately around one, leaving the remoter spaces massed in deeper shadow. The most powerful searchlight cannot utterly dethrone the majesty of darkness. Then there is the zest of possible discovery. At any moment you may break into some treasure chamber of natural beauty never yet disclosed to human eye; you are ever on the tip-toe of expectation. And there is an immense difference between the public shows of a cave that has been open and accessible for years, a crust of dirt and soot covering every inch of the dulled stalactites, and the pure, unsullied beauty of these crystallisations fresh from Nature's laboratory."

All that I have seen of these caves has been the "public shows", so that I cannot write as enthusiastically. Mr Baker describes the Blue John mine as dry, but my recollection is of many drips from the roof and of portions of very muddy floor, though I know, of course, what he means. This is to me the most interesting of the mines because of the amethystine spar that comes out of it, the most beautiful coloured crystalline stone in the world, I am told. Fluor-spar is found in many places, but only here under Tray Cliff with such rich and varied colours.

The Romans, who took lead from this part, knew of the spar and it is said that ornaments of it were found in Pompeii. Pliny mentions vases which are believed to have been made of this spar, for one of the biggest and best of which Petronius gave 300 talents (£30,000). When he was condemned to death by Nero, Petronius broke the vase, supposing that the emperor coveted it. For another vase Nero is reported to have paid nearly £50,000.

From Roman times until the eighteenth century no other mention of the spar has been discovered. One version is that Lord Duncannon in 1743 was riding down Eyam Dale when his horse kicked a piece of rock and the sparkle of the scar catching his attention he put the stone in his pocket and later had an ornament made of it. Another version is that in 1770 a messenger in a cart going up the Winniates noticed some blue stone, and thinking it would look nice in a garden, picked up a number of pieces and took them to Earl Fitzwilliam's gardens at Wentworth. One day a visitor from Rotherham, Mr Platts, selected some of the stones and had two salt-cellars made of them. These were later seen by Mr Robert Hall, of Castleton, who knew where the stone was from and later started the making of vases and other ornaments. This Mr Hall was the father of geology in Derbyshire and on his grave near the south-east corner of Castleton graveyard it is stated: "Born of parents in humble life, and having a large family to provide for, yet he devoted himself to the study of geology for 70 years with powers of originality and industry rarely surpassed." The first ornaments made of the blue spar after its rediscovery were all clumsy and solid, very different from later bowls and ornaments which let light through and show the lustre. The spar is very friable to work, and is seldom found in large pieces. The largest uncut specimen weighed nearly 5 hundredweight and was found in 1813. The largest vase known is 2 feet high and has a diameter of 14½ inches. At one time the spar was very much sought after by the French who called it blue-yellow, that is *bleu-jaune*, which is supposed soon to have been corrupted here to Blue John; though some say the spar was given that name to disinguish it from "Black Jack", the local name for Derbyshire black marble.

The supply of Blue John is believed now to be very limited and the guide who took me down the last time told me that the mine was worked on one day only in the year, this by agreement with some authority, I forget which.

During the war almost every particle of radium used in Manchester's hospitals — £40,000 worth — was stored in the mine in a small cavern known as the New Dining Room. It was lined with many tons of lead bricks and though two land-mines were dropped near the mine entrance the delicate equipment hidden 200 feet below was undisturbed. All the cavern guides were sworn and faithfully kept the secret for over five years. When visitors noticed the locked door and asked what was behind they were told that it only led to some disused workings that were not yet ready for the public to see.

Although the Blue John mine is one of the easiest to visit in its "public shows", even so simple a descent does not suit everybody. I once started to take a relative down and she had only got to the foot of the first ladder when she said she would have to go to the surface or she would faint. We had difficulty in getting her up. I find walking underground very tiring, and have been glad to get out into the open again, even though a blizzard of part sleet, part snow, was blowing. It was this mine that inspired Conan Doyle's short story, "The Terror of Blue John Gap". Probably the author visited the district about 1908. He makes the hero describe it as follows:

"On each side are the fantastic limestone hills, formed of rock so soft that you can break it away with your hands. All this country is hollow. Could you strike it with some gigantic hammer it would boom like a drum, or possibly cave in altogether and expose some huge subterranean sea."

I cannot miss one more quotation, this from Dr Charles Leigh, who wrote in 1700 about Derbyshire's "most amazing vaults in the Universe that are Natural and not Artificial". He says

"it is very probable that these Cavities have continued in those unpolish'd Mountains ever since that terrible Deluge" (described in the Bible) "and in my Sentiments absolutely demonstrates the Veracity of it; for so far as I am able to conceive, it is not in the Power of Human Understanding to give any rational Account of those prodigious Cavities, but either by Earthquakes or that general Inundation; but since there is no Historian that gives an Account of any such Earthquake in this Island, and that by the Experience of those which have happen'd in all preceding Ages in these temperate Climates, we may reasonably suppose there never were any such. I adhere therefore to the latter Hypothesis, and do suppose that at the Universal Destruction, the Strata of the whole Globe were broke asunder, most of them lying in a shelving or dipping Posture, as in all the Quarries we find at this Day they do; it is probable therefore that they tossing to and fro in the Flood upon the receding of the Waters, most of these Strata lying shelving, sometimes Two opposite Summits convened and in that terrible Confusion wedg'd themselves together, and by that means might easily form those prodigious Arches and Cavities which in our Days we observe in these Mountains. These Phaenomenas, if I mistake not, absolutely evince the Universatility of a Deluge."

I had not thought of that before I read Dr Leigh, but there it is.

The oldest lead mine round Castleton is the Odin Mine, believed to have been worked by the Saxons. One of the remarkable things about the early miners is how they penetrated so far. Up-to-date cave-hunters with all the latest aids and appliances are continually coming on signs in the remotest places of men now long forgotten. How they got to and worked in some of these places is a mystery, though it is supposed that there have been subsidences and changes due to water action which may have made big differences in the underground layout, yet one cannot help but feel that some of those early explorers and workers must have been really heroic, defying not only physical perils but evil spirits of the underworld which to them probably seemed even more terrible.

The chief feature of the village of Castleton is its castle, now a "national monument". It was built, says Sir Walter Scott in his novel *Peveril of the Peak*, "upon the principles on which an eagle selects her eyre". On top of its steep hill with the precipice descending to the Devil's Hole on one side and the narrow ravine of Cave Dale on another, it is an ideal defensive position, though I have climbed into it from the hill extension. Very little besides the keep and a broken wall remains, and it seems unlikely that it was ever a castle of great importance or ever withstood any long siege. Sir Walter Scott never visited Derbyshire and he misnamed the castle. Its true name is Peak Castle, not Peveril. How many know that Sir Walter was nicknamed Peveril of the Peak by friends and sometimes playfully signed himself "Thine, Peveril"?

When William the Conqueror made a grant of some of this district to William Peveril, an illegitimate son, as part of his barony, there was only a stockaded town with a ditch all round, which is said to have been still traceable in 1840. William Peveril built a castle there, some of the wall that remains possibly being part of it, but the keep was not put up till 1177. The walls of the keep are eight feet thick and the cost was £135, which Dr Cox puts as equal to £3,000 of our money. Henry II had special apartments made on the hill below so that he could come and supervise the building of it. He seems to have had a liking for Castleton, for he visited it a number of times, in 1157 receiving the submission of Malcolm the Maiden, King of Scotland, here. No doubt the chief attraction to Henry II, King John and Henry III, who also several times stayed at Castleton, was the hunting round about. There were herds of wild ponies, many wolves, and one writer says that the number of red deer was so great that they trampled men and dogs to death in their wild flight. Henry II was so jealous of his rights that the people who lived in the forest hardly dare cut a bough without royal sanction, and death was the punishment for killing a deer. Red deer continued plentiful in the district till James I's time, when a great many perished in an unusually bitter snow winter, but from 1264, when Henry III last visited, Castleton falls out of royal records and it is difficult now to think of the village as ever having been a place of state importance and bustle. The railway is still far enough off to leave it very quiet on most weekdays, though at weekends and holidays visitors of many sorts sometimes monopolise it.

A famous occasion in Castleton is Garland Day, May 29th, known elsewhere as Oak-apple Day. The garland is a big bell-shaped affair, the flowers being threaded on a wire frame. The weight is considerable, and the man who wears it has to have help to get it over his head. Entirely hidden, he then rides on horseback round the village with his queen, usually a youth in woman's clothes. Children do Morris dances round a Maypole and there is a band of sorts, which I have found usually more amusing than musical. The traditional tune (which soon gets on one's mind!) is known as "Pudding Baked in th' Lantern". A man who learnt it in his youth told me that the first verse was:

> Aa dunna know; An dunna care,
> What they do i' Bradda (Bradwell)
> Piece o' beef an' an old cow's yead,
> And a puddin' baked in a lantern.

What the significance is in connection with King Charles II, I cannot suggest, nor have I been able to get information about any other verses. The people of Bradwell, close to, call the tune rather disrespectfully "Th' Roity Tootio!" and a Chapel-en-le-Frith man, asked to describe the festival, did it as follows: "A band playin' nobbut two tunes, th'owd un an' t'other, both alike, and a damn fool sittin' on a 'oss wi' half-a-ton o' flowers on 'is yead." Some say that the Garland

Tune is very similar to the Cornish Floral Dance, and that it was introduced by Cornish lead miners who settled in Castleton district. If so, the slight differences in melody would be explained by its being handed down for some time by ear before being put into manuscript. The Garland Man with his retinue stops at various places as he goes round the village, and if he is offered a drink, then the garland is hoisted while he takes it and you get a glimpse of red and sweaty features. The bandsmen, too, often require refreshment. I have known occasions when the band has dwindled to one fiddler scraping away valiantly at "Pudding Baked in th' Lantern". Sometimes towards the end of its journey the garland, I have been told, sways curiously, and this may be due to the rider's fatigue. Finally the garland is hoisted by a pulley to the parapet of the tower of the Church of St Edmund, where it is left till it withers. During the late war there was danger that the Garland ceremony might be discontinued, but this raised local feeling and the celebrations were improved instead of languishing.

In the vestry of Castleton Church is a library of 600 volumes, including a "breeches Bible" and other rarities. There is a lepers' window looking towards the altar, and the barn at Spittal (Hospital?) Farm, by Spittal Bridge, is said once to have been a leper hospital.

Castleton seems always to have been a place for some good characters who knew how to make the best of visitors. James Croston in *On Foot Through the Peak* tells of "Daft Sammy", who used to levy a kind of blackmail on everybody who went to the Castle. There was a man whom I shall not name who twenty years ago was farming well and always talked genuine, broadest "Darbyshire". Some years ago some friends went down one of the mines and were struck by the guide's rather "posh" speech. "Fancy", he said, "the disappointment of miners searching for lead when they suddenly found this"; and he switched on his power lamp with reflector and everybody stared into the roof of one of the finest caverns. Yet my friends were even more astonished to recognise in the light the farmer whose dialect they had enjoyed so much so many years before. When they had told him who they were and were talking with him later privately he explained that taking visitors round the caverns was much more profitable than farming.

The latest cavern opened to the public at Castleton is Treak Cavern, which is also the easiest to visit. Fuller descriptions of all these underground " shows " will be found in *Caves and Caverns of Peakland.*

set store by the one which was lost?' A farmer's son answered: "'Appen it were th'tup.'"

There it is, slightly utilitarian, earthy, and yet so astute, spontaneous, and, well, good.

In the village school at Combs a boy who regularly arrived with tousled hair and who was regularly reprimanded by the teacher, was asked again: "Did you comb your hair *this* morning, Arthur?" and promptly replied: "Yes, miss, I commed it wi' th' brush."

A farmer and his wife invited to a wedding got there very late, too late for the ceremony but in time for the breakfast. When asked why he was so late the farmer replied: "It were Hannah's fault; oo (she) winna have th' clock fast enough. We keep it three hours fast, but if oo'd let me put it on four, we met 'a get 'ere."

Derbyshire people as a whole do not mind laughing at themselves. Sarcasm is generally lost on them. I well remember a woman leisurely going with cows up a narrow lane from the farmyard to pasture. If a beast stopped to eat, she did not worry. A highly polished, expensive-looking car was behind. Eventually the driver, leaning through the window, said: "My good woman, I hope you're not going to Buxton with them." "I hope so too," said the woman, making not the slightest increase in her speed or any attempt to make way. Eventually the cows turned into the field, the car went ahead with an angry toot and a spurning of the macadam on the seven miles to Buxton, and the woman smiled placidly as she hooked the gate.

This is the kind of humour that you do not hear about till you become one with the villagers. Thoreau says: "If . . . you wish to explore a given neighbourhood, go and live in it, i.e. get your living in it. Fish in its streams, hunt in its forests, gather fuel from its

8* 113

Typical Low Peak country beside the Sheffield–Hathersage road on Millstone Edge

water, its woods, cultivate the ground, and pluck the
wild fruits, etc., etc. This will be the surest and
speediest way to those perceptions you covet." With
this I like to couple that advice from Richard Jefferies:
"To traverse the paths day by day, and week by week;
to keep an eye ever on the fields from year's end to
year's end, is the one only method of knowing what
really is in or comes to them. That the sitting gambler
sweeps the board is true of these matters." So am I
sure that the only way to get to know any county is to
live in it, and more than usually so is this true of such
a county as Derbyshire. A very full and I think very
interesting book could be written on the village of
Combs alone, and in a sense it would be a book of all
Derbyshire, for every true village must be an epitome
of the district of which it is an integral part. And by
true village I mean one inhabited chiefly by persons
who earn their livings there or round about. Too many
Derbyshire villages near Manchester and Sheffield
and other towns have been, since motor-cars were
mass-produced cheaply, invaded by persons who only
wish to sleep and holiday in the country, and who do
not in any real sense partake of the indigenous life of
the villages. These persons never will be anything
more than strangers. They will never be let into the
spontaneous, earthy humour of the villagers, they will
never know all the tales and possibilities of the places
in which they "live".

Twenty-five years ago Combs had hardly begun to be
known by motorists and a record of it as I found
it may serve as a more intimate picture of Derbyshire
village life generally.

The print of a hen's foot suggests the layout of the
village roads. The single back spur is the road coming
in from the Horwich End–Buxton main road. The

three toes are roads that split away from the Green, each road going narrower and poorer-surfaced till they all lead out on to high moorland and become for the general motorist impossible. At the Green, which is the centre of the star of the foot, is the Post Office, merely a wooden hut, lit then by a suspended oil lamp, where groceries and bread and sweets are also sold; and across the road is the substantially built inn, the Beehive, which has a swinging sign painted by Mr T. C. Dugdale which is worth looking at. A very short distance away on the left of the main, or middle, toe of the foot is the small Methodist Chapel which is also the village day-school, used from a year or two ago for primary children only, but previously serving children of all ages. Nearer the Green is a row of three stone cottages. There are two single cottages, a house, and two farmhouses, and these together make the real nucleus of the village. Throughout the valley are scattered other houses and cottages and, of course, farms. Twenty-five years ago nearly everybody in the valley was connected with farming in some way, though there was a local carpenter, a small contractor of sorts, and one or two men who worked on the railway. Two men went regularly into Chapel-en-le-Frith and were employed at the Ferodo factory, the original brake lining that gave that firm its start having been invented in Combs, at Rye Flatt, half-way up the left toe of our hen's-foot map.

The village had its own small, but paying, annual agricultural show, which had grown out of competitions held in the Beehive, where men had bet on who could bring in the biggest swede-turnip or the best cabbage. Hot-pot suppers held in the Chapel were very popular, as were occasional concerts, the players being out of the valley or from no farther off than

Chapel-en-le-Frith, or Whaley Bridge. Beside one of the cottages near the Green was a rather outsize wooden garage, known to many as "Combs Hall", and here on one weekday evening a month a church service was held, and throughout the winter there were regular whist-drives. If the night permitted and there was a crowd, often the wide double-doors had to be left open and some tables would have to be on the gravel path in the moonlight. Episcopalians and Nonconformists attended all entertainments, whether in the Chapel or in the "Hall"; everybody knew everybody else, and if anyone came in from the main road, it was generally easy to guess where they would be going. The inn was a free house, where a good useful country meal could be got at almost any time. The proprietor was homely, genuine, and sufficiently go-ahead to stock the little Brookhouses Brook that runs close by with trout to attract a paying angler guest or two.

Every morning about ten the village woke up, as it were, in a very pleasant way. From all round about farmers and their lads and girls and dogs gathered on the Green with iron-shod traps and carts drawn by shaggy horses. From the near farms men would come trundling churns on two-wheeled iron "dandys", for they all came here to hand over the previous night's, and the morning's, milk to the company's lorry-man. While everybody waited there was gossip and argument and laughter, a little banter among the dogs, and then in the distance would be heard the noisy rush of the motor-lorry and everybody would look up the larch avenue towards the railway bridge. Down would charge the lorry, curving to a sudden stop almost on the Beehive doorstep, for the young drivers liked to show off. Then would begin a bustle and banging and shouting as empties were almost thrown off and carts were backed alongside for full churns to be transferred. Horses were sometimes stupid, dogs got in the way, if there was a holiday children dodging round and under the lorry were nearly sure to bump into somebody at an awkward moment and get scuffed, if they weren't nearly back-broken by a falling churn. For ten minutes or so it would look as busy as could be, till finally the back-board was slammed up, the iron pins were dropped in, and away the lorry went with a heavier roar. The driver, having noticed perhaps a particularly nice girl watching, would spectacularly miss the hub of one of the more ramshackle traps by two inches. The scared farmer would swear competently, but the lorry would derisively splutter blue exhaust fumes and go careering under the larch trees. Then the gathering began to break up. Farmers fished out crumpled papers from cross-pockets and found what they had to buy at the shop, lads grinned and winked, Molly looked away but wondered if Jim would be where he said at night at the time he had said, and what the picture would be like. Worn wheels rolled slowly away, nags clopped thoughtfully up the three lanes, the shop shut, a cat came from the corner and lapped spilled milk. The labrador on the big stone step in front of the inn watched her lazily, let his rear droop, scratched with his left back leg after a flea behind his ear, lay down and went to sleep. It became very sunny and silent, as though all the day's work was done.

That kind of scene happened all over Derbyshire till the Milk Marketing Board began. Now farmers stay on their own farms and milk-lorries journey to them all in turn. It's more efficient, though not nearly as picturesque.

Combs appears more self-contained in its comfortable valley because of the embanked railway that goes across the mouth of it and shuts off the wider strath of Chapel-en-le-Frith. When this line was built—the old L.N.W.R. line from London Road, Manchester, to Buxton—there was difficulty with a bridge known locally as Dickie's. Near by is Tunstead Farm where lies Dickie's skull. How old it is, nobody knows, but when it was examined some years ago by a medical man it was said to show no sign of decay and he thought it was the skull of a girl of about eighteen. One theory is that it may have been taken in the forgotten past from a tumulus on the hillside above. The skull had a reputation for strange powers and when the trouble arose it was at once said that it was because Dickie objected to the line. Eventually the site of the bridge was moved (there was quicksand at the original site) and there has been no trouble since, but twenty years ago it was still possible to find people who would tell tales of what Dickie had done, tales which they told with faith. One which I liked was about the days when farmers had to take their butter and eggs by horseback along the old road by Whitehall to Buxton. The then tenant of Tunstead Farm was riding back with his wife up behind him. She was tired after the long day, but it was her duty at every gate to get down, hold it open, and fasten it again when her husband had ridden through.

"I wish Dickie would oppen 'em," said the weary woman, getting ready to drop off again.

As she did so the gate obligingly opened. The woman could almost have bitten her tongue out for having spoken. After that every gate to the farm opened in the same way, but the good woman instead of being grateful reached home nearly in a collapse.

Higher on the hill above Tunstead is Thornylee
Farm, known locally by the older people as Clog Hall
because of a pair of old clogs which were kept under
the stairs. A woman who often went there as a girl
says that everybody believed that the clogs had similar
powers to Dickie's. Eventually the clogs became so
worm-eaten and dirty that it was decided that they
must be destroyed. My friend remembers how scared
she and others felt, and how after the clogs had been
burnt they waited in suspense expecting they knew
not what. To the surprise of most persons in the neighbourhood nothing dire ever happened. My friend says
that as she remembers them now, the clogs were
exactly like an old pair of Dutch "clumpers", but how
they came to be preserved in the remote farmhouse
she is unable to hazard even a guess.

Beliefs such as these are typical of hill places where
sombre mists, wild storms, and long winters often
enforced isolation and encouraged brooding and
strange thoughts in the days before the wireless could
be switched on to bring in the latest swing music and
how to cook Chinese rissoles.

Thirty-five years ago nobody in Combs and such
villages thought anything of having to walk five or six
miles to Buxton or Whaley Bridge for an evening's
entertainment, and five or six miles back in darkness.
The coming of bus services after 1918 caused a great
change, though the nearest service to Combs remained
a mile and a quarter distant. Now everybody goes
shopping somewhere: then shopping was mostly by
order, or from travelling carts. I do not think that life
is any more enjoyable; it is merely different. Certainly
feeding is not as good as it was, though it is more
varied. They made their own butter and cheese in
those days; sometimes, generally for Christmas, it was

sage cheese (or "Christmas" cheese), which is now almost forgotten. I have not even tasted sage cheese, but those who remember say it looked a bit like gorgonzola though the Oxford Dictionary describes it as "mottled". In 1939 I read that there was still a small market for this cheese in London. One Jermyn Street shop, for instance, had two cheeses for its Christmas season each weighing 10 lb. and like a "Cheshire loaf". The only place where it was then known to be made was Derbyshire, but I have never known it to be made in the last twenty-five years in Combs.

Oatcakes were another of the good old delicacies—yes, I think it is right to call them that. Generally they were made in special outside ovens of brick, which were little round towers with an open top and an iron plate part way down. One day a week, often on a Friday, a fire was lit underneath and a seven-days' supply of cakes was made, a great stack of them, which nevertheless would often be gone long before the next Friday, so that an extra baking would be necessary. There was nothing but oatmeal and water in the mixing. A tablespoonful was dropped on the hot plate, where it spread like a pancake. When nicely browned it was skilfully turned. Taken out hot, spread with yellow home-made butter in clots, or with honey, syrup, or black cattle-treacle, nothing could be more delicious, especially on a fine frosty morning. Although oatcakes are still popular, the outside ovens are gone and the trade has passed to the bakers, many of whom unfortunately think that oatcakes need baking-powder. As a result most modern oatcakes are floury and lack the old nutty flavour. Another excellent way of eating oatcakes on a winter's morning is to have them straight out of the frying-pan browned with good dip from slightly salty home-cured bacon or ham, but the modern cakes soak up too much fat and get greasy in the mouth; the old crunchy cake turned up so crisp and tasty one could go on eating till one felt ashamed.

A tale is told of a Cockney who came to work at Chapel-en-le-Frith and stayed in digs, where he got to like oatcakes so much that he sent a parcel home. When he went on holiday six months later he found the oatcakes set out on the sideboard under the flower-vases: after some discussion his people had decided that they must be mats!

Oatcakes have been eaten in Derbyshire from very early times. John Houghton writing in 1693 (see page 283) said that oatcakes were the bread generally lived on then in all the northern parts of the county. Sir Humphry Davy, the "father" of agricultural chemistry in this country, has an interesting note in his book written in 1813: "I have been informed by Sir Joseph Banks that the Derbyshire miners in winter prefer oatcakes to wheaten bread; finding that this kind of nourishment enables them to support their strength and perform their labours better. In summer they say oatcakes heat them, and they then consume the finest wheaten bread they can procure."

This fact about oatcakes being preferred by miners, among whom, I think, quarrymen are meant to be included, can be confirmed today. There is no work harder than mining or quarrying and the men must have food that will last. With oatcakes they class cheese; there is nothing else as good. After an ordinary meal they feel empty, but with oatcakes and cheese they can work all day. One of the quarrymen's grievances during the war was that they were not allowed extra cheese like farm-workers.

There are no quarrymen in Combs, though there were quarries not far off, but all the old houses and

farms were gritstone-built, many of them from stone
cut close by, as is shown by the holes in the hillsides,
long ago grassed over. All the fields were fenced with
stone and most of the farmers could build a dry wall,
though a preference was beginning to be shown by
their sons for fencing-posts and wire.

A dry wall well put together will last for a century
or more, but in a wet season sometimes the foundation
softens and then trouble starts. The wall loses shape
and balance, lengths fall out, and the remaining portions are weakened. The hill sheep that climb walls as
easily as most persons go up stairs soon topple a
weakened wall, and so there is nothing to do but build
a new wall on a fresh foundation—or put up a fence.
Although the drystone walls look somewhat haphazard
they are all as true as possible to certain standards:
height, say, 5 feet (which is the common height);
width at base, 22 inches; width at top, 10 inches;
similar proportions for other heights. Every joint in a
course should be overlapped by a stone in the course
above, and care must be taken to put in enough
"throughs" or " keystones" regularly, these going
from front to back, that is, right through, binding the
structure. The coping stones, or "copers", are all put
on their edge, binding into one another, and are all
"throughs", giving the top, and the whole wall, its
final strength. Masons used to mortar can very seldom
make a good drystone wall. All the walls round Combs
are gritstone; walls of limestone are even more difficult
to build, limestone being much more irregular in
shape.

So well could experts build in past times that there
is a story of a wall on the Duke of Rutland's estate that
the huntsman's horse could not jump and his followers
could not push down, so that a man had to be em-

ployed specially before the next hunt to lower the wall
at certain parts. Walls built by a certain Wagstaffe
seventy to a hundred years ago in the Biggin-by-
Hartington district can still be picked out because of
their excellence. This Wagstaffe did miles of walling.

It is the old walls with undermined foundations that
are such a temptation to children and others who come
from the towns to find enjoyment in the country. I
add my plea for thoughtfulness and care. Before climbing a wall, test with your hands to see that it will
support your weight. It is not fair to the farmer or
landowner to break his wall and may easily lead to
serious loss. If in climbing a stone is dislodged, put it
back. Walls at the edge of a steep slope are the greatest
temptation and a good many fields have been littered
with stones and made unmowable, but there is another
danger. I once saw stones being pushed off the wall
by the old tramway above Barmour Clough. They
bounced grandly down the steep wooded side and one
crashed only a foot behind a cyclist going down the
road, as he was entitled to, at a fine speed. A second
sooner, and the stone might have caused a death.

A girl born and brought up near Dove Holes, whom
I took round some of the beautiful Lancashire Fylde
country, exclaimed: "Oh, isn't it lovely not to see any
walls." She had tired of them. I have never got like
that. I like to see them in their strange shapes over the
hillsides, netting the farms together. Although I know
that they were not all built simply as fences, but often
as a means of getting rid of stones off nearby ground,
I still cannot understand why many of the walls were
built where they are. Some go up slopes of as much as
one inch in four where there does not seem to be any
necessity. Were they built as the result of a challenge
between men, or between a man and his own building

ability? I cannot say. But there they still stand, examples of craftsmanship at its best.

It is usual to talk of these walls as grey, but that is slipshod. Even the gritstone is seldom true grey. There are pink gritstones, black ones, some blue, and even some lemon tinted; and then on top they soon take fine lichens and dwarf mosses and ferns and such plants as stonecrop and Herb Robert. The limestone walls in particular seem to suit some of the most velvety and greenest mosses and are well worth examining by woodsides.

Mosses, indeed, are one of the beauties of the type of country about Combs. There is a shoulder of Ladder Hill above Long Lane, which I always visited at certain times just for its many colours of mosses mixed with the heather and bilberry. I was not the only regular visitor, for every year it was a favourite haunt of curlews at their nesting time. Curlews go naturally with stone walls and mosses, and to the man who loves hills there is no more inspiring call than that of the curlew heard perhaps in mist or out of thickening twilight. He is the tireless watcher of hills and an alert picture he makes as sentinel on a wall top, occasionally opening his long curved beak to send out his flute-like and long-travelling warning. You must stay still for a very long time to satisfy the suspicions of a curlew near his nest. He is not one who readily accepts the idea that a man may climb a long way just to admire colours on a hillside.

On the hills ever-present friends in summer are the meadow-pipits. They flit up from every heather clump and their quick trill of song, or more common plaintive *Peep, peep!* become a familiar association with thoughts of high country. On the moors there are, too, red grouse and an occasional blackcock, but these fly

straight away, often with disconcerting explosive call
and wing-beat, and show no real interest in men and
cannot be written of in any very friendly way. Nor
can the magpies which with steady flight and long tail
are a familiar sight dropping from view over the slopes.

Combs is typical of dozens of other North Derbyshire villages in having a variety of bird life from
highland to lowland. On Meveril Brook the dipper
may be watched. I have seen several wheatears,
though they are not common. Along Combs Edge in
the cliffs jackdaws and kestrels nest, and there are
occasional sparrow-hawks. Above the station at Chapel-
en-le-Frith South, which serves Combs, there is a
fairly large rookery and I have spent many interesting
hours in spring on the wall by the road up to Bank
Hall watching the excursions the birds make all over
the valley after food; the road gives a kind of front
gallery view. From there you can see Combs Reservoir
glinting between its bushes. This mile-long stretch of
water gives to the valley the last touch of beauty. It
also brings a number of birds that seldom visit other
parts of the county. The great crested grebe is quite
common and is a pleasure to watch. The willows on
the main-road side of the water are very popular with
wild duck (chiefly mallard, with a few teal and widgeon
in bad weather periods), though not so much so as in
the 1920's when the people then tenanting Bridgefield
Farm made great efforts to increase the number of
ducks, actually for shooting, though this was never a
success. Redshanks and sandpipers frequent the water
in spring and no doubt nest near by, though I have
never found their nests. In the alders on the Ladder
Hill side of the reservoir is a favourite feeding ground
of tits, the blue, the great, and the coal-tit, but I have
never seen long-tailed tits there though they visit the

near-by Valley of Goyt in flocks in winter. A flock of siskins visited Combs Reservoir in the winter of 1938.

Every summer a kingfisher or two were to be seen along Meveril Brook, and sometimes could be approached very closely. Half-way along the reservoir side in the brook was a regular standing place of herons, probably because from there they had a good view of the paths as well as a good place for spotted trout. It used to be fun to stalk them, and then see them tumble into the air, as it were, when they found one almost on them.

Bullfinches are so common in the south that they are scarcely noticed, but I shall never forget the pleasure of looking up from work in my orchard hut and seeing a pair swinging among the loganberry canes almost against the window. They stayed about and I watched them for some time, but never saw any in the district again, though a schoolmaster friend told me that he had occasionally seen bullfinches in the sheltered corner of hollies at the near end of the reservoir where the footpath leaves the main road to go by Brookhouses Brook. Similarly, I knew tree-pipits so well in Cheshire that I scarcely thought about them, but the spring that a tree-pipit nested and sang below Bank Hall, soaring from a beech tree above brilliant buttercups, is also a happy memory. And I cannot end about Combs birds without mentioning the wagtails, always favourites for gracefulness and cheerful agility. Yellow and pied wagtails were often visitors on the lawn; but for the grey we had to go farther.

Although jackdaws were not particularly plentiful at Combs, they are too typical of most upland Derbyshire villages not to have special mention. Their querulous crying over the roofs is the most familiar bird sound there. They seem to think that chimney pots are put for their benefit. A contractor in Chapel-en-le-Frith often had a man working on little else for two or three weeks in the nesting season than putting wire-netting over pots to keep jackdaws out. The 'daws go down and build in angles in the chimneys. One householder rang for help and had a nest taken out and his pot wired, and two days later his neighbour rang for help: the 'daws had simply moved next door !

A man working on a roof told me that he watched a pair of jackdaws on a neighbouring chimney deliberately plucking at a newly wired pot all of one day. After twenty minutes or so the birds would fly off for a rest, but as soon as they came back they attacked the wire again. He did not see the birds break the wire, but he did not doubt that they would keep at it till they succeeded.

Often, with warmer weather coming, the fact that birds have nested in a chimney is not found out till autumn when a fire is lit for the first time for months. Then the chimney will not draw, smoke crowds down. Unless the fire is quickly raked out, everywhere becomes saturated with smoke, and tempers hot up. So well blocked was one chimney that a friend of mine went to, that he could not push the obstruction down from above but had to get under the roof and take bricks out of the chimney. He got three full buckets of sticks and debris away. The job took three hours, while the jackdaws stood on the chimney top and protested. Often the only way to keep a seldom-used room free is to burn paper or other rubbish up the grate at least once a week throughout the nesting time.

Sometimes all the jackdaws of a village will fly high above the roofs, usually in an evening, and then they are amusing and interesting to watch, dodging, twisting, turning, diving, and all the time gossiping together at the tops of their voices. Sometimes individuals will close their wings and drop headlong as though about to crash to death, though they never do, but fly up again chuckling about it.

Dr Cox says that Derbyshire has about 235 "well-assured species", but there are many birds and also few birds. The few are the ones that we know best and love for some private reason, and those are the ones I have mentioned. Readers who want more should see *Birds of Derbyshire* by F. B. Whitlock. Good though this book is, unfortunately it is rather out of date, and if somebody were able to add information from 1893, when it was published, up to now, it would be of great interest. Whitlock, for instance, records the commonness of the corn-crake in Derbyshire—and I remember it fairly common round Combs—but it has disappeared. The last I heard was near Baghouse in June 1937.

Goldfinches, which had gone down in numbers when Whitlock wrote, seem to be increasing again; and I read in the *Manchester Guardian* of a great grey shrike being seen in February 1939 in South Derbyshire, a report that would have been very interesting to Whitlock, showing that although it was very rare in his time this bird is not yet to be crossed off. Also to Whitlock's list of visits of the white-tailed eagle to North Derbyshire in 1892, there is at least one more to be added, one being seen in March 1939; and there have been, no doubt, other visits.

W. H. Hudson knew a lot about Derbyshire and there is a good chapter in his book *Adventures among Birds* on "Birds of the Peak", and another chapter telling what he learned, while at a "small hovel of a farm-house" on Axe Edge, about the ring-ouzel. He found between forty and fifty breeding pairs within easy distance of where he stayed. Best of all I like his

Fly-fishing in the Derwent

chapter in *A Traveller in Little Things* where he
listened to a blackbird at the top of the village street
at "Chilmorton":

"In the upper branches a blackbird was trolling
out his music in his usual careless leisurely manner;
when I stopped under it the singing was suspended
for half a minute or so, then resumed, but in a
lower key, which made it seem softer, sweeter,
inexpressibly beautiful.

"There are beautiful moments in our converse
with nature when all the avenues by which nature
comes to our souls seem one, when hearing and
seeing and smelling and feeling are one sense, when
the sweet sound that falls from a bird is but the
blue of heaven, the green of earth, and the golden
sunshine made audible. Such a moment was mine
as I stood under the elms listening to the blackbird."

To complete this brief record of Combs life there
are the fish and wild animals to tell of. In Meveril
Brook, as others besides the herons knew, trout were
plentiful, though usually wary. I often thought how
tantalising they must be, basking in the amber-tinted
water, to the many fishers on the railway side of the
reservoir who sometimes strolled up the bank from
their rods (left in a crotch with bell in case anything
happened!). In the reservoir, nothing; there in the
brook where the club members were not permitted to
fish, trout in dozens. How many were poached under
these circumstances I cannot guess.

The reservoir at one time must have held many
good fish, but though in the years I lived close by I
was very often round the water I never saw a single
fish landed. At one time it was a well-known place
for trout, but then pike appeared; it is alleged that

9   129

*Drowned village—Derwent Church spire as it was in Ladybower
Reservoir*

they were put in by some persons who had a grievance against the then holder of the fishing rights. Pike became so plentiful that I have been told that one man who went round spinning got twenty-seven in the day. Then, just before the 1914 war, came a serious drought. The lake shrank to about a hundred square yards between high banks of mud, and in this area seethed all the fish. It was only necessary to scoop with a net and something would be got out. People came from miles round and great catches were made in various ways. After that for many years it was hardly worth fishing, till gradually the water began to recover. Then it was discovered that the dam had begun to leak, and to enable repairs to be made the water was lowered by opening the special valve. Unfortunately no netting was put down and thousands of fish, especially small fry, were swilled away. I saw the runner down towards Horwich End strewn with stranded, dying fish of all sizes. A few fry were caught to restock Shallcross Pond above Horwich End, but the rest that got to the Goyt would be poisoned below New Mills by effluent. Since then angling at Combs has been very unprosperous-looking.

"If the pool was well stocked with trout, and the coarse fish greatly diminished in number, Combs Fishery would give very excellent sport to the fly-fisher," wrote Walter M. Gallichan in 1905, and I think that is true today, especially the "*if*"! But whether fish are caught or not, the angler can spend a very pleasant day there in beautiful country with Castle Naze calm on the distant height.

"I couldn't wish for a better holiday," said one town weekender, though his wife wasn't as enthusiastic.

A friend, now dead, once shot an otter in Meveril Brook just below the reservoir. He thought it was a poaching cat, otherwise he would not have fired. In the Canal at Bugsworth was shot another otter which no one could identify till a friend of mine saw it. These are the only otters I have heard of in Combs district.

The only common animals are rabbits—there is a "bottomless" breeding-place for them among the tumble of rocks under Castle Naze—hedgehogs, voles, field-mice, and moles, which tunnel the pastures and meadows in spring almost as though purposely to impede the mowers. Occasionally a hill-fox will come into the valley from the breeding holes under the massed rhododendrons at Errwood in the Valley of Goyt, and some of the farmers will join the annual shoot there, but it is more for the fun of the outing than because foxes do them much hurt. A solitary badger was shot some years ago at Furness Vale. A very few hares breed in the bottom land about Marsh Farm and the Chapel-en-le-Frith golf links, and occasionally the High Peak Beagles turn out there, but generally they have a disappointing day. Combs district, in common with most of Derbyshire, is not hunting country. It is best perhaps for rough shooting, though I prefer it for walking and natural observation.

CHAPTER XI

GARDEN MAKING

COMBS gave me my first experience of a Derbyshire garden; my first experience of a garden of my own anywhere. Like most other people, we did not buy our bungalow because of the land that it happened to be standing on; we bought it because we liked it as a bungalow. The making of the garden came afterwards.

At first the garden was very small, twelve yards in front of the bungalow, and twenty yards behind, with enough at either side to allow for a garage at either end . . . if we had ever wanted that strange extravagance. We were so happy and proud that at first the garden seemed quite large enough, and as the fence was made of deal posts simply connected with three lengths of wire, and good fields were beyond, the garden did not seem to end at the fence, and there was no feeling of restriction. For twelve months the bungalow stood empty, waiting, and grass grew round it.

But at last we were married and occupied the bungalow, and I went out to mow and to turn the grass roots under. As farm-hand I had worked on farms that locally were called big, one hundred odd acres up to four hundred. I had often ploughed an acre in a day, so that I went out confidently, with the idea that such a small plot could be tidied in about half an hour. The spade was plunged in heartily. It penetrated two inches and, with a nasty jar, stopped. I tried again a foot to the right. There was a splintering and the blade stopped horribly at five inches. A third plunge, not quite so hearty, went in less than half an inch. I gave up and prospected with a sharp-pointed stick and discovered that nearly the whole area was bedded just beneath with everything that the builder hadn't wanted. The sweaty work of unearthing this jumble made the little plot seem to expand somewhat and I became a little more respectful towards it.

But at last a deep hole took the whole conglomeration, the first beds were finished and the new-turned earth looked healthy and good. Daffodils and narcissi, roots of lupins, golden-balls, and phlox were put in, because we fancied a mixture that would always give flowers. As spring came and the plants thrived we watched them happily. A row of daffodils bloomed nicely along the southern fence. One morning my wife looked and saw a long pink tongue just licking in the last of them; a whole bouquet gone into a bull. She ran out with the rolling pin and the bull tossed his back legs and frisked away and seemed to think that she had come out to play.

After that came worse. First the farmer's eleven geese waddled through the wire and ate all the tender plant tops; then his five porkers bellied under the wire and nosed up most of what was left. Dolly, the shire mare, who seemed to have the reach of a giraffe, helped by tugging lupins and phlox out by their roots.

"Now you know why farmers never have tidy gardens," I said to Elizabeth. "We'll fence all round so that nothing can get in."

So we did . . . and everything was spoiled. All at once the fact that intruders had been successfully shut out ceased to matter; what did matter was that we were shut in. We were as in a yard in town. We saw how very small our plot was and became contemptuous again. The only way was to add to it, and this we did, taking in a piece of the field on the southern side forty yards long by twenty yards wide. There were no spare bricks, slates, planks, laths, and so on under this, thank goodness, so that digging and mowing there were a pleasure. I began to be a little more ambitious about gardening. Close about the house there had not been much scope; but here there was space, and in addition to a round rose-bed and a long bed specially for our favourite long-spurred aquilegias, we decided to put a shrubbery of flowering trees by the roadside wall to take off the bareness.

Before this I had always ploughed, or hoed, or dug, to someone else's orders; now I could give myself orders and I enjoyed obeying myself. But even yet I hadn't quite been cured of the attitude of disparagement, for after the work was done I began to think that the garden did not seem as large as it had done immediately after it had been added to; in fact, that it was still quite small. Elizabeth was afraid of someone coming and building where they could overlook us, so that eventually we extended again, and then again, until we were suddenly inspired to measure our bit of Derbyshire. From that day started what I consider my right respect for one statute acre.

What problems that plot set us! But the happiness that it returned cannot be computed. Now I am convinced that to plough an acre is nothing; one merely turns it over and has done. But really to know an acre one must live on it.

For instance, there was the oak grove that we tried, or more properly that I tried, to grow. In early days I had read with deep pleasure *The Book of the English Oak* by Charles Hurst, and the desire had been born to join the noble band of acorn-planters. Plant not for a month or year, but for two hundred or three hundred years, that was the idea. I went into the valley towards the lake and there searched under the best oaks and filled my pockets. Each acorn was chosen with care. Those that were best, according to Hurst, were the plump and fair-coloured, and those that were dark and lean were rejected. A yard apart all round our first small plot they were planted, also with care, and Elizabeth protested that when all came up we should never get any sunlight. Only I told her that I liked trees more than anything; and that it was unlikely, anyway, that the oaks would ever grow to more than sapling height while we lived; and finally, that if they came up too closely I would cull the weaklings. Of course, there would be one or two that would not come up; those there would not be any need to cull. She gave in, and winter passed very slowly, as it does in the Derbyshire north, and then we began to look out for the first sturdy sprits. The oak is late to start, but when June had come and there was still no sign I began to wonder. Elizabeth asked facetious questions and I had to explain that oaks, taking two hundred years to reach their prime, must not be expected to shoot up like sunflowers. But surely, said she, there should be a bud or something. In August I was driven to confess that the whole matter was queer. Surreptitiously, I probed a bit, and found not even a rotted acorn. A year later when we first enlarged and moved back the fence, Elizabeth pleasantly pointed out that it would be rather awkward when the oaks came up having them in a row cutting the garden in two. In reply I asked whether we should varnish the fence or creosote it. She replied that perhaps we might use two of the oaks, anyway, to swing a hammock. And after that it is pleasing to record that one oak did come up, one that is now a brave sapling. Unfortunately it is nowhere near where any of the carefully selected acorns were put, so that I suppose that a rook must have taken pity and dropped it where he could see that the land wanted it.

Then there was the lily-pond. This was Elizabeth's idea. She said how beautiful lilies were, more pure and fresh than any other flower. I answered that even a lily would have a job to look pure and fresh on a hill-side where there was only water in spate time. She said kindly that she was sure that Johnson and I could manage that—if we really wanted to.

By this the garden had reached its final size and in the southern corner, decently sheltered by an ancient thorn, a tall ash, and three tapered larch trees, was a hollow into which, by leaning on the gritstone wall, passers-by could look. The very place, said Elizabeth; it would be a Christian act to provide the beauty of lilies for weary ramblers, who had just come down the hills and had more hills yet to climb. She looked up into the foliage and said, too, how pleasant it would be for me after a hard day to be able to rest by still water.

"Stagnant, you mean," I said. "Think of the smell, which will surely outdo the lilies. And of the flies! Don't you know that water——?"

She interrupted to ask how it was that I had been eager to give so much trouble to planting useless acorns, yet would not go to this little trouble for her. After that, of course, it became a matter of studying methods and deciding what we should want. Bricks were ordered by the hundred, bags of cement and tiles came, and six loads of prime pink clay were thrown over the wall below the bottom gate on to the delphiniums.

"A *little* trouble," I murmured. "It looks as if we'll deserve a pond when we get it."

"Yes," said Elizabeth brightly. "And as well as lilies we'll have goldfish."

So the bricks became a wall across the lower side of the dell, and the cement was laid over all to take off the harshness of the colouring. The clay was barrowed down and laboriously puddled into saucer form. Tiles were laid from the garage and from the top of the orchard where my revolving sun-hut stood, so that water would flow from the roofs to float the lilies and fish. It was a dry summer. When all was done we could not wait for rain, but borrowed two hoses and added them to our own, and at last the great moment came when water was turned on from the house and a pleasant gurgle started. All of that day it ran and all of the night and all of the next day till we became used to the running, as if a stream had miraculously been given to us. Although the pond during this period was not pretty, being a slow swirl of clayeyness and frothy bubbles, we knew that when the flow stopped it would clear, and even I began to feel glad that we had gone to all our trouble; I imagined myself taking visitors there to see goldfish that would come obediently when we whistled or struck the water.

At last the pond was brimming and the tap was turned off. The garden suddenly went quiet, and it is easy now to imagine that this was the silence of disapproval. Only then we simply felt it strange and soon got used to it once more. Last thing before going to bed we went to the dell, in the warm summer dusk. The pond had gone down somewhat, only we expected that and were not worried. But in the morning less than half of the water remained. With spades we slammed the sides till they were even more compact, and again the tap was turned on and the long pipe squirmed and began obedient duty. After all this we managed to make the pool keep two-thirds full, and reluctantly we decided that this would have to do. We would plant moss and water-side plants to hide the unsightly upper clay, and still everything would be well.

Drought continued, daily the water diminished. We began to spend more and more time noting rain signs, which all turned out false. Three more weeks passed —it was a phenomenal summer—and then rain came with a rush, driven by a happy west wind. We went down to see the tiles gush into the dell and at last everything was a success. We bought three lilies and sank them in baskets which were weighted with stones. We would have bought goldfish, only there were none in the villages round about.

The rain became intermittent, sometimes pelting, then going away in grey waves along the russet valley slopes, but the wind became more determined and veered till there was a south-west gale. I watched the ash, for it is good to see a proud tree tossing defiant boughs under swift-flowing grey; and after a squall had passed the tree gleamed, as if enjoying its battle. The larch trees were not defiant, but leaned away from the wind, streamlining themselves cleverly. After a while I thought I would go down to see if there were waves on the pond. When I got there nearly all the water had gone. I was astonished and went for Johnson. As we talked there was a tremor. Was the earth trying to tell us that it didn't want the pond? Foolish fancy, and yet that was how it seemed. Whenever wind blew and the trees rocked to their root-grip the earth opened its cracks and let the water escape.

"Either the trees go or the pond," I was driven to

say to Elizabeth eventually. "The land won't hold both."

So the pond died and in place a rock-garden was born, and the land was pleased, for it willingly nurtured the rock-garden, and at a certain time in early summer it was the beauty spot of our bit of Derbyshire.

Often people ask why I chose to settle where the year is "nine months winter and three months bad weather", and where on much of the land only hill sheep and grouse and curlews can find a living. Then I reply that with this wild country I feel akin; though, also, I have found here how true is that saying of Mr Boone, the best farmer for whom I ever worked, that there is more satisfaction from making a hard land yield than from harvesting the largest crops in easy country. Our garden was stern land. Many setbacks it gave us. The orchard was a setback. As an experiment we planted trees of twenty-one varieties. A number never matured their fruit and eventually we gave up expecting them to. The land would not have them. But how sweet tasted the apples that did mature! The Lombardy poplars were a setback; the rough wind snapped them every one. But we were only the more proud of the young larches that looked so flamey-green in spring. The carrots were a setback; for five years we tried before accepting the land's verdict that it was not going to have them. We might have persisted with imported sand, but how foolish when the land was willing to grow such good potatoes, peas and beans, turnips, cabbages, cauliflowers, sprouts, and spinnach, far more than we could eat? Yes, against every refusal there was an acceptance. Lettuces failed regularly; strawberries regularly did well. Victoria plums failed; loganberries and raspberries always were excellent.

Fifteen years after our beginning we were still learning what the land did not like, and what it would gladly accept and nurture. What this bit of Derbyshire taught us was that an acre is as interesting and as much to be respected as a hundred acres or a thousand. But isn't that true in every county?

CHAPTER XII

MAN-MADE LAKELAND

ANOTHER rich experience from Combs was watching the making of Fernilee Reservoir. Derbyshire, I believe, has more artificial lakes than any other county, and the transformation I watched has taken place in at least half a dozen other valleys and is likely to be repeated, for the Peak is natural gathering ground.

Before the Valley of Goyt was drowned there was a long sandy road, along which every Sunday, and often on weekdays, a coach and pair was driven from Errwood. The road crossed the bottom by the old powder works, which when I knew them were roofless, though they had been used in the 1914–18 war. When first we heard that the valley was to be flooded we thought that its beauty would be destroyed promptly and for ever; but after the first warning there was a long waiting time during which nothing worse happened than the appearance of long white boards set at a height which we could not believe would be the level to which eventually the water would rise. We often went up the valley then, toying with rather amusing fancies about walking where fish would swim. But the Goyt was very pleasant and we should have liked it to have been reprieved.

Then the first four hundred arrived, hardened pick-and-shovel men, mostly Irish, used to starting reservoirs, roads, railways, and other great works. They were no respecters of beauty, but at once began to slay trees, rip up turf, destroy walls, and turn good

141

earth into quagmire. They drove roads, advancing first
from Fernilee, then bringing a light railway up from
Horwich End by Taxal. Soon dumps of timber,
girders, gravel, sand, coal, and machines, and
mysterious parts of machines blotched the fields; and
one day for the first time since nature began gouging
the valley a steam whistle sent its penetrating blast
from the depths to the moorland heights. It belonged
to a steam-navvy which had been coaxed along the
railway, and which quickly began to scoop away the
foot of a bluff.

A shanty village was built. The number of workers
increased, but for months it seemed as though all their
efforts were to destroy and to produce only ugliness.
The hillsides were torn through and great benches
made along them. A long straight gash was run up the
steep west side of the valley, the use for which I could
not guess. When I asked I learned that an important
part of the plan was that as much use as possible
should be made of local materials. The gash was to
become the track of a cable railway to bring rock and
clay and tree trunks from the tops.

Still more men and machines came in. Electric
power lines straddled the valley, with an under-mesh
of finer telephone-wires. Light railway lines were laid
at what seemed impossible angles, yet soon little green
engines were charging up them with important gush-
ings of smoke and steam, lugging clattering tails of
tip-trucks. There were points and signals and bridges
on long legs that made me think of Rocky Mountain
films. Pumps vomited muddy water all day, cranes
swung spinning loads of stone and rubble non-
chalantly, and from where the core of the dam was to
be came the subterranean boom of explosions. It
seemed impossible that any valley could be more

desecrated. To prevent the poor Goyt from interfering, it was herded between muddy palisades of trunks cut off its own banks, and stole past as though it had done something wrong and was ashamed.

Winter came and electric lights hung on bent and leaning ash poles gave a pitiful light amid rain, mist, and smoke. Men moved unwillingly in mud, or crouched by spluttering braziers, and swore at the Peakland cold. I looked down into the slot where the core of the dam would go. The sides were shored with great timbers, and lights burned sadly far below. There was glisten of clay and dripping water. The crane buckets went spinning out of sight. It was half-past five and suddenly a whistle shrilled and men appeared up ladders out of the earth's mud, a surprising number of shaggy men in waders, brown blotched to the head; and broken lines of men converged on the pay-box, where notes and silver were doled out and counted with clayey hands. There was a dash for the line of shabby buses with engines already warming up to rush off to Stockport. But some of the men stopped with an ancient Jew who had green-and-red check shirts, shoddy vests, and coarse nailed boots displayed over an old saloon car and on a neighbouring wood dump. Then only indifferent watchmen were left and I could wander as I chose. On a notice-board I read: "It has been decided that 2*d.* a week be deducted from all wages to go to Stockport Royal Infirmary, which takes our cases. Anyone objecting to this deduction should see his own works manager." The Goyt was not dammed without taking toll.

As the slow years passed, order began to show. Into the core of the dam thousands of tons of concrete had been pumped. There were strange cracks in the bedrock that swallowed much more than had been anticipated and the cost went up. Liquid cement had to be driven in by compressed air. But the men conquered, and a great embankment began to rise, leaning against the core from either side. It was 130 feet high, made of clay and earth and faced with cut stone blasted from close by. At first I had felt sad and had greatly disliked all the destruction wrought by the workers; then, seeing how they slouched and idled and were careless about waste, I had become cynical; but I began to admire them. Everything that had been done was beginning to fall into place, to have meaning. A round stone tower rose above the upper face of the dam, and I went down from stage to stage beneath it and saw how cunningly all had been done so that the flow from the reservoir could be controlled as desired; and I thought of the simple and pretty stream which had run untrammelled through the valley those few years before. All this labour to hold it and to make it more useful! There was romance in the accomplishment.

And the machinery and the dumps went, the shabby wooden village began to empty and was itself taken away, while the dam filled, slowly, slowly, till at last Derbyshire had a new lake. The old beauty was gone, but here was new beauty. Fortunately very few trees had been felled above the water-line, but the saddest part about reservoir-making is always the destruction of old homes and the exiling of the inhabitants. Where in the Valley of Goyt there were happy families, now there are only water and sheep.

The more recently finished Ladybower Reservoir above Bamford (opened by the King and Queen on September 25th, 1945) ousted many more families and drowned the villages of Ashopton and Derwent, together with fine old Derwent Hall, which once

The Church of "The Capital of the Peak", Chapel-en-le-Frith
Sheep-wash pound and bridge, Ashford-in-the-Water

belonged to the Duke of Norfolk. I hope that more efforts will be made than hitherto to grow woodlands round our reservoirs. Even sheep are held to pollute water to some degree, therefore only limited numbers are allowed to graze, and the shores of most of the reservoirs are extremely uninteresting, almost bare of stock and life of any kind. Trees would improve the picture. Also they help to conserve water, their roots hold the hill slopes together, and they reduce the risks of pollution. But we do not want all conifers. The argument is that broad-leaved trees will not flourish at the elevation required, but this was disproved in the Valley of Goyt higher up than Fernilee, where many years ago about 1,000 acres were afforested, up to 1,700 feet. Although the trees on the wet exposed moorland at the highest altitude failed, the conifers grew well at about 1,500 feet and beautiful beech flourished up to 1,250 feet.

Fernilee Reservoir, of course, supplies Stockport, as does Kinder, but I have asked many persons where the water from Howden, Derwent, and Ladybower goes to and few have known. These reservoirs are controlled by the Derwent Valley Water Board and supply Sheffield, Derby, Nottingham, and Leicester. Ladybower Reservoir is the largest in England, if not in Europe, and has an embankment 1,250 feet long.

Sheep-pasturing in catchment areas has, by the way, its own peculiar problems. As there can seldom be close supervision over so many acres, where walls are usually non-existent or falling down, unscrupulous men sometimes turn sheep on without authorisation and thus get a summer's grazing free. Other sheep disappear, perhaps stolen by persons coming by car from a distance. And always there is the danger of stray dogs. I saw two Alsatians working together cut

10*   145

The Terrace, Haddon Hall
The Font, Youlgrave

out a sheep from a flock and worry it to death down a hillside in a most expert manner. Obviously they were used to it. One of these dogs was shot and the other traced, and when the owner came up in court it was stated that in one season fifty sheep had been lost through worrying in a single catchment area.

CHAPTER XIII

"CAPITAL OF THE PEAK"

CHAPEL-EN-LE-FRITH, nearest neighbour to Combs, which naturally I came to know well, is a typical small market town of Derbyshire north. It claims to be the Capital of the Peak, this arising no doubt from the fact that a chapel was first put up here by the keepers and foresters of the old Forest of the Peak, in 1225, becoming known as the Chapel in the Frith or Forest, which suggests that there was none other at that time in the Peak. The keepers chose a good place on top of a knoll in the wide valley, and the chancel of the present Church of St Thomas à Becket is believed to stand on the site of the original Chapel of Saint Thomas of Canterbury. Round this chapel began the settlement that became the town.

Floodlit at dusk, as it is on special occasions, the present church with its square tower shows finely, and is very suggestive still of a watchtower above a trusting settlement. Nevertheless, the church has been a cause of frequent fierce local disputes. From earliest times it seems to have been the custom of the inhabitants of Chapel-en-le-Frith to elect their own minister to the Dean and Chapter of Lichfield, who then placed him in the benefice. Although it has been said that generally the inhabitants selected "the worst man they can find to the best of their ability", they were jealous of their power, and in Queen Elizabeth's reign when the Dean and Chapter proposed to put a minister of their own in there was an instant outcry and the inhabitants won.

147

About 1574 notorious Bess of Hardwick, Countess of Shrewsbury, tried to put a minister in, but once more the inhabitants won. Again in 1617 there was trouble and this time the dispute went before the Lord Chancellor's Court, but still the people won.

Why or how does not seem to be known, but eventually the selection of a minister came to be made by a committee of twenty-seven members, but if these twenty-seven could not agree on a nomination, then there had to be a general election. The present vicar was selected without dispute, but for the previous vicar an election became necessary. There were six candidates. Nearly everybody attended all six trial sermons, and feeling got hotter than at a parliamentary election, until the Wesleyan minister felt it necessary to preach a sermon about it. An old inhabitant who gave me this information says that this sermon swayed the election, all the Wesleyans who heard it voting for the man whose name was eventually sent in to the Dean and Chapter for licence. All parishioners over twenty-one assessed to church and poor rates had the right to vote.

Until the coming of the present vicar it was the custom of the incumbent to preach in a black gown, but the Rev W. H. Green said that he felt strange in black, and though he did not wish to hurt anybody's feelings he would like to preach in the usual surplice, which he has done since. Similar small customs have died, or are dying, in villages and market towns throughout Derbyshire. To the older persons it seems a pity, but generally the younger people do not care, and one has sometimes to live long in a place before one hears mentioned some custom which perhaps at one time meant a great deal to every one of the inhabitants. Such a custom at Chapel-en-le-Frith was the Wool Fair in the Market Place. The Fair had been held for practically seven centuries, until 1910. The great day was July 7th, and I have heard how farmers brought in their wool to sell and were often measured in the market for a new suit to be made of the wool from their own sheep. Chapel Wakes Sunday is always the first Sunday after July 7th, which suggests that in the old days revelry took place after business and while money was, presumably, plentiful.

When first I went to Chapel-en-le-Frith, Wakes week was still important, most persons spending at least the first weekend at home to attend the fair, also known as "the wakes", where they met friends not seen perhaps since the previous Wakes. But cheap transport and the new wish for different sights lured even the older people into spending the whole of the week away from home and immediately before the war the local fair was very poorly attended.

A custom necessarily stopped during the war, but now continuing, is the ringing of a nightly curfew at eight. A "passing bell" is also rung when anybody dies in the parish, the number of tolls telling the sex and age of the dead person, and from this information, before so many strangers came to live in the town, the old inhabitants could generally tell whose death the bell told of. A "Pancake bell" is rung at eleven in the morning on Shrove Tuesday, to remind housewives, it is said, to put their pancakes in the pan. When the bell is heard the children at the local schools are released for the rest of the day and twenty years or so ago when an attempt was made to stop this holiday, many of the children at the Town End School made a concerted rush for the door and escaped. There were punishments, but the holiday has never been interfered with again.

Pancake Tuesday night was also Mischief Night,

when the young men put rats in milk churns, stuffed chimneys or dropped cats down, lifted farm gates off and hid them, and tied house doors so that the people could not get out in the morning. So much mischief was done that eventually the police had to act, and this custom passed before the 1914 war.

The main Manchester–Derby road runs the length of Chapel-en-le-Frith, is, in fact, its main street, and there seems small doubt that the first settlement was made here because it was a road centre. The great royal forest was in three parts: Longdendale, which included Glossop; Hopedale; and Champaign, which took in part of Bakewell, Tideswell, and Hathersage. So the keepers set up their chapel where tracks from these three parts met. With this in mind it seems strange that the roads about Chapel-en-le-Frith remained poor until almost recent times. When George III was crowned, says William Braylesford Bunting, author of *Chapel-en-le-Frith, its History and its People*, "the direct way to Whaley and Cheshire was over Eccles Pike: to Peak Forest, Castleton and Sheffield up Peaslows; to Edale, Penistone and the Woodlands the way would be by Bagshawe and 'Rushop Yate' to the Stake Road; and to Glossop, New Mills, and Manchester by 'Drum and Monkey Lane'. . . . As late as 1792 Chapel was only served by wagons passing through three or four times a week: 'No coaches to or from this town'."

Perhaps the methods of road-mending had a lot to do with this lack of transport. It was the custom for many farmers to pay their rates in kind, by carrying loads of stone from quarries to wherever the Council thought they might be needed. The stones were tipped, roughly levelled, strewn with some soil dug from the side, and were then left to be rolled by traffic. To ensure that the surface would be rolled all over and to guard against missing the rockiest places, trestles were put part-way across, sometimes from one side, sometimes from the other, so that a journey could become almost like an obstacle race.

Before the first railway (the L. & N.W.) was built in 1863 Chapel was served with one coach per day to and from Manchester, and another to and from Sheffield through Castleton. After the line opened a horse-bus used to take passengers up to the station, but this stopped when the Central Station became available and naturally took most of the passenger traffic.

No book on Derbyshire could be complete unless it mentioned railways specially. I do not think that any other English county has provided as many engineering difficulties, or has lines through more diverse scenery. The line from Chinley to Matlock is a succession of tunnels and embankments with brief tantalising views of dale and river scenery which the passenger never has time to see properly because the train is continually rushing into fresh tunnels and under huge rock walls.

The line from Chinley to Sheffield is only 20 miles long, but $5\frac{1}{2}$ miles of that distance is through tunnels, including the Dore and Totley Tunnel, which is 3 miles 950 yards long (second only to the River Severn Tunnel, 4 miles 636 yards), and the Co'burn Tunnel, 2 miles and 182 yards long. This Chinley–Sheffield line was only opened in 1894, well within memory of many persons still in the district, and listening to them one gets a vivid idea of the greatness of the undertaking and the courage of the men who tackled such difficulties without any modern aids that might make such a task comparatively simple.

My chief informant was a Chapel-en-le-Frith man,

and as such tales are likely to be lost unless recorded now, it is worth telling of the matter pretty fully. The line was started by an independent contractor named Edwards, but he had underestimated the difficulties and the cost and the undertaking failed. The Midland Railway took it over and finished it ten years from the date on which it was begun. Thousands of navvies and "miners" were employed and what happened at the Chapel-en-le-Frith and Edale end doubtless happened also at the Grindleford and Dore end, for both tunnels were being made at the same time. At Chapel and Edale little camps of crude huts were put up for the workers and the two villages found themselves called on to cater for all these additional persons, many of the craftsmen bringing their wives and families till the job was finished. A few even settled in the villages when the line was opened and are still there. Many of the shopkeepers made profits that they had never dreamed of in the days before the railway was projected, and could retire when the work ended.

All materials for the line and tunnel-making were brought by the already existing line to Chapel Central station and there for the whole time that the line was building a ganger and his men were employed unloading and loading into the wagons and carts that went to and from the workings. Two steam traction-engines of the type that still haul a few of the heavier threshing sets, or sectional roundabouts and swings about the country for "Wakes", were employed, taking eleven tons or so at a time, towed on a string of wagons, but for the rest any carts that could be got were used. Farmers would be employed and when there was no urgent work on the land a score of farmers might turn out, generally with two carts, each pulled by a single horse. The farmer would lead the first cart with the second horse tied by a loose link of rope to the tailboard. One can imagine a long procession of carts, some going, some returning, on the Castleton road with one of the "steamers", say, in the midst, perhaps scaring some of the rough farm horses and causing more trouble than their owners would think the engine's worth justified. The road was poor, so that very soon it was all broken up. My friend in wet weather saw the traction-engines lap up the road surface round their wheels in the manner of a sponge-roll, so that always there was work for anyone who cared to come, for when there were no loads from the station, there was always stone wanted from the quarries for the road. Tremendous quantities were taken from the quarry on the hill north-west of Sparrowpit.

One journey from Chapel station to Edale and back was as much as one man and his horses could do in a day, and the most that could be taken in a cart was one ton. No horse could manage more down from Mam Nick. Think how many journeys could be done in a day now by motor-lorry carrying six or seven tons easily! The great slow "steamers" could not go over Mam Nick at all and their tonnage had to be unloaded on the Rushup Edge road where the Edale branch leaves it and horses hauled the freight the rest of the distance, and hard work it was for them, too. Always a boy was at the trough a little back along the road to Chapel and there he had a fire and kept warm water continually available in which was mixed oatmeal which made a stimulating drink. No horse going up from Chapel missed this refresher after the long climb.

As the work got on it was decided that a railway engine would greatly help in Edale Valley, so the colossal task of taking one "mountaineering" was begun. A special sectional length of line was prepared at Chapel station and the engine steamed on to it. When the engine was clear of the back section, the line was loaded on to a long low bogie and towed forward past the engine by a splendid team of horses and then relaid and the engine was able to go another few yards. Thus leap-frogging, as it were, the engine steamed slowly and laboriously up the three-miles rise to Rushup. It was a great sight and people came from all over the district to see it. On Rushup the engine was 1,405 feet above sea-level and had still Mam Nick (nearly 1,700 feet) to go over. This wild road is one to be careful of in a car, and the thought of taking a railway engine over gives one a tremendous respect for the men who somehow managed the job. One cannot imagine the man in charge gazing with wonder and pleasure on the view of Edale's beauty and Kinder's bleakness which comes so abruptly into sight as one goes through the Nick! There must have been many very tricky moments, but eventually the engine was got down safely and resumed its monotonous chuffing to and fro on lines more or less reasonably level.

But the Co'burn Tunnel and line were not made without accident. Several men—I have not been able to learn the exact number—were killed during the boring by falls of rock and other causes. Boring machines were used to make the holes into which the dynamite was plugged, but after the shot had been fired it was all pick-and-shovel work. The debris was taken out by horse power. These horses were specially trained and wore thick pads on their chests to push the trucks into the tunnel, and then were turned round and dragged the loaded trucks out. They were always kept in excellent condition and when work stopped at Christmas and Easter they were paraded for exercise and were much admired by farmers and other judges from round about.

"They had coats just like mowdiwarps (moles)," said my friend enthusiastically, remembering them over fifty years. He meant that their coats were close and thick and had a sheen, which is the sure sign of good health.

One can imagine how the country people enjoyed the talk and bustle and the many novelties that the railway job brought to them. The labourers were a strange race to the villagers, the great bulk of whom had never been farther than Buxton or Castleton. Most of these labourers had been all over the kingdom, from contract job to contract job, railways, reservoirs, canals, and new roads, for it was the time of expansion in engineering and big business. So much did these men crowd the villages that it is said that one woman, big and strong and stout, who kept a lodging house, used to get one relay to sleep, and then go round and lift them out still asleep and prop them against the walls, so that she could take another lot in to sleep in the beds! The truth was that the men all worked on shifts, so that she let the same beds to two or three men, one being up and gone to work before the next arrived back from the previous shift.

One of the most admired permanent officials was a cashier whose task it was every day to go round the workings making a "sub" to any of the men who wanted one. Very many of them did, not being of the type that saved much; but others who had money in their pockets would still take a sub, on principle, as it were, never knowing when the mood might come on them to leave the job and go elsewhere. Many of these men were turbulent and when drunk were hard to manage. A six-foot member of the Derbyshire Constabulary who was stationed at Chapel is still remembered as the only man who could really deal with the worst of them in their bad moods, and when others had done all that they could to settle a row and failed, a runner would be sent to find this constable whatever time of day or night it might be.

In addition to their own constable, so to speak, the navvies had their own parson, a man who went among them continually and held services at meal times and between shifts, whenever and wherever he could gather a few men to listen. Many a time my friend saw little services being held in the quarry up the Castleton road on to Rushup Edge; and doubtless there were similar services in the brickyard which was opened near where Edale station is now. Thousands of bricks were needed to line the Co'burn Tunnel and it was found that some of the Edale clay was suitable for the rough bricks of the inner lining, though blue bricks from away were used for all facing work.

For so long a tunnel I believe Co'burn is unique in having only one smoke shaft, and that this was the result of an agreement with the landowners at Ford Hall. This shaft is now conspicuous on the moor and the sinking of it was in itself a considerable undertaking in those times. A winding-engine was assembled on the moor and a rope railway laid down from the Chinley end of the tunnel and everything was wound up the thousand feet or so on this. The shaft is a very wide one, but does not go straight into the tunnel but a bit to one side, this for safety in case there should be a fall of any kind. Normally it keeps the tunnel clear of smoke fairly well, but on other days with the wind in certain directions the smoke will not clear at all and the gang of plate-layers who are always working in the tunnel have a bad time.

Dove Holes Tunnel on the Midland line from Chinley to Millers Dale, made earlier than Co'burn Tunnel, is not nearly so wide, yet has fourteen shafts in its considerably shorter length. These are not so well constructed, a serious fall having occurred within living memory. Fortunately it fouled a signal wire and the man on duty, a porter-signalman named Chambers, stopped all traffic while he went to investigate. He found the tunnel completely blocked. So shocked was he by this, and the thought of the smash that might have occurred, that his hair went completely white and never got back its colour. The passengers of the first train that would have run into the tunnel were so grateful to Chambers that they took a collection which amounted eventually to about £20, a very good sum in those days.

While the work on Co'burn Tunnel was in hand the great frost of 1895 came and all work was stopped for eighteen weeks. Grave distress occurred and soup kitchens had to be opened in the nearest villages. All over Derbyshire that frost is remembered, for quarrying and nearly all other outdoor work ceased and few working men had money to carry them over such a long period. In Two Dales (Toad Hole), where I write, the then proprietor of the flourishing nurseries here sent out hot meals round the village every noon for anybody who was in need and a fund of £70 13s. 1d. was raised for soup and coal. Similar help had to be given all over the county, but where the railway was being made the trouble was worse because of the very large numbers unemployed in a small area.

I had intended that this chapter should be entirely about Chapel-en-le-Frith, indicative of the many interests to be found in every small market town in Derbyshire, it being impossible to deal with each separately. Although I have wandered far away, I will end with the description of Chapel-en-le-Frith written by Mr M. J. B. Baddeley for the 1883 edition of his guide *The Peak*.

"This town is", he says, "dull and featureless, and the church equally devoid of interest. Agriculture, mills, and calico works provide the staple occupation of the people," and that is all! In the 1908 edition of the guide the first sentence had become: "The town is dull, and the church devoid of interest. Note, however, the old cross and the stocks." What a place has to show and tell is generally only found by patient search, but no Derbyshire market town should be dismissed as cursorily as Mr Baddeley would have us dismiss the Capital of the Peak.

knob of his stick as he tried to remember an old local family that we had asked about. And because the effort of remembering seemed to be too much for him, to take his mind off it I asked how he thought Derbyshire compared with the Lake District. It was as if I had jabbed him with a pin: he leapt up, quivering almost, and explained that Derbyshire was not to be mentioned in the same breath; there was no comparison!

"Then why have you retired here and not gone back there?" I asked, astonished.

He grew calm, rather sad, and said that after thirty years one made friends in a place; nevertheless, he had been born by Windermere and there was nowhere like the Lake District. I did not agree with him, so we left him and went to look at the sheep-bridge, with the fold beyond. A farmer's cart stood in the stream and the man was having to wait while his churns filled. I did not ask whether he was going to add milk to the water, or the water to his milk. We did not have time to go in Ashford Church, but it has some of the few funeral garlands left in Derbyshire. Mr Baddeley says they might be mistaken for five fly-catchers. They were last carried at Ashford in 1870 at the funeral of a girl named Blackwell who was drowned in the Wye, near the marble works. With its low situation and many trees Ashford seemed rather shut in and enervating; not the healthiest place to live in, we consoled ourselves on not having found a house there.

We walked on the main road towards Bakewell. There are many fine trees. Round the bases of some just over the left-hand wall there were rings of concrete for which we could not guess the reason. Before entering Bakewell the road passes by an old cotton mill which once belonged to the Arkwrights of Cromford. There is a big waterwheel which still trundles

Black Rocks, Cromford
Ornamental thatch at Osmaston

over. Closer by the road comes the Wye, beautifully clear, with so many fish hanging easily, almost lazily, it seems, in the current that there is nearly always somebody leaning over the wall to watch, as I have already told. Occasionally a fly-fisherman will make a cast from the causeway. On a sunny day when the road is dusty the water looks very tempting under its trees. Next comes Bakewell, first a narrow, unimpressive street, with two skeleton hands at the end reaching eerily from the door of the Rutland Arms Hotel. At the turn there is the square with the pleasant Bath Garden on the left. Bakewell here has a clean, attractive look; it is one of the prettiest places of its size in Derbyshire.

But that day when we were house-hunting we had no time to visit the church or other interesting places. Instead we stood in the queue for the Youlgrave bus. This took us out by the Matlock road. Here the valley is much wider than on the Ashford side and the pastures and meadows by the winding Wye are rich and satisfying, while the wooded hills beyond could not be bettered as a background. Soon we caught a glimpse of the battlements of Haddon Hall. Nearly everybody who goes this way says how much they prefer Haddon to Chatsworth, but no doubt this opinion is often given because Haddon is never seen entire, but is always tantalisingly partly hidden. There is a fine beech hedge bordering the road, and behind that a long line of hawthorn trees which flower a beautiful blush pink; and then for twenty yards or so there is a gap, through which the tower and walls can be seen above foliage, specially framed, as might be, for sightseers. No wonder that everybody exclaims enthusiastically; and into the minds of most persons come at the same instant romantic thoughts of a

beautiful girl eloping with a handsome lover—Dorothy
Vernon with Sir John Manners. This pair have become traditional lovers, and their imagined romance,
of which nearly everybody has her or his private
version, is just what we should have liked to have
happened to ourselves. I am not writing thus to prove
that Haddon is not more romantic than Chatsworth;
only to show that most persons compare the two with
a considerable bias in favour of Haddon!

Shortly after passing in the bus I asked a local man
which was the true story about pretty Dorothy and Sir
John, mentioning that I had three different versions
each claiming to give the authentic story, and that I
knew there were other versions which I had not read.

"The true story is in the book called *The Heiress of
Haddon*," said my informant with absolute confidence.
On getting home I found that this is one of the books
that I possess, and that it was written by W. E.
Doubleday. I am afraid that I did not trouble to read
it on my unknown friend's recommendation, but I
pass his word on. He was over eighty and had lived
near Haddon all his life, so that his confidence should
be worth something. It has to be added, however, that
though the elopement, if it occurred, must have been
in the closing fifteen-hundreds, nothing was ever put
into writing about it until the early eighteen-hundreds.

At Pichory Corner, just past Haddon, the bus took
the right turn for Youlgrave. Galleries of the famous
Mill Close lead mine at Darley Dale (see page 187)
are said to reach to this corner. The road here was
sheltered by good trees, but many have since been cut
for war use. Where the road from Winster comes in,
the way swings right again and climbs through woods
on to the uplands where Youlgrave lies along one
long narrow street, boldly obstructed part way by its

sturdy towered church. Bakewell is a typical warm market town: here for contrast is a typical exposed hill village. Although on either side there is beautiful sheltered country close by, the village extends up a long ridge, and one cannot help wondering why it grew there. Middleton, only a short distance on, is cosily enclosed in trees and banks, but Youlgrave, no, it stands bluntly on its hill. At one time it was the home of lead-miners and miners are notoriously in-different to weather hazards or beauty. But the people we met in Youlgrave were friendly and we looked at a bungalow in which we could have been happy if only it had not been quite so small. From the front garden we could peep into charming Bradford Dale: but that can be done from the back gardens, or yards, of most of the houses on the south side of the main street. It is surprising and interesting. I remembered from attending a funeral at one of the houses years before. I acted as one of the bearers of a girl of beautiful character who had died of diphtheria. Is there some-thing at Youlgrave that helps to breed girls of that type? I ask because there is in the church a memorial to another maid on which it says:

Fridswide Gilbert to this grave
Hath resigned her earthly part.
Her soul to God that first it gave,
On Angels wings went with her hart,
A Virtuous Maide she lived and died,
Hurtful to none but good to all.
Religious, modest, hating pride,
These virtues crowned her funerall.

That was true also of the girl I knew. While the committal was taking place the sun shone and jack-daws called in the new-green lime trees. The tall, fine

wall built by some wise person now forgotten gave
nice shelter and I thought that no more comfortable and
peaceful a place could have been wished for. I give this
memory to show that Youlgrave is not all bleakness.
We were sorry not to find a home there and thought
that it would have been healthier than Ashford, though
difficult to travel from and back to in snowy winter.

In a search that soon began to seem hopeless, on
another day we took bus from Matlock through Matlock Bath to Cromford. We knew that the first cotton
mill in the kingdom had been built there (in 1771) by
Sir Richard Arkwright, but we had no time to look
for that. But we could not help noticing the artificial
pond in the centre of the village, and with the houses
clustered up the cliff side above it we found ourselves
thinking of such Devon fishing villages as Clovelly. It
all looked quaint and rather attractive, and now that
we live near we often take friends to Cromford. Of
course, many of the houses may not be as attractive to
live in as to look at, but that is because of their age,
for many of them were built for the cotton operatives
before ideal homes for workers had been thought of.
They were not very keen on ventilation in those days
either, judging from many of the windows. They have
metal frames and the panes are in squares or rectangles,
one small piece in the centre generally being the only
one that will open, on hinges. It is a peculiar arrangement that I have not noticed much elsewhere. There
is another peculiarity of much later date. A number of
semi-detached houses have their front windows, down-
stairs and up, clustered together in the centre, and not
spaced out evenly. Presumably all these houses were
built to the plans of the same local architect. What
the advantage of this style might be we could not guess.

Up the steep road towards Wirksworth the houses

might be called good mountaineers, for they cling to the hillside in an expert way, one above the other, like men on a safety rope. The cobbled gutter is so wide and deep (to take the flush when there is heavy rain) that each house has to have its private bridge, generally consisting of one great stone slab, well hollowed from years of wear. Even if there had been a house, my wife did not like the idea of living in such a steep place, and the grind of the buses going up in low gear must be troublesome till one gets used to it.

So after a rest, looking across at the Black Rocks standing impressively on the moor edge eastward, we went on to Middleton Cross and turned right for Middleton, where, according to the *Derbyshire Times*, there was a "desirable residence with seven bedrooms" for sale. We have no family, and we did not know what we could do with all those bedrooms. Still we thought that we had better take a look. Our first impression was that the village was all stone quarries, and secondly that it must be more bleak than Youlgrave. It is, in fact, about 250 feet higher than Youlgrave, being well on the contour of 1,000 feet above sea-level. That is a good height at which to live where there is no shelter, and the only compensation at Middleton seemed to be the views, which are far and extensive. There was an excellent long view from the kitchen of the place we went to—there were windows all along one side like a steamer cabin, and the ground fell away almost immediately outside—but apart from that the house did not seem as desirable as the advertisement had made it out. It was old, and shabby, and five of the "bedrooms" were garrets, and as many houses near by looked about the same, we did not feel much interest in looking farther in Middleton, though D. H. Lawrence, who lived here from May 1918 for a year, described it as a pleasant little place. He says: "It is in the darkish Midlands, on the rim of a steep deep valley, looking over darkish, folded hills—exactly the navel of England, and feels exactly that." He and his wife lived at Mountain Cottage, a "smallish bungalow—with rather pretty little grounds—croquet lawn —and a field attached".

Middleton is the centre of the Lawrence interest in Derbyshire. Although Lawrence was born in Nottingham, it was only just within the border, and no author that I know has caught the spirit better of the adjacent Derbyshire. Writing from New Mexico in 1925 Lawrence told an inquirer:

"The scene of my Nottingham–Derby novels all centres round Eastwood, Notts (where I was born): and whoever stands on Walker Street, Eastwood, will see the whole landscape of *Sons and Lovers* before him: Underwood in front, the hills of Derbyshire on the left, the woods and hills of Annesley on the right. The road from Nottingham to Watnall, Moorgreen, up to Underwood and on to Annesley (Byron's Annesley)—gives you all the landscape of *The White Peacock*, Miriam's farm in *Sons and Lovers*, and the home of the Crich family, and Willey Water in *Women in Love*. *The Rainbow* is Ilkeston and Cossall, near Ilkeston, moving to Eastwood. And Hermione, in *Women in Love*, is supposed to live not far from Cromford. The short stories are Ripley, Wirksworth, Stoney Middleton, Via Gellia (*The Wintry Peacock*). *The Lost Girl* begins in Eastwood—the cinematograph show being in Langley Mill."

In *The Virgin and the Gipsy* Woodlinkin is Middleton-by-Wirksworth and Amberdale is Ambergate.

Writing to a friend in 1926 Lawrence still remembered Derbyshire lovingly, for he advised his friend "to do a hike",

"Langley Mill to Ripley, Ripley to Wingfield Manor (one of my favourite ruins), Crich, and then down to Whatstandwell and up again to Alderwasley and so to Bole Hill and Wirksworth and over Via Gellia, or keep on the high ground from Crich and go round Tansley Moor round to Matlock Bridge, or where you like. But it's real England—the hard pith of England. I'll walk it with you one day."

Lawrence was never to do those walks again, but when he wrote undoubtedly he was remembering how he had gone round in his youth. His sister Ada in her book *Early Life of D. H. Lawrence*, and "E. T.", who was the Miriam of *Sons and Lovers*, in her "personal record" of Lawrence, both tell of the "memorable outing" they had with Lawrence one Easter Monday, going by train from Eastwood to Alfreton and then walking by Wingfield Manor, Crich Stand, finishing at Ambergate. They had hoped to catch a train at Whatstandwell, but found the station there locked, and were all very hungry. They pooled their money and after taking out their fares from Ambergate to Langley Mill found that there was just sevenpence left. Lawrence, the leader, went to a cottage to buy bread and butter. "It was astonishing how much he got for so little," says his sister. They had only water to drink, but were all very happy.

When Lawrence went to live at Middleton in 1918 he seems to have been happy at first and to some extent to have got over the unfortunate experiences with spy-hunters and others that he had had in Cornwall. He had come to Derbyshire in the best of all months and he enjoyed the many flowers. In his collected letters there is one to Catherine Carswell written on June 3rd, 1918, in which he says:

"I got you such a lot of flowers—but am so afraid they will die this hot weather. I love the yellow rock-roses: but they are so frail, I wonder if you'll ever see them as they really are. I'm afraid they'll be all withered. They are pure flowers of light—and they cover the dry, limey hills. The little blue and red bunch is milkworts; the wild columbines are wood-avens, I believe: the yellow pansies are mountain violets—they grow sprinkled close all over the tiny meadow just under the house, and so glittery standing on the close turf—like a Fra Angelico meadow. There is a bit of wood-ruff with a few forget-me-nots. We call it new-mown-hay. It smells like that if you crush it."

Lawrence found other local things interesting. For example (December 20th, 1918):

"We went to Matlock yesterday and got you this bit of the Derbyshire underworld. It is Fluor Spar —mined just near, and cut in Matlock. It is very difficult to cut. There is a purple sort—the common name for this stone is Blue John—but it was too expensive to buy you a purple bowl. And I like this yellow one. It is a golden underworld, the rivers and clearings—do you see it? For some reason, it is like Derbyshire."

But unfortunately the military could not let Lawrence alone in his bungalow on the brow of the steep valley at Via Gellia. He got an order to go to Derby for another medical examination. He went on September 21st, and was put in Grade 3; it was an unpleasant ordeal for one of his extremely sensitive temperament. He told in *Kangaroo* something of his feelings when he had to submit. However, after Derby nothing further happened with the military, and Lawrence was able to live on in his own way. He went to Matlock again, where, he says, "The Derwent rushes very fast. This for some reason gives me extreme pleasure." He had some pleasant walks round about the bungalow till winter began to draw in. Then he found that Mountain Cottage was a "wind centre", and he was very quiet there, "strangely quiet, though the wind blusters, and the rain beats on the little house". In November he wrote to Katherine Mansfield:

"This morning I find the world rather Macbeth-looking—brownish little strokes of larch trees above, the bracken brown and curly, disappearing below the house into shadowy gloom. But the trees to the well are blue-green and luminous almost like stone. On the lawn the moles have turned up a circle of strange black mounds, very magical. But I regret it."

His mood got worse and in December he wrote, "England is gloomy. I think I shall go to America." Later in the month it was:

"The weather continues dark, warm, muggy and nasty. I find the Midlands full of the fear of death —truly. They are all queer and unnerved. This 'flu is very bad. There has only been one flicker of sunshine on the valley. It is very grim always. Last evening at dusk I sat by the rapid brook which runs by the highroad in the valley bed. The spell of hastening, secret water goes over one's mind. When I got to the top—a very hard climb—I felt as if I had climbed out of a womb. The week-end I was at Ripley. Going, on Saturday night, the train runs just above the surface of Butterley Reservoir, and the iron-works on the bank were flaming, a massive roar of flame and burnt smoke in the black sky, flaming and waving again on the black water round the train. On Butterley platform—when I got out —everything was lit up red—there was a man with dark brows, odd, not a human being. I could write a story about him. He made me think of Ashurbanipal. It seems to me, if one is to do fiction now, one must cross the threshold of the human people. I've not done *The Fox* yet—but I've done *The Blind Man*—the end queer and ironical."

Before leaving Middleton he finished *The Fox*, and the essays on education which were printed in *Phœnix*. Several of his *Studies in Classic American Literature*, including the essay "The Spirit of Place", were also done at Middleton. One wonders if the dark man on Butterley platform became Mellors in *Lady Chatterley's Lover*.

The hard weather in that winter among the hills was too much for Lawrence's weak chest. He had a bad attack of flu, and went down again to stay with his sister in Grosvenor Road, Ripley; but he found it very shut in there and soon wanted to get back to Middleton. The last of his letters before he left Middleton in April 1919 to go into Berkshire are of snow in Derbyshire. Lawrence's genius was for descriptive writing, therefore I quote him, for these letters are little known, and give much more vivid pictures of this part of the county than I can hope to do.

Sunday, February 9th, 1919, to Katherine Mansfield:

"It is marvellous weather—brilliant sunshine on the snow, clear as summer, slightly golden sun, distance lit up. But it is immensely cold—everything frozen solid—milk, mustard, everything. Yesterday I went out for a real walk—I've had a cold and been in bed. I climbed with my niece to the bare top of the hills. Wonderful it is to see the footmarks on the snow—beautiful ropes of rabbit prints, trailing away over the brows; heavy hare marks; a fox, so sharp and dainty, going over the wall; birds with two feet that hop; very splendid straight advance of a pheasant; wood-pigeons that are clumsy and move in flocks; splendid little leaping marks of weasels, coming along like a necklace chain of berries; odd little filigree of the field-mice; the trail of a mole—it is astonishing what a world of wild creatures one feels round one, on the hills in the snow. From the height it is very beautiful. The upland is naked, white like silver, and moving far into the distance, strange and muscular, with gleams like skin. Only the wind surprises one, invisibly cold; the sun lies bright on a field, like the movement of a sleeper. It is strange how insignificant in all this life seems. Two men, tiny as dots, move from a farm on a snow slope carrying hay to the beasts. Every moment they seem to melt like insignificant spots of dust; the sheer, living, muscular white of the uplands absorbs everything. Only there is a tiny clump of trees bare on the hill-top—small beeches—writhing like iron in the blue sky. . . . It is beautiful to cross the field to the well for drinking water—such pure sun, and Slaley, the tiny village away across, sunny as Italy in its snow."

On Friday, December 27th, 1918, he wrote to Katherine Mansfield:

"I wish you could have been there on the hill summit—the valley all white and hairy with trees below us, and grey with rocks and just round us on our side the grey stone fences drawn in a network over the snow, all very clear in the sun."

And then in an undated letter:

"It is snow, snow, snow here—white, white, white. Yesterday was the endless silence of softly falling snow. I thought the world had come to an end—that I was like a last inhabitant of the moon, when the moon shed all its snow and went into a white dream for ever, slowly breathing its last in a soft, dim snowfall, silent beyond silence. Nobody comes, the snow is white on the shrubs, the tufts of larches above the road have each a white line up the trunk. Lord, Lord! Only the rabbit feet and bird feet are all over the paths and across the yard."

Then a little later, to another friend: "The sun shines —the snowdrops are out in the garden, under the bushes. I long to begin life afresh, in a new country." So Lawrence, the restless genius, left Derbyshire once more and the following year was in Italy, from where eventually he went to Australia, New Mexico, Mexico. But in his last novel, *Lady Chatterley's Lover*, obviously he was still remembering his native district and per- haps the dark stranger seen on Butterley platform in 1918.

Having decided against taking a house in Middleton,

despite D. H. Lawrence having lived there, my wife and I returned to Cromford. Coming down the long steep hill we noticed the view, one of the best and most unusual in the county. We saw at once why Matlock Bath and round about has been called "Little Switzerland", for there below is High Tor, the mountain limestone of which it is made suggesting snow. At its foot, as it seems, is Willersley Castle among its woods, and beyond is Darley Dale, the whole picture enclosed with higher hills ending in skylines that suggest more and more hills. There is beauty and impressiveness, and if visitors could arrange their first visit to Matlock Bath and Matlock from Ashbourne, coming over the bleak limestone plateau above Brassington, through Wirksworth in its mountain hollow, and down this long road to Cromford, they would see many extraordinary contrasts and appreciate the wooded loveliness of the gorge under High Tor much more than it is possible to do when seeing it in the usual way travelling from prosaic Matlock.

CHAPTER XV

THE SUNNY SOUTH

HAVING failed to find a house anywhere in the Bakewell and Matlock areas, we determined to try south
of Derby, and having travelled by train down the
beautiful valley of the Derwent—nowhere more beautiful than between Cromford and Ambergate—we left
Derby by bus for Melbourne. I am told that the whole
of Derbyshire should properly be classed with the
Midlands, though I hold that down to Derby it more
naturally belongs to the North. But about that part
south of Derby there can be no argument: it is of the
Midlands truly. How far Derby itself stretches out on
this side, as if reaching for the southern sun! Then
there is the Trent, a broad lowland river; how great
a contrast from the highland Wye. And yet there is
romance here too, particularly at Swarkeston. It was a
pity to rush over the bridge that first time by a bus
that almost seemed to have difficulty in getting past
the many twists between the narrow walls.

For Swarkeston is most certainly a bridge that
should be walked over, though I hope that before long
a new bridge will be built for cars and lorries, leaving
the old bridge as an "ancient monument" over which
it will be possible to stroll at ease and think of times
past, instead of always of the hooting, ever-dangerous
present.

Dr Charles Cox was very annoyed about many of
the strengthenings and other alterations made to the
bridge, which he said absolutely disfigured it, but to one
like myself with a very poorly developed architectural

conscience, the bridge still looks quite attractive. I agree, of course, that the use of stone instead of bricks would have been more in keeping. It is a bridge that suggests old tales at once, and what could be better than the tradition that it was built by two sisters whose lovers were lost when trying to cross the Trent by boat or ford to meet them? That the expense left the sisters paupers is understandable, for the bridge is three-quarters of a mile in length. The actual river span is only 414 feet, the rest being more of a causeway, though with many arches to let flood water through. The part of the bridge spanning the river is, says Dr Cox, "quite modern", but it was built in 1796–7, the earlier part being smashed in 1795 by timber from a yard higher up being swung against it by flood. In pack-horse times Swarkeston was the only bridge across the Trent between Burton and Nottingham, and was of great importance. In the Civil War the bridge was first held by the Royalists, but on January 5th, 1643, they were routed by Sir John Gell, of Hopton, and the Parliamentarians then held it firmly to the end. Two centuries ago the bridge was held for two nights by the last invaders who ever penetrated England as a marching army. And that I think of most, for no picture could be stranger than that of members of a Highland army patrolling here in the very midst of England.

Thousands of persons who have come to see the bridge must have thought of the guard as men dressed somewhat like those of our present Highland regiments, but it seems more likely that they were mounted, probably Lord Pitsligo's Horse. There are in existence extracts from the Order Book of Captain James Stuart, of Lord Ogilvie's Regiment, which give the order of march for Prince Charlie's army. On December 3rd

Melbourne Hall, as seen from the Pool
Sudbury Hall, which has a village to match

and 4th, 1745, Derby being entered on the 4th, the order was: "A field officer and 50 of Pitsligo's Horse to be in the van of all. Cluny to be the van of the foot." The order for December 5th and 6th gives, "Pitsligo's the rear of the whole Army", which would have been correct had the march to London gone forward as was then intended, leaving them to guard the bridge till everybody and everything else was across. Pitsligo's men were described by the *Derby Mercury* of the time as "likely men" who "made a good appearance", being "cloathed in blue, faced with red, most of 'em had a scarlet waistcoat with gold lace". Probably the guard numbered about sixty or eighty, and there may have been a few foot among them. If so, they would have on the usual dress of their kind at the time: a shirt and a long plaid, so wrapped as to form a crude kilt, with hose of plaid. It is said that the Duke of Cumberland intended to blow up the bridge, but that the Scots beat by four hours the party sent out to demolish it. Obviously it was best for the Prince to send troopers when it was a race to get there first.

It is even possible that the Prince visited the bridge outpost on the second day of his stay in Derby, for there is a tradition that he went to Calke Abbey, which is only four miles farther, to see Sir Henry Harpur, to persuade him to join his cause. If he did go, he failed in his purpose, so that it is permissible to imagine him riding back dejectedly across Swarkeston Bridge to attend that black council meeting which decided that his army must retreat. Had Sir Henry Harpur and one or two other influential Derbyshire men agreed to come out for the Prince, the retreat very probably would never have taken place. Despite the lack of open alliances, the Prince, think many men, should still have gone on and not back, and Major Eardley-Simpson,

12*   177

Cubley
Darley Yew

after very carefully considering all the evidence, gives in his excellent book, *Derby and the Forty-Five*, "the emphatic and unhesitating view that, if the army of the White Rose had marched over Swarkeston Bridge on that morning of December 6th, 1745, within a week James III would have been proclaimed in London, while Newcastle and Bedford encouraged an enthusiastic populace to welcome Charles not only as the Prince Regent of the Kingdom, but as the victorious leader who had restored the native House without the aid of a foreign bayonet".

Well, what might have been we can only guess, but, as John Buchan wrote, the critical moment of the Forty-Five was not Glenfinnan or Prestonpans or bloody Culloden, but that December day when the tide of the adventure reached its farthest point at Swarkeston Bridge and then mysteriously ebbed.

In Melbourne there is a tradition that before the Jacobite retreat was decided, orders were sent for preparations to be made there to billet the army on the next stage of its way to Leicester, and that the orders were obeyed. If, as is to be presumed, these orders were taken by special messengers, they must have gone by King's Newton, for the present main road from Swarkeston to Melbourne was not then made. We got down from the bus at the corner for King's Newton and went by the same way, which is well worth while. For there is a warmth of weathered brick and a quiet shaded picturesqueness about King's Newton that make it a pleasant introduction to the villages of this southern end of the county, which contrast so with the more strenuous villages of the north. When the pack-horse track went through to Swarkeston, King's Newton was much more important than now, and there are ruins of a big hall where Charles II

once stayed, and a fine, high wall still standing.
Melbourne sprawling on the low hill behind looks un-
attractive despite its age and the honour it holds of
fathering the Australian Melbourne. Among trees, as
at King's Newton, red brick looks attractive, but on
the bare hill it is garish.

Melbourne, or most of it, instead of mellowing,
seems to have deteriorated as time has passed, and we
found it difficult to imagine it with a famous and
important castle. The most prosperous feature of
Melbourne now is the open-field "market gardens"
round it, which looked well and faithfully kept. We
decided that if we were to find a house here we should
never want for good vegetables; but that generally all
other shopping would be best done in Derby. We
thought that life would be sleepy, too, without the
invigoration of the hills. Perhaps we were not really
sorry that the house we had gone after was unsuitable,
yet our first sight of this part of the county made us
wish to see more.

In Derby I had been asked which did I think were
the prettiest Derbyshire villages. I was unprepared.
My instant inclination was to say, "Combs", because
I had come to love it so much during all our years
there, but I knew that that was no fair answer.

"I am sure about the third," said my questioner
while I hesitated. "But I am not sure about the first
and second."

"Tissington first?" I hazarded.

"Third," said he promptly. "Tissington is just a
bit too . . . too precious, if you know what I mean."
I believed I did. "Ashford, I think I place first—really
charming—and after that, Sudbury."

"Sudbury?" I repeated. "I'm afraid I've never even
been there."

"Oh, you must. It's red brick and tile—not your grey north—but it's so much all in keeping, unspoilt."

So off to Sudbury we went, this time by car, taking the road through Melbourne for Ashby-de-la-Zouch. It happened that I carried a letter from a woman born ninety years before and still able to write legibly and wisely. As we drove on into the gently undulating, beautifully wooded country I thought of this letter and eventually we stopped in the shade of an excellent oak and I took it out. It was dated from Sudbury, not, however, the Derbyshire one, but in Suffolk. I read:

"It is many years since I saw any of that part, and have seen so many other lovely scenes in Devon and some parts I cannot even remember the names, but the dales and Matlock, also Buxton, have a soft place in my heart. I sit and think of many happy times I have had. Then there is Kent—some call that the Garden of England. Father always said Derbyshire was the Garden of England. Wish I could see it once more. It must be seventy years since I stayed with a friend of Mother's and made her a black silk dress out of hat bands worn by her sons. They drove the hearse and carriages at funerals. The hat bands were about half-a-yard wide and two long, worn round their hats, tied in a huge badge at the back, ends hung down. . . . I hope you will not be too tired with my muddley letter— set it down to old age. Am thankful to be as well as I am; never thought to reach my ninety years, but one can live too long. All one's real friends are gone. . . ."

Rather a sad letter, an exile thinking lovingly of her birthplace and childhood home, but I thought of her

father, so long dead, calling Derbyshire the Garden of
England. Actually he had lived in Ashford, that other
village my Derby questioner had mentioned, but if
any part of the county deserves the name of Garden,
it is where we were as we read under the oak: as
beautiful as Kent, lacking only the white cowls of oast-
houses peeping among the trees.

From Ashby-de-la-Zouch we crossed the southern-
most arm of the county to Swadlincote, a name to
dream over, but a place bigger and more urbanised
than we liked; and thus on and over the border again
into Burton-on-Trent. Shortly afterwards we got on
to the Roman Rycknield Street (from Birmingham to
Chesterfield through Derby) and saw it stretching
straight ahead; but shortly after entering our own
county once more, near Monks Bridge, we turned off
the Street to look at Repton. Slim, tall and shapely is
the tower of the church seen over the foliage across
the level water-meadows. Repton, like King's Newton,
was once much more important than today, and despite
the activity being displayed on the cricket field by
scholars of its famous school, the place gave an impression of retirement after a life of labour now nearly
forgotten. Its busy days were in Saxon times when it
was one of the first towns of the Kingdom of Mercia,
with an important abbey. Later a priory was founded
and the picturesque arch by the church was the
entrance to the priory grounds, now taken over by
Repton School. The old market cross on its high flight
of steps in the centre of the square opposite church
and archway completes an old-world scene. Going up
the hill towards Bretby we hoped to get a bird's view
of Repton, with church and school spread together,
but we did not, though there was a good view of the
gently rolling country around. All farmhouses and

cottages hereabouts are of old brick, and after so
many years in the north we had to keep reminding
ourselves that we were still in Derbyshire.

Returning across the Trent, a mile from Repton,
we passed through Willington again, quite forgetting
to inspect the church tower, which is said to have cost
only £86. Then over Rycknield Street, which in spite
of its Roman origin did not look very interesting. We
made for Hilton and were soon on the main Derby–
Uttoxeter road, running parallel with the River Dove,
which hereabouts is the county boundary. But is it
Dove? Very different it is from the tiny stream that
rises under Axe Edge. And very different, too, is the
country through which it flows. Here the roads are
muffled with thriving trees and hedges, every cottage
had its roses and brilliant spired delphiniums, every
farm its stack-yard of a size that would make an Earl
Sterndale or a Monyash man smile, though perhaps
rather wistfully. There were one or two small collections of cottages which we thought might be the beginnings of Sudbury, but past them we ran through more
good country until I began to wonder whether we might
not have missed the village. And then we came to a
signpost which pointed to "Sudbury station, 1 mile"
leftward. I looked at the map and saw that the station
is actually over the Dove in Staffordshire, though Sudbury village is a mile within the Derbyshire border.
What a pity if there had been any doubt about which
county this pretty village belongs to! For Sudbury is
pretty in the genuine English way, old and good, and
yet not blatant. There were big United States Army
camps all round, but even these had interfered only a
little with the beauty, being very nearly hidden by the
great trees. The village proper consists of one short
main street, if street it should be called, every house

of mellowed brick with tiled roof to match; and then
the road runs out in front of the level lawns of the big
Elizabethan hall with its fine range of windows and
central arched doorway. It is not hidden, as so many
halls are, but seems to be part of the village, watching
over it benignly. It was sad to find the lodge, built to
match the hall, empty and falling into ruin. Over the
road the hall looks on to the tree-studded park, and
some way back is an ornamented deer shelter, which
also is part of the picture. Many of the U.S. Army
men who were stationed near here must have taken
charming photographs to show to the folks at home
what the old country still looks like. From my one-
inch-to-the-mile Ordnance map I had expected to see
a lake in front of the hall, but I was disappointed, the
lake and the gardens being hidden by a high wall
which starts beyond the hall.

Sudbury is the ancient seat of the Vernons. The
hall was built in 1615–20 by the widow of John
Vernon, and it has been suggested that it was the
example of Bess of Hardwick that started her on the
work. From 1840 to 1843 Queen Adelaide, widow of
King William IV, lived here. Coming from the south,
no doubt she liked it, for the prevailing spirit of Sudbury is of the south. Therefore, even allowing for its
quiet and charm, I do not feel that it can be put first
on any list of Derbyshire villages. After all, the greater
part of the county is greystone country, so I put
Tissington first, despite my questioner, Ashford
second, and then Sudbury. I add, however, that anybody who sets out to see Derbyshire's villages must
not miss Sudbury.

But is it not invidious work, judging among
villages? Even such exposed places as Brassington,
say, have each their own particular charms; and what

about such pretty, sheltered places as Middleton-by-Youlgrave? Because I have listed only three villages in order, I do not want it to be thought that there are not many others with nearly equal claims. Derbyshire is, indeed, rich in its villages.

Take Cubley, for instance, through which we passed on our way back from Sudbury on the Ashbourne road. Here are beauty and history together, and nobody having caught sight of the little church on its hillside can help feeling a desire to stop and go in. And a look inside repays the time it takes. Close by one can trace the moat of the ancient home of the Montgomerys, otherwise completely gone, and imagine the times when Cubley was Great Cubley, and had a weekly market and a noteworthy annual fair.

But we had no time for further loitering and ran on quickly to Ashbourne. Sight-seeing is pleasant, much less tiring than house-hunting, only it does not get one a house!

Chapter XVI

CARNIVAL CENTRE

When we set out to find a home in the Bakewell or Matlock district we were very dogmatic on one point: we did not want to live in Darley Dale. We thought of Darley Dale only as a long straight road, with a few dull houses beside it, a kind of pause between the variety and beauty of Chatsworth Park or the Wye Valley past Haddon Hall, and the romantic gorge under High Tor. Older people at Chapel-en-le-Frith told us that we were wrong; that Darley Dale was not only beautiful, but gay also. However, we thought their opinions were due to nostalgic memories, for we learned that years ago, whenever a day's outing was planned, usually they went to Darley Dale because of the convenience and facilities provided by Whitworth Park there. We had been told of the gay rides they had down the dales by horse wagonette; and some spoke of childhood trips when they were carried in springless farm carts, and trundled home singing through summer's dusk. It all sounded quaint; nice to be told about it, but had the actual thing been very exciting? Well, there was the time when young Bertha fell full length, all white frills, into the paddling pond in the Park, and was pulled out all green. That was exciting enough, of course; it would be—for young, proud parents! It did not make us change our minds about Darley Dale as a place to live in. We were inclined to class the joys of these trips with the joys they talked about at the old Wakes. We had been to the modern Wakes and found the steam-yachts and swing-chairs rather tame and second-handish. If one wanted thrills of that kind, wasn't Blackpool several per cent better? Anyway . . .

And then a house came empty in Darley Dale, and it had so many attractions that we simply had to have it, and we found ourselves trying to settle in the place that we had despised. Again we learned the truth, that what the motorist, or the day-tripper, sees of a place does not amount to much. Darley Dale has its long straight road, but there are fine lime trees along it. There is some line-building of not very picturesque houses, but here and there on the hillsides are some of the most attractive old stone houses, for the main road is very emphatically not all of Darley Dale: it is merely the quickest way of letting motorists through!

The first thing that everybody should see in Darley Dale is the yew in the churchyard, though local people do not think as much of it as they should. It is the veteran of England, reckoned to be 2,000 years old, but it cares nothing for man's reckoning and carries itself as upright as a youngster, in summer putting new, bright tips to its boughs and in autumn decking itself with pure, bloomy red berries, as though it intends to live for ever. A friend who came from north of Preston, a farmer and passionate admirer of healthy crops, having seen the yew said that it was well worth his long journey if he never saw anything else. About twenty years ago a Darley-born man who had gone to America offered £200 to the church if he could be buried under the yew, but his offer was declined.

There are many things round and in the church that suggest great age more so than the yew, among them a number of stone coffins with lids, one made for a very small child. There is a tale that when this coffin was dug up by some workmen draining or doing other work, a girl was found inside looking almost as though she had only just been put in. One of the men ran to bring a doctor, but before he got back the figure had fallen to dust.

Round the south porch of the church are a number of gravestones of unusual shape, somewhat like ornamented chests with wide tops. These bear dates about 1750 and belong to Protestant exiles from France, Huguenots, who brought with them from there their trade of spinning and weaving. On the sides of some of the tombs can be found carvings of shuttles, spinning wheels, and a weaving frame.

Although there are a number of interesting epitaphs in the graveyard one in particular I like to read regularly to my wife. Other husbands may like to do the same. It runs:

A virtuous, careful, and industrious wife,
Each duty fill'd thro' every stage of life:
Attend ye females of the rising race,
Her virtues copy, and her footsteps trace.

Inside the church there is an effigy of a man in armour, John de Darley (about 1325), of the family that gave the place its name; and incised effigy-slabs to members of the Rolleston family, whose name lives on as Rowsley. More interesting to the ordinary visitor is the Burne-Jones window, with twelve pictures illustrating lines from the "Song of Solomon" most graphically and sometimes amusingly. It must be very helpful when there is a dull sermon.

Wandering through Darley Dale it is impossible to miss the unsightly mass of white debris across the river from the church. This marks Mill Close Mine.

No county, I think, can have more abandoned quarries and mines than Derbyshire. Always I wonder what stories they could tell. I have an old friend at Chapel-en-le-Frith and remember his telling me quietly as we passed a certain large, well-built house: "I carted that house there, every bit, out of Barmour Clough Quarry." He had been a horseman and lorry-man in his younger days. The house is likely to stand for a hundred years and more, but already the quarry is deserted and done with.

No mine in the county has a stranger history than this of Mill Close between Darley and Stanton. At one time it was the richest lead mine in Great Britain, producing a third of the whole country's output. The mine was opened more than a hundred years ago by Mr E. M. Wass, for whom and his successors it made fortunes. During the 1914–18 war, however, the ore began to run out, many miners were suspended, and Winster and other villages suffered. Yet old miners had faith in the mine and after the war a number of local men were induced to invest and the mine was reopened. More rich ore was found, four hundred men were employed and the mine prospered. In 1929 the ore began to give out again, and the company which had done so well eventually had a debit balance of more than £31,000.

Then the New Consolidated Goldfields of South Africa, Ltd., and the National Mining Corporation, Ltd., began to take an interest and put in the largest electric pumps in the world up to that time. Water had always prevented mining below 70 fathoms, but these pumps drew up 30,000,000 gallons a week and it soon became possible to go deeper. At 125 fathoms ore richer than any previously known was discovered and once more the mine became a great money-maker. At

one time work was going on 500 feet below the level
of the near-by Derwent and more than eight hundred
men were employed, but the ore was going deeper
and deeper and becoming more costly to get out
because of the steady increase of water.

One Friday afternoon in February 1938, following
the firing of a shot, water burst into all the lower levels.
Fortunately, owing to previous evidence, it had been
thought possible that something might happen and the
men had been warned and no lives were lost, though
the pumps were overwhelmed. It was estimated that
500,000 gallons of water were pouring in every hour
from some unknown reservoir. Three hundred miners
were thrown out of work, but within three days the
management put in extra pumps to take another
30,000 gallons per minute and gradually the battle
was won, and that May the galleries, though filled
with mud, became workable again. Misfortune, however, seemed determined to keep her hand on the mine,
for just after the reopening four men loading a motor-
lorry at the "slime" tip were suddenly buried by an
avalanche. Thirty men went to their rescue but three
of the men were dead before they could be dug out.
The fourth, though badly injured, survived. Shortly
afterwards the mine was stopped again by an inflow of
water so immense that the whole labyrinth of workings
was flooded within a few hours. This time many men
only just managed to escape, though again nobody
was lost. For several weeks the great pumps were kept
at work night and day but the water remained within
a few feet of ground level, scarcely showing any
alteration, and the mine that had paid hundreds of
thousands of pounds to so many royalty owners had
eventually to be given up. In May 1945 all the expensive pumping machinery, electric motors to a total of

some 3,000 h.p., switchgear, filters, and the flotation plant were sold for dispersal.

In the early days of the mine's history the ore was taken to Lea beyond Matlock for smelting, but later smelting was done on the site. After the mine had finished producing, the "slime" or residue was found to be worth re-treatment for lead deposits that had been missed by earlier methods. But already wild plants are beginning to encroach and soon many parts of the famous workings will be green, and passers-by, noticing the unusual conformation, may idly wonder what once happened there. How many other industrial romances as interesting are hidden and forgotten under grassy mounds elsewhere?

Just after one in the morning of March 4, 1945, while the smelting night-shift was at work one of the last piloted German planes to raid this country circled Mill Close several times, and swooping, fired two bursts of machine-gun bullets. Although a warning had been sounded it had not been heard and the works were still lit up. The roofs of one or two of the sheds were broken but no one was hurt.

From Darley Dale our nearest shopping place is Matlock. Much has been written about the beauties round Matlock and of the town's own ugliness, and the ugliness of the buildings and quarries between Matlock and Matlock Bath. But it is so easy to forget that everything has some cause or reason for its existence based on real life, the working part of life, which is very different from the leisure of life which includes rambles and holidays. The so-called ugliness of Matlock and Matlock Bath, the lack of planning in the building and in the opening of quarries and other industries, seem to be the results of a sturdy independence rather to be admired than belittled. I did not realise this till I came to live near and began to talk with people there.

Matlock is on the edge of the Dukeries, that wide stretch of country claimed by big landowners. Hemming Matlock in are the estates now held by the Dukes of Devonshire, Portland, and Rutland. Think what this meant in the old days. Men had either to be obedient to these landowners, or there was no work and no homes for them. Only this bit of land round Matlock and Matlock Bath was free, a kind of island, and so here gathered independents and the fighters and poachers of a vast district. They lived how they could on free crafts, and they built where they could, wherever they could make foundation. In the day when town-planning first came to be thought of Matlock and Matlock Bath consisted of little blocks of grey-stone houses put up anywhere, owned by all kinds of people, all of whom were self-reliant and self-willed, the very last type to agree to regimentation. Matlock Bridge is a cold place. Winds draw up the narrow valley and up the gorge to Cromford, and it was not the pleasantest of places to live in. That is probably why it had not been taken into any of the estates, and life was hard there. The people did not consider the beauties of the place when they were going about making a living, and so when they found that money was to be made out of visitors they set out to cater for them in a business-like way. Many things the people did are to be regretted now, yet it is only fair that some record should be given of how they were driven to it.

Many of the native-born have still their own peculiar spirit of independence, inherited from parents who had refused to lift a hat or make a curtsey to any duke or lord whatever. A stranger who went into a pub and threw a pound note on the bar and told the man to give everybody a drink would very probably find that not all the company would accept. One or two would be most likely to ask: "Who the hell. . . ? What I want, I can pay for. Let him keep his bloody money." Once a landlord came from Devon and when he was asked for a drink, said "Yes, sir," and "No, sir," as he had been accustomed to. But his pub soon lost custom. The average man hereabouts when he goes into a pub wants a drink; and all he wants of the bartender is that he should take his money and give him a drink. He doesn't want any extra politeness; he hasn't been used to it. Nevertheless, I am wrong if I give the impression that he is rough and crude. He is just quietly, resolutely independent to those he does not know; but very friendly indeed with those whom he does know.

The best thing I can think of to illustrate the difference of the Matlock district character from the character of men from other parts of the county is what I was told by a man there who had served for twenty-four years first in the old Derbyshire Volunteers and then in a territorial battalion of the Sherwood Foresters. At each annual camp he met men from every other part of the county, and, of course, for the time being lived with them. What struck him was the quiet good-nature of the men from Chapel-en-le-Frith and the north. "I never heard one of them fall out with another; they were all a grand lot of pals together. The men from Claycross and the mines were just as different—always rowing and swearing. They couldn't keep quiet. Good pals all the same; it was just their way."

What the Matlock man did not realise was that he represented a different type again, and that was why

Matlock Bath, from the Fish Pool Hotel
Cromford Bridge, which has round arches on the other side

he had been struck by their ways. The men from the north are independent, but it is very many generations since Peak Forest was broken up and since then the inhabitants of that part have lived as small farmers and quarrymen, working for themselves or for whom they chose. They have not had to assert their independence. They carry it naturally, knowing very little about it. The Claycross men come from generations of miners who have always had to fight for wage increases and better conditions. They have been in constant conflict with bosses and have had to assert themselves. But the Matlock men were never in such close conflict with anyone. They had escaped, or walked off from the estate bosses, though they were still fairly close to them, and there was always danger of clashes. So the Matlock district man is intermediate between the other two, but which type is most typical of the county as a whole it is futile to try to decide.

It is only fair to end this subject with an anecdote about men representative of those who have lived for generations on the estates. In the Sherwood Foresters during the 1914–18 war, when an inspection was to be made by any big man, some of the Chapel men used to twit the Calver men by saying: "Hats off, lads! The Duke's coming." But the Calver men never took it amiss. They grinned and stood to attention with the rest, showing that though they knew of their dependence on the estates, they had their private opinions about it, nevertheless.

There is a good deal of loyalty among all Derbyshire men towards the local regiment, the "good old Notts and Jocks", as there is also a good deal of county loyalty. While living near Chapel-en-le-Frith, almost on the Cheshire and Lancashire borders and only twenty miles from Manchester, I was often surprised

13   193

The Moot Hall, Winster
A peep in pretty Beeley

that there was so little interest shown in Manchester City and United football teams and in Lancashire county cricket. Papers came much quicker and more regularly from Manchester, and transport there and back was much cheaper and easier than with Derby, yet the later papers from the south were preferred and the county teams were the only ones much thought of.

There is no particular rivalry against any other county, as between Lancashire and Yorkshire, but there is still much healthy rivalry between villages inside the county boundaries. The Volunteer movement was very strong in Derbyshire before the 1914–18 war and it was an excellent thing for men from different parts of the county to camp together for a fortnight to get to know and respect each other. Between the wars the Territorial movement never had the same popularity, but it would be a good thing if some other movement could be started, say with some peace aim, that could get men from all over to meet not for a day, but for a minimum of two weeks annually, long enough for them to get to know one another, just as they did in the old Volunteer days, which are still remembered thankfully by many men all over the county.

We have come a long way from Matlock and the mix-up of its buildings, but that kind of thing seems inevitable in a book about a county in which so many different things jostle one another so closely. Matlock having been defended, this seems the point to defend much other building. It is so easy when looking at an asbestos bungalow, or a cheap brick house, to exclaim against its unsightliness, but not nearly so often do we stop to consider the circumstances. Many persons have retired into Derbyshire to these little houses built at their own charge. Had they been able to afford houses of local stone, no doubt they would have done so; but they put up the best that they could afford. It is difficult to see how this can be stopped without autocratic methods. What should be stopped is the wholesale erecting by speculative builders of shoddy, inappropriate houses from which they hope to make big profits out of people who can ill afford to pay. What is even worse is the setting up, by persons with money and luxury cars and good homes elsewhere, of wooden bungalows, and the depositing of garish caravans in beautiful places which are thus disfigured all the year round, although the accommodation they give may only be used for a fortnight or perhaps half a dozen weekends in a season. The good country round Whatstandwell has suffered sadly in this way. I do not think there is any other county as suitable as Derbyshire to become a national park. Now that it has been put first on the list for this use, this weekend joy-house habit should be controlled. It is not that one wishes to stop weekending in the country, but then sites could be set aside in healthy and pleasant places, where the huts, or whatever might be put up, would not be planted higgledy-piggledy in the centre of the best beauty spots to mar them for everybody else.

Now we must get back to Matlock. It cannot be claimed that the town is beautiful, though about the surroundings there can be no challenge. The commanding building of the town is Smedley's Hydro. It commands because of its position, high on a terrace of Matlock Bank, but looks something like a mill, though now fortunately it has become covered with Virginia creeper, which sometimes transforms it with many colours—almost a rainbow effect—into a thing of beauty. John Smedley, the builder, also built Riber Castle, the other dominating building of Matlock.

This was his private residence, and cost him over £70,000. It was finished about 1860. There was a danger some time back of the building going into the hands of speculators, but Matlock Urban District Council bought it at an auction sale in 1936 for £1,150, though what is to be done with it I do not know. Riber Hill without the Castle would seem bare. There is a very wide view from the towers, yet it seems an exposed spot to choose for a private residence when there was no question of ever being attacked. John Smedley, however, was eccentric in many things, though he made money very readily. Smedley's was the first "hydro" in this country. There is a story that Smedley first noticed the good effect of the local water on some cattle, either of his own or belonging to a neighbour, and then offered free treatment to any of his work-people (he was first a stocking manufacturer) who might care to try it. This led to the establishment of his hydro, which became immensely successful, even though no intoxicating drink was ever served there, Smedley being a Primitive Methodist and a teetotaller, refusing even to allow guests to bring their own liquor. He soon gave up making stockings, the hydro being much more profitable.

The road from Matlock Bridge to Matlock Bath gives splendid views of the wooded banks of the Derwent and the limestone cliffs of the High Tor—I do not think that at one time it would have been possible in Britain to have found a road giving views of more beauty and grandeur—but now the road is spoilt by far too much traffic, unsightly industry, and far too many advertisements, beginning at the railway bridge where on one side we are told that Bass is good for us and on the other that it is a sheer joy to drink Worthington. So I prefer to walk to Matlock Bath by the path that leaves Matlock Bridge on the left and goes by the side of the park and under the trees of the river bank. Near where the little brook comes in from Matlock Green there is a boulder of gritstone with a metal plate to tell of a policeman drowned in trying to save a boy from the flooded river. When the Derwent is at anything above summer height there is a great flow at this corner and it is easy to understand the brave man's loss. The path, after crossing the brook, swings rightward at the base of cliffs that lean forward as though threateningly, but are made picturesque by ivy and the fringe of clinging trees above. Where the rock is less sheer trees cover the slopes, and so-called "Lovers' Walks" go up and down among them. It is worth while climbing the twisting path that goes to the War Memorial standing clear on its escarpment, for there is a good view to which the traffic and the industries give interest without entirely spoiling things.

At the footbridge one must cross the river to see the best of the quaintness of Matlock Bath itself. There is something suggestive of the Wye Valley below Symond's Yat in the houses at different heights among the trees under the Heights of Abraham. The village, once thought quite a stylish place, now seems a bit too Victorian in its shops and amusement offerings. The Blue John ornaments shown in the shop below the premises where the stone is turned and polished are attractive (and expensive!), but the days are past when many persons are eager to buy old shoes and fans and toy trumpets which have been left in the "petrifying well" opposite and been coated with lime. They are curiosities of rather too crude a type. More worth looking at are the fish in the roadside pool fed with the authentic Bath water. There remained only one or two golden carp when last I was there, but there were many trout, and strange they look when they crowd, in front and behind, above and below, all together at the mouth of the low tunnel through which the water flows in, bringing with it, of course, eagerly awaited food. The fish interest children and others by rising for crumbs and are as tame as any fish I have seen.

While I was looking into the pool one winter afternoon a policeman came up and asked if I knew a very strange thing about it. When I said "No," he asked if it wasn't true that in 1940 all signposts and milestones were taken away so that our enemies might not get information from them. I said that I believed that that was so. The policeman chuckled.

"We had an inspector came round, and when he'd finished, I asked if he was satisfied as there was none left. He said he was. And the sergeant that was with him said as he was. So I told them there was a milestone within six yards of them—and there it is," ended the constable triumphantly, and in the wall of the pond near the tunnel we saw it. "One of the very few in England as was never disturbed," added the constable. "I've won many a bet on it."

"Chatsworth 10 mil, Bakywell 10, Manchester 45. 1801 A.D." says the milestone. No distance is given to Derby, for the simple reason that the road past here when the milestone was cut did not go to Derby. It was not till 1815 that Scarthin Rock at Cromford was blasted through and the present road made southward. Previously the road to Derby went over the hills by Cromford Common, Wirksworth and Kedleston. Matlock Bath has quite a short history. Defoe, who visited in the eighteenth century, wrote: "The Bath would be much more frequented than it is, if a sad stony way which leads to it, and no accommodation when you get there, did not hinder." The making of the road through Scarthin and the opening of the Midland Railway to Ambergate (known then as Matlock Station), from where visitors travelled the remaining six miles by carriage or wagonette, soon made Matlock Bath more popular. When the railway was brought through to Rowsley and eventually to Manchester the Bath really came into favour. What it was like in its heyday is best left to a writer of 1879, Edward Bradbury, whose style seems appropriate to his topic:

"What Carnival time is to Rome, what the Derby Day is to Epsom, what the Goose Fair is to Nottingham, what the St Leger is to Doncaster, Good Friday is to Matlock. To assert that Matlock Bath is crowded on Good Friday is really to extenuate circumstances. To say that it is lively is to convey but an elementary idea of the hillarious jollity which prevailed. Rudely aroused on the buniferous day from her winter's rest, Matlock receives visitors from half-a-dozen counties. There is a crowded train from remote Bradford and Leeds. Sheffield and Chesterfield call for two 'specials'. Manchester and Stockport send ten excursion trains to Matlock, and three extra trains of sensational length hardly satisfy the demands of Derby. Birmingham by special train sends her button-makers, Nottingham her bleating 'lambs', and Leicester her mill-hands; while dog-carts and traps contribute a large auxiliary traffic. Matlock is ready for the invaders, and resists their demands with boiled ham and mounds of beef, sufficient to victual an army corps. She lays in oceans of explosive beer, and makes barriers of buns. The supply of eggs for tea speaks libraries for the industry of the Derbyshire hens; while the professional

commissariate of the place is strengthened by half
the private houses boiling 'hot water for twopence
a head'. The main thoroughfare is one sweeping,
swaying crowd, whose greedy lungs soon consume
all the fresh mountain air in stock, and leave the
valley close and oppressive. . . . To complete the
bliss of the bona fide excursionist, he must be sold
with a purse containing half a sovereign for the sum
of sixpence. He must be supplied with one of the
cheap canes with gay knobs, hawked by lusty-
lunged itinerants. He must upset his stomach with
a packet of the bilious-looking gingerbread from
the basket of the man whose face seems made out
of the mould Nature patterned for Bill Sykes. He
must prove himself a 'crack'-ed shot at a gaudy
rifle-gallery. It is necessary that he should strain his
lungs by blowing down a tube, ascertain his fighting-
weight by sitting in an impossible arm-chair, agitate
his nerves by pennyworths of galvanic shock, and
show off his pugilistic prowess by punching a grinning effigy of the late Sultan 'below the belt'. It is
also a *sine qua non* that the cheap tripper should
display his generosity by copper contributions to
the begging-box of the sham sailor, with the sham
medals and the sham wounds, and the sham children; or to the supplicating hat of the sturdy vaga-
bond whose card announces that he was 'blinded by
blasting', but whether by dynamite or damning is
left to charitable conjecture. The wants of the
'tripper' in this direction are well supplied. . . .
The bulk of the multitude is doubtless seen in the
main street, but holiday-makers invade every inch
of Matlock."

Bradbury goes with the crowd to the petrifying

wells, on the Derwent "in boats that might be used in the transport service", up the Lovers' Walks for six-pennyworth "of shuddering sensation" by gazing down from the top of High Tor, and into the miners' caves which become "natural caverns" where he found a guide "as wonderful as the cavern". The guide gave a lecture "in which diluted Latin, geology, and botany, are so marvellously blended that you become ashamed of your own ignorance". But that is enough. Attractions such as that may be all right for Blackpool which has so little natural beauty, but they seem out of place under the magnificent strength of High Tor and the rich "cloudland of green" which is Masson. Fortunately, although Matlock Bath still has its busy days, it is never quite as thronged as it must have been when Bradbury went.

Between Matlock Bath and Cromford the gorge becomes more sylvan, and then opens out on the left to show Willersley Castle, finely placed looking down on the Derwent. The original house on this site was begun by Sir Richard Arkwright, inventor of the spinning jenny, but he died before it was finished, and then it was burnt down and had to be rebuilt. For many years it was the home of the Arkwrights, the grounds being open to visitors on two days a week, providing a favourite walk from Matlock and Matlock Bath. One of the Arkwrights had 350,000 trees planted round about, and horticultural history was made here by a gardener who was the first in this country to rear the grape vine in plant-pots. There was a wall gooseberry tree in the gardens with a bough which in 1841 measured 40 feet, and grew abundant fruit. Willersley Castle is now held by the Methodist Guild as a Guest House.

Scarthin Nick, just past the Willersley entrance, is

as romantic a gateway out of the Derwent Valley as any sightseer could wish for. The famous Arkwright Mill, built in 1771, is on the road which goes leftward down to Cromford Bridge. It looks somewhat like a fortress, at the gateway particularly, and it has been suggested that it was built like that in case it should be attacked, the introduction of the spinning jenny raising at the time many fears of unemployment which led to machine-breaking and rioting, though, so far as I know, nothing of the kind ever happened here.

Although Richard Arkwright was a Lancashire man, it is not generally known that he was helped in his starting of the modern cotton trade by the Derbyshire inventor, Jedediah Strutt, who was born in 1726 at South Normanton. Strutt served a seven years' apprenticeship to a wheelwright at Findern, and then took over a farm at Blackwell, and continued there for eight years before being asked by a brother-in-law if he could suggest how certain difficulties in manufacturing ribbed stockings on frames could be got over. Strutt studied the problem and two years later took out two patents which worked and became popular. He later suggested improvements in Arkwright's spinning jenny and went into partnership with him in 1769, as a result of which the mill at Cromford was built and then one at Belper. In 1782 when the partnership came to an end Arkwright kept the Cromford and Matlock Bath mills and Strutt those at Belper and Milford. It is strange to think that the vast money-making but also extremely noisy and smoky cotton industry should have had its beginning in such a remote tree- and hill-sheltered spot as Cromford, but this was because there was water to give cheap power. The water that drove the first wheel came from a sough which drained some lead mines, and the flow was so steady and good that it never froze. It seems likely that Strutt, who most probably knew the district, would be the partner to suggest Cromford as the best place for the first mill.

Cromford Bridge, below the mill, at a most picturesque corner, is a fine old piece, unique for having pointed arches on one side and rounded arches on the other. On the downstream parapet an inscription reads: "The leap of RM. BH Mare June 1697." This is said to mark where a roan mare ridden by Benjamin Hayward, of Bridge House, Cromford, leapt over for some now unknown reason, landed safely in the river and carried her rider out unhurt. A remarkable jump! At the near side of the bridge there are the remains of the old chapel of Cromford, just recently renovated; and, beyond, the road climbs to Lea village prettily scattered along the hill looking across to Riber. Below the village is Lea Hurst, the occasional home of Florence Nightingale, before and after the Crimea. What a relief and pleasure it must have been to get back from the pain and stink and squalor of war to this wooded park; and one cannot doubt that she must sometimes have thought of it in the wearying night-rounds with her lamp through the crowded wards in frost-bitter Russia. Lea Hurst was occupied by the Nightingale family from the eighteenth century till 1946, when there was a three days' sale which included several of Florence Nightingale's things. The house was bought as a memorial home for nurses.

This part of the vale of Derwent is so beautiful that I do not think anybody would object to having to retrace the same route to Cromford to catch the bus back to Matlock. While waiting in Cromford square I like to cross to the old smithy and look over the half-door and have a chat with the smith. His place is hung

with shoes, but it is seldom that he is making more.
Few farm horses are shod now. They are kept for land
work and can do without shoes, most road work being
left to motor-cars and wagons. Therefore the smith
usually is fashioning long curved bars, which are new
leaves for broken springs. In the old days springs
didn't often break, but modern high speed has made
a difference.

"It is chiefly this sort of thing that keeps me busy
now," he says.

Chapter XVII

"REET DARBYSHIRE"

DERBYSHIRE retains a good bit of dialect. To those who are used to it, naturally it is homely talk, though to strangers it may seem crude and harsh. It has many similarities to good "Lancashire", a fact that was pointed out amusingly one hot summer day when I had motored to Kidderminster. Getting out I exclaimed to a car-park attendant: "By gum, but it's hot!" He said at once: "You come from Lancashire." He was surprised when I told him that he was wrong.

How this similarity came about I am not expert enough to say, though I hold a theory that the considerable interchange of workers caused by the cotton industry must have had something to do with it. As explained in the previous chapter, cotton spinning was begun at Cromford, but by a Bolton-le-Moors man. Doubtless he would bring one or two other Lancashire men; and as the cotton trade grew, becoming more established in Lancashire, but with many spinning mills and bleach sheds continuing to be put in different Derbyshire dales where water-power and fuel invited, there would always be Lancashire people coming in. Most of the firms that eventually had their headquarters in Manchester, when they opened a new Derbyshire mill, would probably send a foreman and one or two good workers from Oldham or Bolton or elsewhere to instruct local people. Thus the two dialects would meet and assimilate each from each a little. Nevertheless, in some words both dialects still keep distinct. "Gradely", for example, is much more Lancashire than Derbyshire; while "sithee" (probably a corruption of the old-time "sire", but used now generally with a more affectionate, or at any rate friendly, intention) is more characteristic of Derbyshire. I hesitate to venture further into this subject, but it is one of deep interest, and anyone with an urge to study it should begin at once, for the B.B.C. and other influences are working here as elsewhere to lower all talk to one level.

Dialect with which one is unfamiliar can be tiring to read, so I give a taste of "Darbyshire" in the form of a tale. It is based on a true incident, and illustrates as well something of the local character, for dialect and character are dual, as indivisible as a man from his skin:

SHORT CUT

His face reminded me somehow of an apple. I mean a green apple, smooth, and crisply curved. When he spoke only his lips moved and the rest of his face was unchanged. His eyes dwelt deep behind still, dark lashes, so that one saw not his pupils but only the gleam of them. And the gleam did not flicker but was like the steady gleam of silica in our own Derbyshire gritstone. Yet despite his appearance of stillness and self-containment he turned out to be voluble and aggressive.

I first heard of him from our Dad, who said to my Ma: "Yo' know yon mon as 'as teken th' place bi ar lane—'Oodseed is name is,—'ee's a cheeky young brat. Aa just seed 'im crossin' ar medder as brisk as a turkey-cock."

"He's a reformer, or summat," said Ma, "an'll soon be puttin' up as M.P.—so Sarah Adams towd me."

"'Im M.P.!" scoffed our Dad. "Why 'ee's nobbut size o' two-penn'orth o' copper."

"Still," said my Ma, "I dunna know as they measure 'em fer size at Westminster. It's brains, they say, as counts theer."

"Brains or no brains, if 'ee starts trespassin' reg'-lar 'ee's goin' ta be towd abaat it," threatened our Dad.

This, of course, made me interested, and when I went by the solitary house that stands like an island in our fields on our lane I looked out. He stood by the gate, and the scent of his smoke puzzled me till I saw that it was a thick cigar. I thought to slip by, but he called in a quick, sharp bark "Hi, son!"

This was high mastery, not to be disobeyed; and I saw him, still and smooth, staring with a coldness that seemed to strike across the space and prickle.

"What's your dad, son?" he asked.

"A farmer, sir."

"Is all this land his?"

"Yessir."

"Is it?" said he, and blew a puff of smoke that seemed to say "Bluff!"

I was dismissed and felt it; as if I had done wrong. At first, for no reason, I felt ashamed, then angry, and after a bit I wondered why.

But his effect on our Dad was quite different. When they met, for all his apparent smoothness, Mr Hood-seed appeared to act like a file. He rubbed up our Dad the wrong way proper.

"'Ee's dang well mekin' a path across th' medder from 'is gate," Dad cried angrily to my Ma one night. "If Aa cop 'im Aa'll tell 'im what's what."

"It's 'is short cut to th' station, I guess."

"Short cut or lung cut, it's my medder. If 'ee'd

change 'is route a bit it wouldna be so bad, bur 'ee's wearin' a path yonder like a paved street."

"I should tell 'im," said my Ma.

"Aa will," said our Dad; and the way he said it made me feel sorry for Mr Hoodseed. Next morning we left milking and went down the lane and to the far side of the meadow where the trail of broken grass and footprints led to a gap in the drystone fence.

"Even took th' wall daan ta suit 'issel'," said our Dad, sniffing.

Then the house door opened and out came Mr Hoodseed as smart as my Ma's thimble and turned across the meadow with a prim, swift stride.

"'Ere, naa," said our Dad, "Mester 'Oodseed, this is my medder, an' Aa'll ax yo' ta stop usin' it i' future. Th' grass is growing', an' trampin' it does it noo good."

"Your meadow?" barked the dapper little man. "I like that!" And his voice seemed to laugh; but his face was just as firm and still as that green apple.

"It is my medder," said our Dad, very truculent.

"Not it," said Mr Hoodseed, very pat.

"Then done yo' reckon as it's yo'r's?" asked our Dad, taken aback.

"Yes," said Mr Hoodseed, "both mine and yours, and your little lad's, and everybody's. I'm right glad of this opportunity to talk to you, Mr Kirk, and show you the common error which you share with nearly everybody. The land belongs to the people. It is as much mine as yours; and it is as much everybody's as ours. Therefore I have as much right as anybody to cross it. You use the land for growing crops, I intend to use the land by crossing it. I shall only cross it twice a day. You use it all the rest of the time. Therefore, if anybody had the right to complain, it lies with me—certainly not with you. Good morning."

208

Baslow : "probably the smallest toll house in England"

If the little man had been bigger I think our Dad would have skittled him into the ditch. But the size of him and the way he said his stuff was a bit too much even for our Dad. In fact, he was left gasping.

"What the ——!" he said. "'Is land—everybody's—what done th' silly runt mean?"

But I knew Dad didn't want any reply from me, and for two days he hardly spoke. I kept pretty mum, too, till the third day when we'd been ditching beyond Mr Hoodseed's house.

"Come on, Ben," said our Dad all at once; and his voice was glad, as a man's is when after much doubt he's made a great decision. "Come on, Ben, Aa think us'll goo whoam this way."

Then I wondered if he were mad, for he began to climb Mr Hoodseed's wall. He dropped from sight in the garden and shouted: "Naa, Ben!" in a voice in which was the excitement of challenge.

So I climbed the wall and found him with hobnails in the soft mould of a bed. A short distance to the left was a gravel path, but he said authoritatively: "Foller me," and began a steady tramp through a phalanx of ripening tulips. Tremblingly I followed, for this was desecration. Where he set his feet I set mine. When a flowering almond impeded his straight track to the opposite wall, he stopped and tugged it up by the roots.

Angry shouts came from the house, but our Dad went on and swift steps pursued till Mr Hoodseed, with face lit up at last, placed himself very fiercely in our path.

"Get aat o' mi way," shouted our Dad with a great laugh; "'ow dare yo' obstruct me on mi own land?"

"It—it isn't," stuttered Mr Hoodseed. "You're doing damage. I'll . . ."

14*   209

Chesterfield Church spire

"This land," repeated our Dad solemnly, as if it were a lesson he'd learnt very carefully, "is as much my land as thy land. It's as much everybody's as ourn. Therefore Aa 'ave as much reet as onybody ta cross it. Therefore Mester 'Oodseed, Aa intend ta cross it. Yo' use th' land fer growing flowers. Aa shall on'y cross it twice a dee. Yo' use it mony hours. Therefore, if onybody 'as th' reet ta complain it lies wi' me; certainly non wi' yo'." He paused for breath. Then: "Stop crossin' my fielt an' Aa'll stop crossin' yo'r garden," said our Dad, astride for a moment on the wall top. Then he dropped down beyond, and I followed as quickly as I was able.

Mr Hoodseed never crossed our meadow again. Nor, by the way, has he yet become an M.P.

Chapter XVIII

A LOST INDUSTRY

We have seen pass in this generation a fine county industry, second in age only to agriculture. The story of the last large lead mine worked is in Chapter XVI (page 187). There is still much lead elsewhere, but it is deep, and there is too much water to cope with, so that the working of it has become uneconomic. Throughout the nineteenth century the mines had to be driven deeper and deeper, and when enormous deposits were found in Australia and America, the local trade was taken away.

Lead is believed to have been worked in Derbyshire before the Romans came. It is possible that some of it was sold in the marts of Tyre and Carthage. Under the Romans mines at Wirksworth and Castleton were worked vigorously, and pigs, or blocks, of lead have been found stamped with the reigning emperor's name, and one with the name of an individual, probably that of the supervisor. Odin Mine at Castleton may have been worked by Romans and Saxons, with convicts and slaves. Saxon monks later got hold of many of the mines and the profits could be used to build their religious houses. In 714 the Wirksworth mines belonged to an ecclesiastical house at Repton, but before the Norman Conquest the mines had been seized by the Danish kings, and William I kept them for the Crown.

Domesday Book mentions the mines. The Castle of the Peak, built about that period, had a roof of lead.

Until Queen Elizabeth's reign the Crown continued to hold the mining rights, but she granted them to a society or corporation and many of them passed afterwards to the Devonshire family, who got great wealth from them.

The rights and customs of the lead-miners have their "roots in antiquity, to the contrary of which no man knoweth". By these rights any man, or men, could dig for lead anywhere in the King's Field (which covered the greater part of the mountain limestone area) without permission of owners or tenants of the land, or liability for damage. They could not dig, however, in churches, churchyards, places of worship, burial grounds, dwelling houses, orchards, gardens, pleasure grounds or highways; and if no lead was got within fourteen days, the land had to be levelled and left as found. The first mines, where the limestone was covered with light soil, were shallow, and the ore was got out by driving wedges between the vein and the spars which enclosed it. An old miner told me the lead was like the lean in fat bacon. Later, fires of wood were used, the heat breaking the ore. Such fires had not to be lit between eight and four o'clock, the normal working hours. Some shafts went in horizontally, others vertically, and from these the ore was drawn by hand windlasses, or "stowces", in short stages. When the shafts got deeper a large drum was used turned by a horse gin.

These old miners must have had great hardihood and pluck. All over the Wirksworth district shafts of their mines remain. Some are covered with mounds of stone, others surrounded by drystone walls to keep cattle away. Within the walls, undisturbed, trees, often sycamores, have grown, and if a stone is tossed into the dark hole under their shade, it is generally a moment or two before the stone hits bottom. I should not have liked to go down such places. The shafts are cleverly lined with dry stones, but there were subsidences, of course, and then there was no modern rescue equipment. There is a story in Glover's *Peak Guide* of a Cromford mine where two men were entombed, one using a windlass at a depth of 60 feet and the other getting ore at 132 feet. The one below was killed, but the upper man was got out after eight days and recovered. He had four pounds of candles and had swallowed one or two, but had found them too loathesome to go on. This kind of experience must have been fairly common. Most early miners worked on a share basis, but often the shares were very small.

Miners had the right to carry ore to the nearest highway, and if the owner of the land between objected, the Barmaster was called. With two of his jurymen, one on either side with arms out, the Barmaster would walk direct from the mine to the highway, driving in pegs or stakes at the limit of the hands, and between these pegs the miners could carry, whether it was through corn or any other crop. The explanation of these apparently unfair laws is that when they were made most of the district was waste and men bought the land knowing these laws.

The Barmaster was the president of the Barmote, or Great Court, which met in the Moot Hall, Wirksworth, and decided whether mines were being worked rightly, if a miner had struck a new vein, or settled claims when the workings of two miners met. The Court was held twice a year, with a jury of twenty-four experienced miners. In the Moot Hall is kept the Low Peak Miners' Standard Dish, a brass measure containing fourteen pints, which was made in Henry the Eighth's reign and ordered to remain "hanging by a cheyne so as the merchantes or mynours may have resort to the same at all times, to make true measure after the same". The High Peak Miners' Standard Dish, kept at Monyash, used to hold sixteen pints.

Every May 13th the miners would decorate their windlasses with oak leaves and flowers and have a Festival Dinner at which the Barmaster was chairman. As well as men, women worked in the mines, wearing a dress something like a fisherwoman's.

As the mines went out of use, whole villages lost work. In 1830 there were 2,280 lead-miners; in 1891, 803; and in 1901, only 285. Although this figure went up during the later prosperity of Mill Close Mine, the industry now seems at an end, though recently high lead prices have tempted a few men to try a little mining here and there. Clarence Daniel (in *Pinnacles of Peak History*) tells a good tale of one of the last miners of Eyam to be thrown out of his job. He held a house near the Royal Oak Inn and one day met his landlord, who told him he was sorry but he would have to raise his rent.

"Aa'm glad, sir," said the miner, "'cos Aa conna raise it."

In the time of worst poverty many of the older men were allowed to stay on in their old homes rent free.

An interesting picture of lead-mining is given by Nellie Kirkham in *Unrest of Their Time*. This novel is a curiosity, printed in red and black, but has much serious descriptive writing.

Chapter XIX

CYCLING AROUND

It was from Darley Dale that I first visited Millthorpe, for forty-two years the home of Edward Carpenter, already mentioned in Chapter VII. I went by cycle on a pleasantly diversified route which I recommend to anyone who is not afraid of some walking up steep hills.

First I went along Darley Dale to Rowsley where for twenty years, before the difficult country through to Chinley was mastered by engineers, the London railway line ended. I may be asked why it should have been brought here and not ended at Matlock, a place of much greater importance. The answer is that from Rowsley the line could serve Chatsworth House, and I took the road by which guests would be driven from the terminus, through pretty Beeley, which has a pleasant little church among trees. The guests would be taken into the park past the lodge on the east side of the Derwent, but ordinary travellers must cross the river here, and so I did and went through the park by the road, which was cleverly made to keep just outside the range of anyone looking out from the great house. Then on through Baslow, which is a clean, stone-built place, perhaps a bit too decorous, though not nearly so much so as Edensor. At Calver Mill I kept to the east side of the river, surprised and a bit disappointed to find that the track that I remembered from the Froggatt holiday as sandy and rutted with turfy ridges had been prisoned in macadam and made to act as a normal road. And then I found that the Froggatt hillside, which had been a bracken-grown wilderness decorated with mossy boulders and dainty birches, had somehow spawned a remarkable crop of bungalows and houses, no two alike, all shapes, made of all kinds of materials. I was told that most of these belong to Sheffield people who have retired here. They must have some strange ideas about architecture in Sheffield and find great difficulty in agreeing with one another. Nevertheless, most of the houses appeared to be well looked after.

I went on into Froggatt village because I wanted to see if the old lead-miner's cottage remained and to look at the bridge. All the way from Matlock there are good bridges across the Derwent, all of them with individuality. It has been claimed that there are more bridges scheduled as national monuments in Derbyshire than in any other county, and when you see these along the Derwent it is easy to believe that that is true. The Froggatt bridge is well worth the short detour that was necessary. Then I had to climb the steep hill to the main Calver–Sheffield road. It is best to continue walking when you reach the main road, too, and there is compensation in looking down into the valley and up the strath towards Hathersage. Thank goodness the many houses round Froggatt cannot spoil the rugged majesty of the Edge. Stopping to look more carefully down into the valley, I saw a lot of Froggatt Wood, where the pheasant chicks had been, had gone and that more was being cut. Sheffield Wood had gone also. A lot of the land hereabouts is now National Trust property.

Farther up on the left is the often talked-about Longshaw Estate and even here pit props were being cut. I know that trees are grown to be used, and I agree that they should be used when they are ready and are needed, but too many trees were felled in the 1914 war and never replaced. A fine beech wood was cut at Two Dales in 1940 and the hillside where it stood has become a wilderness of elderberries, brambles, and willow-herb that blows everywhere. There is apparently no intention of replanting there, so that one wonders if the same is going to happen elsewhere. On Longshaw replanting was begun in 1945, but I was disappointed by the high proportion of conifers.

At the Standing Pole I took the road to Owler Bar, where the Peacock Inn faces into the Cordwell Valley. From the Standing Pole one crosses the typical bleak plateau of this country: long gradual moor slants black with heather plants and wire grass, their edges sliding off into blue-grey mist. Overhead was a grey sky with a faint incandescent blur of lemon and white for sun. In the lap of the moor was a slab of grey as dull as the sky, the water of Big Moor Reservoir, but without a suggestion of reflection. With this picture still in mind I plunged into the road to Millthorpe, and at once what a change! Here were pleasant banks and knolls decked with bracken and rhododendrons, and many topped and clothed with fir trees. A stream fell from ledge to ledge under the trees and rocks and a peewit skirled, so that I knew at once why Carpenter put one in his poem:

"The little red stars appear once more on the hazel boughs, shining among the catkins; over waste lands the peewit tumbles and cries as at the first day; men with horses go out on the land—they shout and chide and strive—and return glad at evening; the old earth breathes deep and rhythmically, night and day, summer and winter, giving and concealing herself."

It is easy to understand that being written in the Cordwell Valley and it is easy to understand why Carpenter was so fond of this place. At Millthorpe, though wider, the valley is still sheltered, and holds the sun. The soil is good for farming and of a warm colour. It is the sort of place that feels genial, just right for fostering that genius for friendship that the writer had. Undoubtedly this valley had a lot to do with the quiet compassion that is in all Carpenter's work. "Of course I could not help rejoicing in the lovely necessity of living in such a place—the charming brook running at the foot of my three fields, the beautiful wooded valley, and the close proximity, a mile or so off, of the open moors," he says.

I have wondered if Carpenter and Murray Gilchrist ever met. Although I can find no record of their having done so, it seems likely that they would do, for Holmesfield, where Gilchrist came to live after leaving Eyam, is very close to Millthorpe. He made Cartledge Hall his home, and there he died, being buried at Holmesfield. Cartledge Hall is a romantic-looking old country house of the type that Gilchrist liked to put in his books. A fine decorative ceiling has just been uncovered.

Neither the builder nor war has yet spoilt Millthorpe, but nearer Chesterfield there was some new disfigurement due to the getting of outcrop coal. It was still, however, a nice cycle run all the way into Chesterfield. Though generally thought of as a coal centre, actually the town is only on the edge of the real mining country, and there is quite an air of a market town about it. There is a fine open square where stalls stand every Saturday. Some of the best farming land in the county is within easy reach. It is a town with a very long history, though few old buildings remain. It is a town of bricks and red-tiled roofs. That it once had a wall is suggested by street names: Glumangate, Knifesmith Gate, St Mary's Gate, and Saltergate. No map or other trace of any wall remains, however, and it seems unlikely that there ever was one.

The crooked tower of the church dominates Chesterfield. It is so very crooked that every stranger notices it at once, even if their stay may only be for a moment or two in the station while a train is putting down and taking up passengers. In addition to its twist the spire has a lean over to the south from the perpendicular of 6 feet and of 4 feet 6 inches to the west. The crookedness, according to local tradition, is due to the devil. This is how Dr Charles Cox tells it:

"The devil when flying over Derbyshire was overcome with fatigue, and paused on top of the recently erected spire for a rest, unaware of the character of the building. . . . He alighted at the time of high mass, and a whiff of the incense, creeping up through the interstices of the spire, so tickled his nostrils that he sneezed ere he could untwist his tail; and the present condition of the spire is the result of the diabolical spasm."

Actually the crookedness is probably due to unskilled workmanship, an attempt at a spiral spire. The frame is wood covered with lead in diagonal ribs. Two hundred and twenty-eight feet high it is, says Dr Cox, "by far the largest example in England of a timber and lead spire".

In Chesterfield I inevitably think of that short, simple, but strangely moving book, *Miner*, by F. C. Boden, and particularly of the opening when "the hills of Watch-hill were lost in a clammy, rainy mountain mist that writhed down the old Roman roads into the valley of the Rother and clung round the town of

Chesterfield like a pall". When I first read *Miner* in
1932 I was excited. I thought that Boden would become
the great Derbyshire author; as vivid as D. H. Lawrence but with a saner outlook. I got at once his two
earlier little books, *Pit-head Poems* and *Out of the Coal-
fields*, and liked them, and when in 1933 *Flo* was an-
nounced, I bought it eagerly, but it was disappointing;
it lacked the intensity of the first novel. *A Derbyshire
Tragedy* in 1935 was too self-consciously would-be
tragic; but *Miner* remains original and poignant, one
of the best books inspired by the county written since
Lawrence died (March 2nd, 1930).

Boden was born in Chesterfield, son of an L.M.S.
goods-porter. He went to Chesterfield Elementary
School, leaving at thirteen to work in a pit. At first he
was where there was a very narrow seam. Stripped to
the waist he crawled about all day in passages only two
and a half feet high collecting coal cut by the miners.
At eighteen he got transferred to the pit-head, and
preferred the night-shift so that he could do his reading
in daylight. His first book of poems (1927), with an
introduction by Sir Arthur Quiller-Couch, was published when he was twenty-four and still at the pit.
Much of the background for his novel *Flo* obviously
came from what his father had told him and from
experiences he had shared with him. Boden's first
poems roused so much interest that the then Poet
Laureate, Dr Robert Bridges, and others made arrange-
ments by which he was able to leave pit work and go
to the University College, Exeter, and it was from
there that he wrote the introduction to his second book
of poems.

In 1945 a novel was published written by Mr W. E.
Richards, entitled *Mother Hubbard*, also about the
Chesterfield–Ilkeston coalfield. When I began it I

thought it might be a good successor to Boden's *Miner*
—even Lawrence's *Sons and Lovers* came into mind—
but from chapter ten the book lost its hold. Nevertheless, it contains some true feeling for this district.
Although born at Kettering, Northamptonshire,
Richards married a Derbyshire girl and lived two years
in Chesterfield and three in Bakewell. As Excise Officer
and Old Age Pensions Officer, he says, he "penetrated
every nook and cranny between Buxton and Cromford
and between Earl Sterndale and Bolsover, visiting
countless homes from Chatsworth House to the company houses of Grassmore and Claycross". He now
lives in Somerset.

When I asked a bus driver in Chesterfield which
was the best way to get on the Matlock road he smiled
rather as though it was a leg-pull, and after a moment
said: "Whichever way you go there's some hills to go
up." I told him that I suspected so, and seeing that I
was serious, eventually he gave me very full directions
which I couldn't follow.

The long climb out of Chesterfield is through good
country, much of it good arable land with strong woodlands for shelter. The road climbs to nearly 1,000 feet,
and from near the Red Lion, which is almost at the
highest point, there is a broad spread of valley towards
Wingerworth which it is good to look on. Wartime
ploughing has increased the diversity and interest in
many places like this. Just near the Red Lion also
there are the rough and extensive remains of a quarry,
such as are to be found on many of the moors hereabouts. Much money was made out of some of these
quarries, which were well known in their prime. Along
this same road which branches off the Matlock road
at the Red Lion and drops eventually into Rowsley
(the last two miles or so as a cart-track only) there are

the remains of Beeley Moor Quarry, once known all over Derbyshire for grindstones. They were finished at the quarry and sent out over a very wide area, the stone having a peculiarly fine texture. It was very good for needle grinding and a needle factory was opened at Grindleford. Then carborundum was invented and trade fell off suddenly. Moreover, labour was becoming more independent and men refused to tramp or cycle (there was no other method then) up the long climbing roads on to the desolate moor, and so eventually the quarry was closed though much excellent stone remained. In a neighbouring unused quarry above Hall Dale several finished grindstones still remain, unsold, abandoned. The Beeley Moor Quarry was used during the late war as a training ground for bombing, but there are still good craftsmen in Derwent Valley who would be willing to pay generously for a new grindstone from there, the ones they got years ago being nearly worn away. The synthetic stone of today is not nearly as "kindly" to their chisels and other tools and does not give the same "silky" finish to a steel edge.

Another well-known quarry is Stone Quarry, Grindleford, out of which in 1936 was taken a stone weighing 1,200 tons, claimed to be the largest ever quarried in Britain and to contain enough material to build a dozen houses. It was cut up for wood-pulp stones for Norway and Sweden.

Probably the most profitable of all the quarries was Stancliff, in Darley Dale. This gave excellent "free-working" stone that could be cut almost any way and yet was extremely durable. Chatsworth House was built of this stone and Trafalgar Square, London, was paved with it. Every stone for the Square was dressed with fine accuracy, and if there was the slightest deviation the stone was rejected and kept for other work.

Stancliff has supplied stone for special work for Canada and as far away as New Zealand, and even today builders in such a stone district as Chapel-en-le-Frith send to Stancliff and pay haulage because they save when the stone comes to be cut. But Stancliff also is past its best, for it is very difficult to get men for quarries nowadays, the work besides being hard sometimes bringing on disease from silica dust getting into the lungs. I was told by a builder that only two stone-dressers remain at Stancliff, and that with the present rush for houses it may be impossible to get stone even in this district and the use of brick may become inevitable. Ground or powdered stone is now being moulded to resemble cut stone, but is, of course, much cheaper.

From the Red Lion corner above the Wingerforth view the Matlock road goes more or less straight for two miles and then descends into Kelstedge in the Amber Valley with a sight of the church tower of Ashover about a mile away leftwards. From Kelstedge there is another climb before the final run into Matlock. This round trip is about thirty-five miles only, but those who do not cycle just to cover distance will find that it makes a nice full day, leaving time to look about at the many different interests.

CHAPTER XX

A CHANGED LAND

IMPORTANT though the Bolsover, Chesterfield, Ilkeston area is commercially, it is not an area to which one would go for romance, yet anyone who would know Derbyshire must go there some time, if only to see how great are the differences within the county.

It is well to go by car to cover distance easily. The road through Alfreton for Ripley, Heanor and Ilkeston gives as good a general view as any. Alfreton has a war memorial of a soldier going forward hand in hand with a little girl, an unusual and pleasant idea. Without being distinguished, Alfreton is a not altogether unpleasant place. There are good trees about, and there is the suggestion of a market town, especially on Friday, when stalls line the main thoroughfare. But on the way to Ripley the country deteriorates. There is that air of poorness associated always with mining districts. It is rolling country, with rows of brick houses lying blatantly on shoulders and ridges. Where there are trees, they seem stuck upon the landscape and not natural to it. The children look older than one suspects they should; the grown-ups look pale. Men go about in the queer pit hats that quarrymen also use in the county, though you will not see quarrymen go home in them.

But perhaps I am being unfair to this area, being used to greener, fresher country. No doubt the people are content and happy, because the pits have as good a production record as any anywhere, and it is very

Bolsover Castle—aged magnificence and modern industry

seldom that pit disputes start here. Nevertheless, I should not choose Ripley, Codnor, or Heanor, if I were asked in what place in Derbyshire I should prefer to live.

One person who would have disagreed with me about that is Mr Joseph M. Severn, author of *My Village*, published in 1935, which is all about "Owd Codnor". Mr Severn loved Codnor, but his memories are of eighty or so years ago and it is strange now to read of it as "really a delightfully unspoiled, quiet country place" with "verdant peaceful roadsides". They had a queer way there in those days of keeping people in order. It was known as "rantanning". If a man beat his wife, or was cruel to his children, or persistently fell out with his wife or his neighbours, or made himself a nuisance in any other way, other villagers got together at an agreed time, usually in the evening, with trays, bits of sheet iron, old kettles and frying pans, and pokers or strong sticks, and went to meet the culprit. He was surrounded and everybody made as much noise as they could, parading up and down every street and road and giving him no chance to escape till they chose. This public advertisement is said usually to have made a man change his ways, and Severn says with pride that there was no record of any murder having happened in Codnor, and only one suicide.

At the turning off the Manchester–Buxton road for Combs, where I lived for so long, there is an inn with the sign of a hanging gate on which you may read:

> This gate hangs free,
> And hinders none;
> Refresh yourselves,
> And travel on.

Staveley Church : a tribute to the men of the pits

I was interested to learn that the Codnor Gate Inn had a second verse:

> Turn in at the gate,
> And taste at the tap;
> Be merry and jovial,
> But keep off the strap.

This verse is no longer there. Perhaps it was thought that it might upset the feelings of some travellers.

Farm workers, men and women, from all round this district used to hire themselves out at Ripley Fair. On the first day of the fair they paraded in their best near Derby Road and the Market Place. At some fairs a neat button-hole of a twisted wheat straw indicated that a person was for hire, but here they used to carry a coil of plaited whipcord round their hats. Hirings were for twelve months and agreements were sealed by slap of hands. Now you may think about such scenes, as you pass through, but you will no longer see them.

In Ripley was born Walter Brierley, author of *Means Test Man*. The chief character is a Derbyshire miner, as it might be Brierley himself, for he was out of work for several years before he got a job as time-keeper at a Derby engineering works and began to write. He educated himself at evening classes and later at Nottingham University where he won the Marsham short story prize. *Means Test Man* spans only a week in the life of an unemployed man, but it is a simple and very effective book.

During the war a flax factory was put up at Ripley and the local people have taken to the work well. But this is really only a revival of what was once quite a thriving Derbyshire industry, for there are old flax mills to be seen at various places, one within half a mile of where I write, at Two Dales, now used as a corn mill. Was flax grown locally in those days? There is none grown now. The flax used at Ripley comes out of other counties.

Heanor Church has a memorial to Samuel Watson, who did most of the carving at Chatsworth House. He was born in Heanor and died in 1715. The epitaph says:

Watson is gone, whose skilful Art display'd
To the very life whatever Nature made;
View but his wondrous works in Chatsworth Hall,
Which are so gazed at and admired of all,
You'll say 'tis pity he should hidden lie,
And nothing said to revive his memory.
My mournful friends, forbear your tears,
For I shall rise when Christ appears.

The main street of Ilkeston is a continuous climb, with the town centre at the top. It has grown tremendously during industrial times, and there is not much left to remind one of ancient Ilkeston, which John of Gaunt granted the privilege of paying half tolls at any market or fair anywhere in England, provided that the inhabitants kept a gallows always in working order. This would be for robbers out of Sherwood Forest.

It was at Ilkeston, as has already been noted, that D. H. Lawrence attended the pupil-teacher centre from 1903 to July 1904, taking from there the King's Scholarship Examination, in which he came out in the First Division of the First Class, and then the London Matriculation Examination. A friend who knew him intimately says that those were very happy days. Lawrence was in the garden one Saturday when he said unexpectedly: "I'd much rather be describing that rhubarb than sitting for matric." The following year he taught as an uncertified teacher in the British School at Eastwood, only four miles from Ilkeston, but just in Nottinghamshire, and began the first draft of his first novel, *The White Peacock*. There is most about Ilkeston in his fourth novel, *The Rainbow*: "Whenever one of the Brangwens in the fields lifted his head from his work, he saw the church-tower at Ilkeston in the empty sky. So that as he turned again to the horizontal land, he was aware of something standing above him and beyond him in the distance."

All roads in this part seem to lead either to Nottingham or to Derby, and if one wishes to keep in the county it is a good plan to take the road by Dale Abbey for Spondon. Ilkeston is industrialised enough, but Spondon seems to be all one sprawling works, yet, in between, Dale Abbey remains surprisingly remote-seeming. First came a hermit here before the abbey was built, and a modern hermit might find peace here, on the edge, though it is, of the iron and coal region. The original hermit's cave in a cliff of sandstone is still available! But the last time I was in this area I fled back to the north via Eastwood, Selston, and Alfreton. It was hot August, with willow-herb in bloom, giving an etching-stipple of colour to many of the pit banks. Occasionally we caught the sun behind the flowers and briefly, surprisingly, they glowed with a clean pink delicacy. I thought how Lawrence would have appreciated this beauty born out of ugliness. It is remarkable that from such a district he should have given us some of the most beautiful prose pictures of countryside that we have.

From Alfreton I took the road past Wingfield Manor. There is a pit bank now in view from the Manor on the Alfreton side, but before industry encroached it must have been a fine stand. The moat is so deep that it is more like a natural ravine. The gate on the main road was locked, and a notice, nearly obliterated, said, "Closed for the Duration", but it was easy to climb over. How much more securely was it guarded in 1569 when the sixth Earl of Shrewsbury, on the order of Queen Elizabeth, brought Mary Queen of Scots here! Her retinue and guards numbered 250 persons, and I imagine that the manor must have been crowded. After a bit the prisoner was taken to Tutbury, but in 1584 back she was brought to Wingfield, and somehow Anthony Babbington, from his home at Dethick, only four miles away, got into communication with her and began planning her escape. The plot was discovered, Mary was taken secretly to Tutbury again, and eventually Babbington, with six others, was executed. Five months later Mary was beheaded in Fotheringay Castle. These are sad thoughts to have at Wingfield, for it must have been a magnificent place. Dr Cox classed it among "the finest and most interesting manorial ruins" in all England.

There was a climb from Wingfield and then we saw on the skyline rightward the slim lighthouse that is Crich Stand. Crich is a straggling village, chiefly noteworthy in an all-stone district for the brick chimneys on its stone houses old and new. There is a motor road and a park and turning place just below the Stand, but it is sacrilege to drive up. It is a place for pilgrimage on foot, for the top of the hill has been dedicated to the 11,409 Sherwood Foresters who fell in the 1914–18 war, and to the honour of the 140,000 who served during that war in the thirty-two battalions of the regiment. A tower was built near by in 1788 and rebuilt in 1851, but in 1882 a tremendous landslide took a great slice off the hillside and nearly took the tower too. Then lightning split it from top to bottom and it became a danger to anyone who went near. Eventually it was taken down and the present tower was built in a safer position. Just above the door is an old stone marked "F.H. 1851", the initials of Francis Hurst, of Alderwasley, builder of the second tower. From the platform round the base of the present tower a tremendous spread of country can be seen all round. Strong eyes on a clear day may even see Belvoir Castle and Lincoln Cathedral. There is no limit but distance, except in the north and north-west, where the higher Peak stops the view. Why Nottinghamshire, which has equal claim to the regiment, should have agreed to the memorial being at Crich, I do not know, but it was a nice choice, for when the revolving light is working, its flash reminds a thousand homes of sacrifices made in good faith, with courage; and it should be a symbol of war's futility, and an encouragement to those who hope for world peace. I know of no better-placed regimental memorial than this, except in Scotland, where they honour the martial spirit more than we do in England. Alone on the height by the tower one can think great thoughts, and it is a good thing that the quarry just below is completely hidden.

I have a belief that I was once told that Crich Stand is the geographical centre of England, the point farthest from every border, though I have not been able to confirm this. But here, at least, one has the feeling of being at the very heart of our land. Long may the light flash!

To complete a view of the Derbyshire coal district one must take another trip, say, by Staveley, Clowne, and Bolsover, ending for pleasure with a look at Hardwick Hall. The main road from Chesterfield to Staveley gives an extensive view of coal and iron industry, railway lines and sidings, smoke and steam. It is country

that one allies in mind more with Sheffield and Rotherham than with Derbyshire generally, and yet it is
Derbyshire and a very valuable part. Somehow, so
close to all this—well, really in the midst—Clowne
still manages to retain a bit of a country town feeling,
very different from some Lancashire coal districts.
There are trees at Clowne, and one can look about
sometimes and not see any pit banks, but they are
there. I have asked, as have many more who love
beauty and would like to see as much as possible even
where the heavy industries are most concentrated (and
isn't that where beauty is most needed?), are pit banks
unavoidable? The reply is that shafts must be sunk (in
Derbyshire to an average depth of about three hundred
yards) and that the debris thus got out obviously must
be put somewhere on the surface. Further, that with
every load of coal raised there is much dirt that can
only be sorted out economically on the surface. That
sounds right enough, too, yet why cannot much of this
dirt be sent back underground? To this the reply
usually is that it cannot be done: what is meant is that
the job would be too expensive, but perhaps now the
mines are nationalised the matter will be reconsidered.
Some of the larger coal companies had already experi-
mented with tree-planting on pit banks, but with small
success, and experts told them that at least fifty years
must pass before there is enough humus on the banks
to allow trees a fair chance to grow. I am not convinced, however, that everything has been done that
might have been. The experts think generally only of
timber trees from which profit may come eventually,
but the disguising of these heaps could be hastened
by the sowing of elderberry, gorse, and broom seeds,
for these shrubs are so hardy that they will grow
almost anywhere, and their branches would arrest

more dust and attract birds with all the minute seeds and other debris that they carry, and the leaves from these shrubs would build a humus supply far quicker than if the banks are left. Of course, this scrub would have to be cleared when it was judged that there was enough humus to make the planting of timber trees reasonable, but for beauty's sake, surely the little extra trouble and cost would be justified.

Running through the spoilt country to Bolsover it is difficult to imagine what this country was like when the original Norman castle was put up by William Peveril, the same who built the Castle of the Peak. As at Castleton, he chose a fine defensive site. Now all of the Norman castle is gone except the foundation which is under the present keep, built in the early sixteen-hundreds.

Although not as wild as in Norman times, the country would then still be beautiful, and Bolsover a market town. Anyway, the Earl of Newcastle, son of Sir Charles Cavendish, who finished the great house, was proud to entertain King Charles I and his Queen here several times. Thinking of those lavish days, it is depressing now to approach the castle up the long main street of the town and down the neglected drive to the rotting gate. The whole place has been given by the Duke of Portland to the National Trust, and already much has been done to preserve the old buildings, but the once splendid riding-house immediately on the left when one gets in the great central yard has its walls splitting and its tile roof patched, and looks worse than if it were roofless and to be regarded merely as a ruin. In fact, it detracts from the stateliness remaining to the chief building which is nothing more than ruin.

This must have been a fine place when completed.

The great stone front, with its double staircase from the central entrance, and great windows, made a satisfactory calling-place even for a spoilt Stuart King, and one can imagine Charles and his lady and their attendants walking on the great terrace looking over the rolling country far below. Now the first thing one notices is a great industrial plant, and the depression of one's approach to the rotting gate is confirmed. Bolsover Castle today cannot be classed among the great inspiring sights of the county.

From Bolsover we sped for Pleasley, and then began to search for Hardwick Hall, and it was a search, for the lanes wind and are narrow, often deep between thorn-hedges, and the country is well wooded, so that to see far is impossible. Even though the hall is on one of the highest ridges of the district and has six towers each 100 feet high, it is hard to get any clear view of it. The hall is now open to the public on several days a week in summer, and holds many priceless antiques and treasures of art. The front of the hall is unique:

> Hardwick Hall,
> More glass than wall.

Lord Bacon, after staying there, declared "one cannot tell where to become to be out of sun or cold". Hardwick was put up by the notorious "Bess the Builder". Begun in 1590, it took seven years. Whether she was satisfied with it when it was finished, I do not know, but as she is calculated to have had rents worth about £60,000 coming in to her every year from the jointures of her four husbands, if she was disappointed with Hardwick, it did not much matter. Anyway, very soon after it was finished she began another great mansion at Oldcotes, but she died (aged eighty-nine) while the work was going on. Her mania for putting up houses is said to have been due to her having been told by an astrologer that she would never die as long as she went on building, and there is a tradition that when she died, building at Oldcotes had been stopped by keen frost.

After an interesting and thoughtful hour in Hardwick we returned past the Hardwick Inn to the crossroads a little lower down and there under the trees that reach over the oak-pale estate fence we ate sandwiches while I read more about the strange life of Bess of Hardwick. She was the fourth daughter and co-heiress of Squire John Hardwick of Hardwick, but became the ancestress of the Dukes of Devonshire, Newcastle, and Kingston, and of "earls and barons by the score". She first married when only fourteen; her husband was Robert Barlow of Barlow, only a bit older than herself. He died a year after the marriage, leaving her all his estates. She remained a widow then, we were surprised to find, till she was thirty-nine, when she became the third wife of Sir William Cavendish, of Suffolk, but soon induced him to buy a large estate in Derbyshire, the Chatsworth estate, of course, where she began her first great house, forerunner of the present Chatsworth House. This time there was only a very brief widowhood before she married Sir William St. Loe, of Gloucestershire, and when he died it was found that she had induced him to leave her all his estates and leave his brothers and his daughters by an earlier marriage penniless.

In 1568 Bess married the greatest subject of the realm, the sixth Earl of Shrewsbury. The following year Queen Elizabeth gave Shrewsbury the keeping of Mary Queen of Scots, and the poor man began as harassed a time as probably any of his standing ever had. Queen Elizabeth, hating Mary's greater beauty, was for ever worrying about her safe custody; Bess became jealous of her husband and Mary, and nagged him and spread scandal about them, until in the end Shrewsbury separated from his wife; and when he was relieved of his responsibility of Queen Mary as well, he wrote to Queen Elizabeth thanking her for relieving him of "the two devils". The Earl, however, died before the Countess, and she spent her fourth widowhood, according to Dr Cox, in great state and magnificence at Hardwick, "feared by many, courted by her numerous progeny, but loved by none".

Of the five great mansions Bess was responsible for —Bolsover, Chatsworth, Hardwick, Oldcotes, and Worksop—only Hardwick Hall remains. When she started these mansions she could have had no suspicions of the mineral wealth that would be found under the ground round about, and of the industries that would grow and besmirch the countryside. But had she known, the thought of the riches that might accumulate would have ousted any regrets about the possible spoiling of the country, for, after all, money was her chief ambition. All her wealth she left to the only children of all her marriages, the Cavendishes. Horace Walpole calculated that by his day the income from her estates had grown to £200,000 a year. How much this figure jumped up when coal and iron were found and townships quickly began to develop we can only guess, but I can imagine the ghost of "Bess the Builder" gloating over it with chuckling glee.

Well, she must have been a remarkable woman, though I would rather read about her than have had dealings with her. Eventually we drove on past the lake with the great oaks behind it on the slope below the hall. Nearly all the way back to Chesterfield we ran through fields of oats, wheat, and barley, which looked clean and in good condition. It was a pleasure to see so much land under arable crops, and I thought that this was very much how it must have looked about 1652 when Walter Bligh put Scarsdale among "as gallant Corne countries as be in England".

CHAPTER XXI

THE FARMER'S LIFE

DERBYSHIRE generally is not thought much of agriculturally nowadays, yet in any farming history the county can put in many good claims. Even before the Romans, much of the area which is now included in Derbyshire must have been as important agricultural land as any north of the chalk downs of the south. Or how could the quite numerous population have lived? In no other district are there more earthworks, barrows, and circles, and the pre-Roman peoples who made them could not have existed by hunting alone. They kept sheep at least, and have left crude hoes and digging sticks. When many areas of England now famous for production were still swamp or under great forests or scrub, the much more open limestone and chalk districts were probably the only ones where the early peoples could set up their homes and grow crops in tolerable safety. So in those days the district was much better thought of agriculturally.

Going about even now after our second great war with Germany, when we imagine that we have ploughed all land that could possibly be worth it, one can still see many fields green side up which must have been ploughed in some earlier time, for the hummocky old butt formation is there. When these fields, which we now call impossible, were turned over we do not know, but there are some people who think that they remain from Roman times when Britain was a granary of the Roman Empire; if so, then Derbyshire must even have been one of the great corn areas of the country. That it was noted for corn very much later is proved in Walter Bligh's *The Improver Improved*, as stated in the last chapter. In the *Boke of Husbandry* by Fitzherbert, 1523, farmers elsewhere are advised to do as Derbyshire farmers do. "They lode not theyr donge tyll harvest be done . . . and that I calle better thanne uppon the falowe, and specyally for barley."

This *Boke of Husbandry* is famous as the first book on agricultural practice to be published in English. The author, Sir Anthony Fitzherbert (some say his brother John wrote it, but the evidence in favour of Anthony is very strong), was born at Norbury in 1470. He died on May 27th, 1538, and was buried at Norbury, where in the centre of the chancel there is a large flat blue marble stone and brasses to his memory. In the jargon of today, Sir Anthony's primary occupation was that of Justice of the Court of Common Pleas, and his farming was largely experimental, done as a hobby, but one cannot think that a man of his legal standing would write a book on farming unless he considered that he knew his subject thoroughly. He had three farms, two in Derbyshire—How Grange at Norbury, and "the fferme of the parsonage of Castleton in the Peeke"—so that it is reasonable to assume that he learned most of what he knew about agriculture in Derbyshire, and though, as is to be expected, he has a lot to say about "shepe", he also gives full instructions about "hey", "all maner of cornes, beanes, pees, and fytches", and about "falowing" with "fyrste and seconde sturrynge" (ploughing), and it is to be assumed that all this he learned also in his own county. His book seems to suggest that he considered that the best corn grown in the county came from "the farther syde

of Derbyshire, called Scaresdale", that is, about
Chesterfield and Dronfield, which was the "farther
syde" from his home near Ashbourne. He gives two
glimpses of the northern parts of the county:

"And for the poore housbande of the Peeke, or
suche other, that dwell in hylly and hyghe groundes,
that haue no pastures, nor common fieldes, but all-
onely the comon hethe, Symon and Jude daye
[October 28] is good tyme for theym [to put the
rams to the ewes], and this is the reason why. An
ewe goth with lambe xx wekes, and shall yeane her
lambe in the xxi weke; & if she haue not conueniente
newe grasse to eate, she maye not gyue her lambe
mylke: and for wante of mylke, there be manye
lambes perysshed and loste: and also for pouertye,
the dammes wyll lacke mylke, and forsake theyr
lambes, and soo often tymes they dye bothe in suche
harde countreys.

"And the poore man of the peeke countreye, and
suche other places, where as they vse to mylke theyr
ewes, they vse to wayne [wean] theyr lambes at xii
wekes olde, and to mylke theyr ewes five or syxe
wekes, etc. But those lambes be neurer soo good as
the other that sucke longe, and haue meate
ynoughe."

Fitzherbert believed that a husband cannot thrive
unless his wife helps. Here are the things that he tells
the farmer's wife she should do. Love her husband, at
rising bless herself and make the sign of the Cross,
sweep the house, milk the cows, dress the children,
send corn to the mill and measure it before it goes,
make butter and cheese, gather the eggs, put the
garden in order, make sheets, towels, and shirts, dry
the flax, make clothes and blankets from sheep wool,

winnow corn, brew, wash, make hay, sell the butter, milk, eggs, cheese, hens, geese, and corn, buy everything that is necessary for the household, keep a true reckoning of all that she spends or gets, and never deceive her husband.

"May fortune sometime," says Fitzherbert thoughtfully, "that thou shalt haue so many thinges to do, that thou shalt not well knowe where is best to begyn. Than take hede, which thing shulde be the greattest losse, if it were not done . . . and there begyn."

To the husband the author says:

". . . go to thy bedde and slepe, and be vppe betyme, and breake thy fast before day, that thou mayste be all the shorte wynters day about thy busynes. . . . That is to say, Erly rysyng maketh a man hole in body, holer in soule, and rycher in goodes. And this me semeth should be sufficient instruction for the husbande. . . ."

I do not know how many editions there have been of Fitzherbert's book, but the number is large; nevertheless many of the editions are very rare. The first edition is so rare that even the Bodleian Library has not got a copy. What was probably a third edition— published by Thomas Berthelet in 1532—was mentioned by a Mr Wallis in the *Derby Mercury* of November 1869, and it would be interesting to know whether any early editions of this precious book by a local author still remain in the county.

In reading many books about Derbyshire I have been surprised never to find anything about the county's connection with the famous Thomas William

A gritstone ram

Coke (pronounced Cook) of Holkham, one of the greatest agriculturists who ever lived. His work and example transformed barren Norfolk into the granary of England. He popularised the growing of potatoes, improved the rotation of crops, encouraged the common use of the drill for seed sowing, and had great influence in bringing about the general adoption of more profitable types of livestock. His "clippings" (sheep shearings) were the beginning of our agricultural shows. They were held annually for forty-three years, and at the last one, in 1821, there were representatives from every county in England, from all parts of Scotland and Ireland, and from America, France, Nova Scotia, Poland, Russia, and Sweden.

This famous Coke was the eldest son of Wenman Coke, of Longford, six miles south of Ashbourne. Longford Hall is near the church at the bottom of a gently sloping park. The walls and buttresses are believed to have stood since the Norman Conquest. Although Tom Coke was born in London (May 6th, 1754) he was brought when very young to Longford Hall and there he spent much of his boyhood. A. M. Stirling, in *Coke of Norfolk and His Friends*, says:

"At Longford he always rose before daylight. . . . He first made his way to the dairy, where he coaxed the dairywoman to skim the cream for him till he had filled his basin. He then adjourned to the bakehouse, and as soon as the oven was drawn he broke off the corner crusts from the loaves, which, steeped with cream, formed his breakfast. Thus fortified he went off for the day and was usually at his destination, four or five miles from home, before dawn broke. Directly it was daylight he began his sport, which he continued till darkness fell, con-

16*

Chee Tor

triving, if possible, to leave off near his home. No weather ever deterred him from being out all day. His naturally strong constitution was thus confirmed by the life he led, by his habits of early rising, simple food, long days in the fresh air, and hard exercise. So, too, he developed the passionate love of country life and country amusements which never left him throughout the whole of his career."

At Longford his father instilled into him the maxim: "Stick to your friends and disregard your enemies", and this together with the motto which he adopted later, "Live and let live", was the commanding rule of his life. At the age of seventeen Coke left Derbyshire on a three years' grand tour, then reckoned to be an essential part of a young gentleman's education, and arrived in April 1772 in Italy. There the Young Pretender, who in December 1745 had led his Scots army through Ashbourne close by Longford, was married on April 17th, 1772, to Princess Louise of Stolberg, then only twenty, a very attractive, clever girl with a very English look. Charles Edward Stuart signed the marriage register as "Charles the Third, King of England", and many festivities followed the ceremony, including a grand fancy-dress ball in Rome which young Tom Coke attended. Charles Edward was then 52, already coarsened by drink and other excesses, and his young bride was at once attracted by the tall, handsome youth from Derbyshire. Whether they ever met again, though it seems very likely, there is no record, but the Princess afterwards gave Tom Coke a life-size portrait of himself in fancy dress painted by Battoni and in the background is a statue of a reposing woman which is said to be a likeness of the Princess. Although he wore a white cockade at the ball, young Coke was no Jacobite, and later having been induced by a friend in London to join a club called the Cocoa Tree and then discovering that it was in fact a secret Jacobite club, he never went there again.

Coke came back from his tour to Longford in July 1774 to attend the wedding there of his younger sister, Elizabeth, to James Dutton, of Sherborne, in Gloucestershire. The wedding took place at Longford and there Tom Coke met the bridegroom's sister, Jane, whom he had known slightly before he went abroad. But now he fell in love, and married her on October 5th, 1775, against his father's wishes. The ceremony took place at Sherborne and one paper refers to "Mr Coke's wonderful ride to Shireborne", and it seems likely that he rode off from Longford like a true knight of romance and got his bride in face of firm opposition, as none of his own family seem to have been at the wedding.

In the general election of 1774 young Coke was asked to stand for Derby and agreed very unwillingly. A brisk canvass showed that he would inevitably have been returned, but an opponent, also called Coke, though no relation, asked if he had reached his majority. Young Tom had to say, "No." "Then I shall oppose you," said the other, "and if you are elected, you must understand that your election will be declared void." So Tom Coke stood down, but he got a friend, Mr Gisborne, to stand. There was a hard contest, accompanied, as was common in those days, by rioting in which young Coke was hit on the head and stunned and got badly bruised. Mr Gisborne got in by a small majority.

Tom Coke became the holder of the great Holkham estate in Norfolk on the death of his father on April 10th, 1776, but even that did not end his association with Derbyshire, for he continued also to hold the Longford estate and lent it to his brother Edward. In the general election of 1806 Coke was elected, as he had been for many years, to represent Norfolk, but a riot having occurred during the poll an inquiry was held by a Committee of the House of Commons which eventually decided that Coke had not been duly elected. Edward Coke, who had been elected for Derby, at once resigned and stood for Norfolk, while Tom Coke was elected in Edward's place for Derby. This exchange caused a lot of amusement all over the country, and quite a lot, one imagines, in Derbyshire. On March 23rd, while Coke represented Derby, the Bill for the Abolition of Slavery was passed. But three weeks after the committee had given its decision against Coke, the government resigned, and then Coke was elected for Norfolk again, without opposition.

Coke died at Longford, but was buried in Norfolk.

At Holkham, Coke's Norfolk home, of which it was said that "there is no other house in England like it", the splendid hall, measuring 38 feet by 31 feet, with a dome 50 feet high, supported on 18 fluted Ionic pillars, is all done in tinted Derbyshire marble.

Remembering Coke's world-known "clippings", it is interesting to find that similar meetings were held in Derbyshire, the idea probably starting from Holkham. The Derbyshire "clippings" were held by W. B. Thomas, of Chesterfield, who had farms at Baslow, Boythorpe, and Brampton. He introduced Merino sheep into the county, probably about the same time that Coke was trying in Norfolk, and, says *Farley's Derbyshire*,

"to excite attention to the progress and advantages of breeding sheep, Mr Thomas had invited the agriculturists of the county to be present at his sheep-shearing when he exhibits the live animals in their several stages of growth, their wool, their mutton; and cloth, also, both for ladies' and gentlemen's wear, manufactured from the wool grown on his own farms. In Mr Thomas's family no other habit or broadcloth, but this of his own growth is worn; and many competent judges have pronounced this cloth to be equal in quality to the best that can be made from imported Spanish piles."

In 1810 King George III gave Thomas two fine Merino ewes for his patriotic efforts. In 1812 off the Thomas farms 386 fleeces brought £340 7s. (besides £22 5s. 6d. for lambs' wool), an average of nearly 17s. 8d. for the wool of each sheep through the whole flock.

In the eighteenth century Derbyshire took up the Shire-horse. This animal had as its ancestor the old English blackhorse, or "great horse", which up to the early seventeen-hundreds had been kept exclusively for knights and battle. The great horse was a weight carrier, for a knight in full armour was heavy, but in the Civil Wars when armour started to go out of use, the warriors began to want lighter horses, and so the great horse was at last allowed to pass to the farmers. It was a lumbering animal and to improve it Lord Chesterfield imported six mares from Zeeland, in Holland. Derbyshire led in the careful breeding from this stock and Leicester and other Midland counties followed.

For some unfortunate reason Arthur Young, first secretary of the Board of Agriculture, when he made his famous tours to report on the condition of British farming round about 1770, did not show much interest in Derbyshire, though he noted an out-of-the-ordinary pigsty there with a stream running through. Possibly it was the shocking state of the roads that deterred him, though for a man of Young's character that does not seem very likely. William Cobbett in his "rural rides" missed Derbyshire, as did Sir A. D. Hall on his "pilgrimage of British Farming", in 1910–12. It is good to find, therefore, that Sir James Caird, when he was "commissioned" by *The Times* in 1850–51 to report on the agriculture of the country—then seriously depressed—did not forget Derbyshire, and he seems to have been pleased that he did not.

He visited the estates of the Dukes of Devonshire and Rutland and was particularly interested in the system at Chatsworth, where he found the best part of the park

> "being reserved for the cows of the cottagers and labourers on the estate. The rates paid by the labourers for joisting a cow are from 50s. to 55s. which are very moderate, and must add much to the comfort of a labourer's fireside. Another part of the park, about 300 acres in extent, is joisted to the tenants, who are thereby enabled to ease their farms of young stock in summer, and to reserve part of their grass for hay. The rate charged to the farmers for year-olds is 25s.; two-year-olds, 35s.; for young horses, 50s. each; and for a mare and foal, £5. We are persuaded that this is a plan which might be advantageously adopted on many large estates."

Sir James was not too pleased with the farming he found "some miles farther on to the north" of Duffield, where it was "not uncommonly cropped in this barbarous manner:—1, oats; 2, wheat; 3, oats; 4, fallow; 5, wheat; 6, seeds; 7, wheat. Good green crop land is fallowed when it becomes too foul to bear a crop. It is then limed and cropped again. Many farms have no turnips whatever; and the accommodation for stock is generally defective." But here is his conclusion:

"Before ending the description we may mention the general impression made on us, and the contrast afforded with the county we had previously visited —Northumberland. The situation and soil of the two counties are certainly very different, but not more so than the state of agriculture. The rate of rent, wages, and taxes of all kinds, in Derbyshire is higher than in Northumberland. The farms are better cultivated, and the farmers infinitely more prosperous and contented. In Derbyshire the land is chiefly in grass, carefully managed, and the small proportion of ploughed land receives minute attention. The farms are small comparatively, being from 100 to 300 acres, and the farmers superintend their own business. They are not encouraged by their landlords to add farm to farm without being provided with adequate capital. They depend for their returns more on the produce of the dairy, breeding, and sheep stock, than on corn. . . . Derbyshire is a pleasant, picturesque county, in which landlords, tenants, and labourers seem mutually content, where the pastures are well managed, the ploughed lands neatly cultivated, and the stock suitable to the soil and carefully tended."

Remembering Walter Bligh's inclusion of Derbyshire among "the gallant corne countries", it is noteworthy that Sir James Caird showed Derbyshire as having the highest average wheat yield in 1850–51 of the thirty-three counties that he toured. This was 33 bushels per acre. Nottingham came next, together with Norfolk, Suffolk, Huntingdon, and Cambridge, all with an average of 32 bushels. The average over the thirty-three counties was only 26½ bushels per acre. The average rent over Derbyshire in the same years was 26s. per acre, and the average wage of the farm workers 11s. a week. By 1867, according to the Royal Commission inquiring into agricultural wages and conditions, wages had gone up in the county to an average of 15s. a week. About the same time the price for hoeing and singling turnips was 4s. 6d. an acre. By 1911 wages were 20s. 7d., lower only than Durham and Northumberland, and level with Lancashire. These figures show an agriculture progressive and able to pay for its labour.

Large areas of Derbyshire, I think, must always remain primarily agricultural. Distance from the sea has no doubt in the past had a lot to do with the slowness of the development of any great manufacturing industry, that added to the hills, which have always made transport more or less difficult. Even should the aeroplane become the chief means of carrying passengers and freight, Derbyshire, because of the scarcity of wide level spaces for landing grounds, and the prevalence of low cloud and mists, is not likely to be developed for manufacturing any quicker than in the past. I hope this forecast is correct, anyway!

Farming in the county can be divided roughly into three main divisions. There is the rich mixed farming of the south, and the upland farming of the centre and north, divided between the gritstone and shale, and the limestone districts. Of the south it is only necessary to say that farming there is similar to anywhere in mid-England; but only those who have worked on both can appreciate the differences between upland farming on gritstone and limestone. Most farmers would prefer

248

to work on gritstone, for there water is generally pure and plentiful. On limestone, rich though grass will grow, it soon burns off, and water is nearly always a worry.

These limestone areas are pre-eminently suited for cattle, but in these days of increased cleanliness and of milk cooling, the water problem has become worse. Those who know how many reservoirs Derbyshire holds to supply large cities may think it queer that in the county there is often grave drought. This is due, of course, to the water percolating very rapidly through limestone, and a shower every morning (with plenty of sunshine afterwards!) is the only kind of weather that would really suit the limestone farmer.

In gritstone country farms are generally reasonably compact. On mountain limestone the farms are very often much more awkward, the land reaching long distances due to the fact that when the enclosures were made it was understood that every farm must have some water, therefore the homesteads were mostly put in the dales where the water was, but the land ran up to the hills and every farmer got a bit of every type of land from lush bottom to arid top. On these tops were developed the meres (called wrongly sometimes "dew-ponds"). How these meres first came to be used is not known, but how to make them is inherited knowledge. Possibly ponds somewhat the same were known to the earliest inhabitants, the remains of whose earthworks are on Harthill Moor and elsewhere, for a hollow dug for any purpose would hold water for a time at least, as a modern mere does, if the bottom happened to be clay. But though it is possible that the value of these meres has been known for hundreds of centuries, there is still something strange, almost uncanny, in finding a silent pool on an exposed hilltop where there is no

spring and where there seems to be no area for drainage.
Yet meres in such positions keep their water, enough
at least usually to supply such sheep and cattle as are
left on the upland pastures.

How these meres are maintained is even yet not fully
agreed among scientists, and Alfred J. Pugsley, in
Dewponds in Fable and Fact (1939), gives three meres in
Derbyshire which he suggests that anyone interested
might watch. They are:

Alsop-en-le-Dale. Two ponds N. of Station, W.
side of Ashbourne–Buxton Road. Either side of
pt. 1184 (1-inch O.S., P. 7).

Burnt Heath. At top of lane running S.E. to Burnt
Heath from Houseley, 3 miles to Tideswell
(1-inch O.S., N.7).

These ponds were chosen out of a number which
Mr Pugsley inspected in Derbyshire as being unaided
by surface drainage, without trees near, and on level
ground, high up. If it can be proved how they keep
their water, and whether the water level rises overnight
even when there has been no rain, then valuable information will have been gained applicable to similar
meres all over the country. Mr Pugsley, after studying
all the evidence available, believes that neither dew nor
mist helps, but that the meres are entirely rain fed, and
keep water so well in drought simply because the early
makers unconsciously evolved a method that makes
the most of rainfall and reduces evaporation to a
minimum. Thus round a mere measuring twenty yards
across its water surface there is usually a collecting
margin of at least four yards, which gives an evaporation area only about half the collecting area. If the
water surface falls to sixteen yards across, it leaves the

collecting area roughly three times as great as the evaporation area. Add to this that annual rainfall is above double the annual evaporation in this hilly region, and Mr Pugsley's theory sounds about right.

I inspected a mere at Middleton-by-Youlgrave which had only been reconditioned in the spring of 1945. This was about twenty yards across with a four yards collecting margin, increased on one side to six yards by a kind of alcove in the drystone wall which entirely surrounded the pond. The sides sloped evenly and gradually to a centre point and were covered with a six-inch layer of smoothed concrete. Beneath was a basin of well-puddled clay supporting a bed of close-set stone, foundation for the concrete. A pipe from a barn twenty yards away brought in roof water, and a pipe near the bottom of the mere led to a trough a little lower down. This trough was set in a wall so that it served two fields for cattle drinking, and the supply was controlled by a ball-tap, no water being let run to waste. It is interesting to note how this pond conformed with the best plans that the scientists can suggest, even though the men who made it most probably did not know anything about the excess-of-rainfall-over-evaporation theory. The wide, inverted conical shape gave a much larger collecting area than evaporation surface, and was best for reducing the possibility of breakage due to ice expansion in winter. The well-made bottom prevented the likelihood of any leak. The wall all round kept sheep and cattle from getting in and so perhaps breaking the concrete and reducing the holding capacity of the mere by treading in mud and soil and vegetation. The wall also kept wind off, wind being a great evaporating agent. And white concrete was the best material that could have been chosen to cut heat absorption to a minimum, white surfaces reflecting radiant heat better than any other. The whole arrangement seemed to me excellent and the farmer was very satisfied, for he had previously had to drive his lying-off stock downhill nearly a mile every day for watering.

To many outlying farms on limestone, water has to be piped long distances from the few permanent supplies. While the pipes remain intact all is well, but should a pipe be broken by subsidence, or get choked, then there is great difficulty. On gritstone, water will usually surface, giving at least some indication of where the trouble lies, but limestone will swallow all the water, so that if a pipe-line is old and liable to more breaks or stoppages, it is often cheaper to lay an entirely new line than dig perhaps for miles to locate the trouble in the old one.

So much about water may seem unjustifiable to some readers, but to understand its importance to a limestone farmer, show him a well in gritstone country with water gushing in and running gaily off all day, and watch his face as he exclaims: "My god, I wish I had that on my farm!"

Chapter XXII

SEE THE DALES!

Unless at least four of the best dales have been visited, do not claim to know Derbyshire. In no other county have I seen scenery quite the same, quite so varied. The dale which I tell my friends to go through first is Chee Dale, taking it from Topley Pike or Buxton end to Millers Dale. Most writers mention Chee Dale, though I think I am alone in putting it first. But for limestone scenery, and for its unusualness, to me it has no equal.

The railway which runs through, with its engines gushing out squealing at unexpected and unhappy moments, spoils the dale to some extent, as do the bridges that take the line over, but the makers of the line did their best to interfere with beauty as little as possible and it was their obvious route from Buxton to Millers Dale. In the deep part of the dale, under Chee Tor, where the overhanging cliff is nearly three hundred feet high, the railway is out of sight and mind.

Chee Dale should be gone through in spring, when the trees that somehow find footing in the cliffs and hang from above are at their best; or in autumn, when their beauty would equal spring were it not for the sadness that it suggests. In the depths of the dale there is often a suggestion of sadness, anyway, without the autumn hint of the trees. The dale must be gone through when the Wye is not too full or the pathway will be drowned. Under those conditions I have been glad of the railway, climbing up and passing some of the worst places through the tunnels; not a wise way or one that I advise. R. Murray Gilchrist, who knew and loved Derbyshire as well as any writer I have come across, said that to see Chee Dale to perfection one ought to go through at night when the moon is at the full. I accept this, and can imagine the effect of moonlight on the high white rocks and gleaming on the limey surface of the Wye, though I have not seen it under those conditions. Coming out from the narrow gorge into the wider beauty and easier walking of Millers Dale gives the walk the charm of a contrasted ending.

Lathkill Dale I place second for a very different reason. Here the water has magic and the river-plants and fish look as I have seen them look nowhere else. Lathkill Dale from Alport to Conkesbury Bridge is a place of calm, where one must wander pensively; as different from Chee Dale as can be thought of. The water shows its views best in the artificial pools under the rocks and trees below Over Haddon. Everything glows with peacock brilliance, and it is hard to understand why some famous painter has not made a picture of the river bed with its weeds and trout and beautiful gloss of water. Perhaps there are streams in Devon its equal, though I have not seen them, but I remember some illustrations to a presentation edition of Henry Williamson's *Tarka the Otter*, done by C. F. Tunnicliffe in Devon, that showed the same colourings. Had Van Gogh come to Lathkill he would have left some oil-paintings with the real magic in them.

Unfortunately the Lathkill is not as merry as once it must have been. Liking the water as well as the great trout do, weed has grown rampantly and threatens to choke the stream, though a lot is dragged out each year. The trout are said to be very difficult to take, which is not surprising, for they must be able to see through that water as through magnifying glass.

Above the fish pools the character of Lathkill Dale is different and can cause disappointment, though there are some good woods. Disappointment is due to the lack of water, for the Lathkill is one of those mysterious limestone streams that gushes full-size from underground, but in times of drought forgets to come out. In fact, there is often no water from the true source, a cave about a mile and a half from Monyash, and at those times the stream begins about Cales Dale, and then very hesitantly. I have seen it nearly dry as far as above the mill below Haddon village, though the fish pools are always full and there there is always beauty.

Conkesbury Bridge, over the Lathkill between Over Haddon and pretty Alport, is one of the most curious bridges in the county. It looks like a wall until one is nearly up to it and sees the low arches. The stream has to step down to get under them. Unfortunately Conkesbury at weekends is a too popular parking place and there may be half a mile of cars. It is surprising how many of the occupants remain crowded inside to eat their sandwiches. I have often thought that many of them might as well have run their cars out on the lawn at home and had their meal there, for all they seem to wish to see of the demure and blameless Lathkill.

That Dove Dale is beautiful nobody can deny, but I put it third. It has been so often praised that perhaps one goes with too rich expectations, and then finds too many people, and the path too well made. Then, to Derbyshire pride, it is rather a pity to have to admit that half the dale at least belongs to Staffordshire. The Derbyshire side has the better rocks, but Staffordshire undoubtedly has the better woods.

Dr Baddeley says that Dove Dale is "simply the most beautiful and harmonious blending of rock, wood and water within the limits of the four seas", so we will leave its beauty at that, except that I must stress that to see Dove Dale is not enough. The walk should always go on through Beresford Dale, which belonged to Charles Cotton, Izaak Walton's friend, who brought him to this "uncivilised" country and taught him fly-fishing. By the way, four editions of *The Compleat Angler* came out really incomplete, for the second part, Cotton's, only appeared with the fifth edition, which was the last issued during Walton's lifetime. How many editions there have been since then I don't suppose anybody knows.

In Dove Dale there used to be an old woman who carried a big basket every day through the summer and spread camera-films, post-cards, and bottles of "pop" on a big flat stone by the water edge below Reynard's Cave. On a weekday, sometimes in drizzle when the dale was almost deserted, I have found her there and stopped beside her novel counter to chat. She was glad of companionship then and told me that she had been there every summer for more than forty years. She had an armchair built of rocks and at mid-day she lit a fire of sticks in a little hole in the rocks and brewed tea. "I couldn't live without that," she said. She walked from Mill-dale every day. I used to think she knew Dove Dale better than anybody else in the world. If only she could have written all she knew! Anything that I can say beside what she could have told is simply claptrap.

Murray Gilchrist thought that the most startling

Conkesbury Bridge, Lathkill Dale

view in all Peakland was that from "Headstone Edge", now called Monsal Head, at the curve of Monsal Dale. This was a favourite spot of Ruskin's, though the railway in the dale so annoyed him that he wrote a most extravagant protest which now only raises smiles. But it is a view that is an integral part of Derbyshire. One comes to it from the sheltered comfort of Ashford or from the long clean limestone heights of Longstone Edge. But either way it is the same, a sudden opening of the ground beneath one and there below, the bend of the clear stream between soft green fields, and grey smoke from stone cottages toy-like for size. The whole view often has that strange, almost unreal, clearness which one used to get crouched in darkness in the old camera obscura huts gazing at mirrored reflections of life outside in the sunshine.

Existence in Monsal Dale must be very calm, the chief events outside of domestic routine the periodic passing of the trains, those northbound ejecting fierce volumes of steam and smoke and roar, and those southbound gliding as smoothly as toboggans, to disappear with an eldritch shriek into Headstone Tunnel. However much Ruskin's ghost may object, I think I should rather like the trains if I lived in Monsal Dale.

When my home was at Combs I used to take the bus to Monsal end in Taddington Dale and walk home. After the quiet, domestic charm of Monsal, Millers Dale is rather open and ordinary, but between these two dales there are the very different Cressbrook and Water-cum-Jolly Dales. Coming from Monsal Dale, it is a surprise to find round a bend the Cressbrook Mills blocking the way, though if all mills were built like Cressbrook the countryside would be much less disfigured than it is. When first I came on the mills in this way, seeing the Big Mill with its clock, I

"*The most startling view in all Derbyshire*" : *from Monsal Head*

thought it was a hospital. At Cressbrook at one time
pauper children let out on contract from Boards of
Guardians used to be employed, but generally they
seem to have been better looked after here than in
many places. Most of them would be town children,
and one wonders how they liked the loneliness of this
enclosed place. There appeared in a local paper ten
years or so ago the following verse, remembered as
having been sung by orphan children from a mill a
little farther on:

> Mitton Mill stands in a hollow,
> Water porridge for us to swallow,
> Rotten potatoes every day,
> It's enough to make us run away.
> Five o'clock the bell does ring,
> Old Gully he comes rolling in,
> With his paper cap and his hair turned up,
> "Now, my lads, come pick 'em up!"

On Sundays when it was fit the children used to be
taken the three miles walk from Cressbrook to Tideswell Church. That would be a change, though not the
kind of entertainment that modern children would
much appreciate.

By the way, local people tell me that if you place a
finger on the inside wall of Tideswell Church and draw
it along, tracing into every corner and along every wall
till eventually you come back to where you started,
your finger will have moved exactly one mile. I have
never tested this, but if any reader has the curiosity to
do so, I should like to hear about it.

In Tideswell churchyard there took place within
living memory a burial which raised hot local rivalry.
The body was that of a certain very popular sergeant
of the local Volunteers. He came from somewhere just

outside Litton. It had been decided by somebody that he should be given a military funeral and a band and firing party were provided out of the Chatsworth Company of the Derbyshire Volunteers. They waited in Litton village where the coffin had been brought in a farm spring-cart with the backboard down. The proposed order of the procession was band, firing party, carriers, nearest relatives, and then representatives of the local lodge of one of the friendly societies, then very strong in the county, and of which the sergeant had also been a popular member. When the procession began to form the lodge members put themselves before the carriers and refused to move away, though the officer in charge of the Volunteers read them his orders. Excitement grew until the officer ordered the firing party to advance with muskets at the ready. The lodge members stood till the last minute, when one of them asked a Volunteer whom, of course, he knew well, what he was going to do with his bayonet.

"Stick it into your stomach if you don't move," said the Volunteer, and so grim did he look that the lodge members all at once gave way.

So the procession moved off in the planned order. There were twenty-four bearers, carrying in three parties of eight. Two thousand persons watched, and, said my informant, one of the firing party, "I dunna think there were one dry eye among 'em." This, he explained, was not all because of their love for the sergeant, but because of the great sadness of the band's playing of the Dead March.

The way through Water-cum-Jolly Dale is private, a small charge being taken at Litton Mill at the far end for charities. Under the rock wall there is a still pool, really a dam, with a green slope marked with rock outcrops beyond; and then where the little gorge narrows I remember finding the waterwheel placidly pumping, chug, chug, chug! I do not know if this wheel still goes round, but it was a place then in which to dream of old-time romances. There were some wide-spaced stepping stones about which a nice tale could have been written. To find the mill so close round the corner was rather a damper.

Millers Dale, with its tiny limestone church under tree-dressed rocks, is a picture for all rail-travellers; but on the road one is rather too aware of the railway and the quarries on the steep behind it. My way home to Combs was by Monks Dale, Peter's Dale, Hay Dale, and Dam Dale to Peak Forest. This was tres-passing, and is not a route I would have mentioned, only that the upper part of Monks Dale has seemed to me so much like what a great part of the old Peak Forest must have been when wolves and bears and wild cats went freely nearly everywhere. There is a thicket of blackthorn, ash, hazel, and brambles, all growing from among mossy limestones, very slippy and awkward to walk over. Dead weeds reach shoulder high and there is the silence of a deserted world, unless one comes on a school of tits or hears the cawing of rooks overhead.

Peter's Dale, a meadow dale, and the higher dales grow shallower and seem full of walls. Rising out of Dam Dale through a winter's dusk, it is pleasant to see ahead the constellation of lights that is Peak Forest village, and then to hear children's voices or the singing of a girl. This pleasure must be somewhat the same as that which the old-time keepers had when they got back from a long day's duty.

Derbyshire has very many other dales, but anyone who has seen those that I have mentioned has seen one of every variety. Not that other dales are not worth visiting; they are. The dales are a feature to be proud of and it is greatly to be hoped that industry will not spoil any more.

I have read that up to the eighteenth century salmon were plentiful in Derbyshire's dales, spawning in the upper Derwent, Dove, Lathkill, and Wye, but pollution—that great disgrace still permitted—thwarted the fish whose hereditary urge it was to breed in these streams, and now the dales are known only for trout and grayling. The best angling book is *Fishing in Derbyshire and Around*, by Walter M. Gallichan, who lived at Youlgrave in the centre of the best area.

In answer to the question: "What should be the fisherman's guide as to the mode of fly-fishing in Derbyshire?" he says that "you should try either method, wet or dry, on the same day if need be". That was his own plan.

I am no angler, but have tried what is locally known as "tickling" in some of the smaller dale streams. This is quite unlike the tickling done in southern streams as described by Richard Jefferies in *The Gamekeeper at Home*. The fish are not soothed in any way, but are felt for under stones and roots, and when touched are grabbed whole-handedly. A friend who is an expert says there is more skill in this than in fishing with fly, but I fancy that those who use rod and line will not agree.

CHAPTER XXIII

ART AT THE WELLS

WELL-DRESSINGS take place in other counties, and yet are also special to Derbyshire. That seems right, for what other county has water of such colours, lustre, and purity? After a period in London washing in scum and drinking the airless fluid that is understood there to be water, what a delight to feel the clean touch of gritstone spring water, or to drink from a glass white and sizzling with oxygen bubbles!

Each village that has kept up well-dressing has its own tale of how the custom began, but there can be little doubt that the real beginning in every village was in pagan days, when the primitive inhabitants understood little about the real nature of water, only that it was good and that without it they could not live. And so they invented a water-god who had to be pleased, and worshipped, lest he should withdraw his favour. When Christianity came it wisely adapted the old water-worshipping customs to its own purposes; instead of bowing to the wells, the priests blessed them; and the presenting of sacrificial flowers became a ceremony of dedication.

Down the years the dressing of wells has become an art. Nearly always there is a picture, usually biblical, though sometimes a local picture or patriotic one. The foundation is a board which is "lathed" with clay into which salt has been kneaded to keep it moist. On this clay the design is drawn with a sharp-pointed tool, and then comes the long and careful task of filling the whole design in with appropriate natural things. Often the main background is made of fine rice gently pressed into the clay, and surprisingly it all looks like mother-of-pearl. Green or grey moss also makes an effective background, according to the subject which is being depicted. In the centre-pieces and borders where brilliance is wanted petals of roses, geraniums, violas, cornflowers, bluebells, aubrietias, and other flowers are used. Buildings are done as substantially as possible with haricot beans, Indian corn, oatmeal, berries, linseed, and fir cones. The best well-dressers can indicate degrees of light and shade as skilfully as if they were working with oil-paints, and when newly put up the pictures have a rich, natural freshness, and will keep their glow for days.

In the villages where the custom has continued for generations the art of well-dressing runs in families. Son has followed father at the work and all the children have helped. Within the past two decades there has been an increase in the number of places which have taken up well-dressing. These generally have been called revivals, though there has not always been proof that the ceremony had been held in all the places before. At Buxton, though it is possible that the wells were dressed in far-back time, the first ceremony of which there are authentic records took place only in 1840, and was simply a picturesque tribute to the then Duke of Devonshire for having water piped into the market-place for anyone's use. The ceremony now seems to be kept up more as an advertisement than anything else, a Festival Queen being crowned and taken in procession through the main streets. A wood-cut of 1864 shows St Ann's well decorated and a may-pole with dancers and a band in the Crescent, and there is no sign that the ceremony had any religious character then.

When in 1936 it was decided to start well-dressing at Stoney Middleton there was no native-born person to do the work, and it had to be directed by Mr Ted Shimwell, who had had fifty years' experience as a well-dresser at Youlgrave. The vicar in his address at the ceremony said that though White's Well had given the village a plentiful supply for more than three hundred years, that was the first time that they had had the decency to meet and thank God for His gift.

Youlgrave well-dressing, temporarily stopped in 1940, is one of the older ceremonies. At the revival in 1945 there was not enough help to dress all the wells and so the Fountain in the main street had to do as token. This is a round stone building with a tap put up in 1829 and was the village's main water-supply for about forty years.

The oldest well-dressing is that at Tissington. Some persons claim that it began as far back as 1350, when there was a service of thanksgiving for all the inhabitants of the village having escaped the Black Death. The Tissington people believed that their immunity was due to the great purity of their wells. There was a tradition that one year, in Puritan times, the dressing was missed and that the wells at once dried up, though they had never dried before and have never done since.

Tissington is an appropriate place in which to retain an old ceremony, for it is aside from the rush of modern life, typified in the main Ashbourne–Buxton road which is so short a distance away. The stone gate-posts, and the avenue of limes behind, suggest the entrance to a private park only, and as one passes under the trees the rush on the road falls away into little more than a murmur. And there under its fine trees

in the hollow the village lies unspoilt, the old houses
dropped, as it were, just where the builders happened
to fancy. The main piece is the Hall, remaining largely
from Elizabethan days, and it would really be no
surprise if one were to see women in flowing skirts and
men in breeches and ruffles walking the smooth lawn
in front. Almost opposite it is the Hall Well, chief of
the five wells dressed up to 1939 every Holy Thursday.
The Hall Well has several pools under a fine stone
arch, and it is pleasant to pause and listen to the low
gurgle and tinkle there. Three of the other wells are
within sight from the Green, and the fifth is in a narrow
garden behind the church. This well has the un-
romantic name of the Coffin Well, from its shape. The
others are the Town Well, Hand's Well, from the
family who have for generations been tenants of the
land where it lies, and Yew Tree Well.

At Tissington till the war stopped it the well-dressing
kept its ancient character as primarily religious. First
there was service in the little church standing over the
Green and afterwards a procession was led by the priest
and choir. At each well prayers were said, a psalm read, a
hymn sung, and then the well was blessed. In the church
—a homely and beautiful little place—there is a font
of Norman times with figures still traceable that link
primitive religion with the present just as the well-
dressing does: the Lamb of God, an animal holding a
man's head in its mouth, also a bear, a bird, and a wolf.

There was always a crowd at the well-dressing, and if
the day was fine those who could not get into the church
stood round the wide-open doors. Sometimes the
offertory plate was passed outside and one wondered if it
would ever be returned, though it always was. After
the ceremony the day became a holiday. Stalls were
opened to sell toffee and soft drinks and there were

donkey rides for children. Unfortunately the crowd often left papers and other litter, which was a pity, for normally the village is as tidy as can be and the wells are kept as though everybody is proud of them. Readers who wish to know more about the unique craft of well-flowering may find it in *The Beauty and Mystery of Well-dressing*, which contains many excellent colour-prints of dressed wells.

Too many Derbyshire village houses still have no water laid on, though the wells have generally been improved with a tap. It is one of the strange though quite common scenes of the country to see a girl in fashionable dress, with painted lips and fingernails, smoking a cigarette, waiting patiently while a bucket fills in the ancient way.

CHAPTER XXIV

"STONEHENGE OF PEAK"

ASHBOURNE has always reminded me of what Dr
Gordon Stables said of Berwick-on-Tweed, which belongs neither to Scotland nor to England: "It is neither
fish, flesh, nor good red herring."

Somehow Ashbourne has always seemed a town
apart from the rest of Derbyshire. Although it is so
close to the hills—really among them—it is as different
from Buxton and other High Peak places as can be.
Nor does it go with Bakewell, Matlock, or Chesterfield. It is on its own, with a character of its own. It
has a certain old-time sedateness which I associate
with thoughts of Izaak Walton and Dr Johnson. Izaak
Walton doubtless came by coach through here when
on his visits to Charles Cotton, at Beresford Hall; and
Dr Johnson often stayed with his friend, Dr Taylor,
of the Grammar School. J. B. Firth, in his *Highways
and Byways in Derbyshire*, gives a full chapter on
memories of Dr Johnson and Ashbourne, which should
be read by all who are interested. Dr Taylor's house,
near the church, seems little altered since Dr Johnson
stayed there; and there is probably little alteration also
at the Green Man Inn, whose Mistress Boswell found
"a mighty civil gentlewoman".

Ashbourne had its heyday in coaching times when
it was on the main route to London. The road from
Buxton and that from Leek met here and continued
on to Derby. The Green Man, which has since added
Black's Head to its title, was one of the coaching inns.

It is a curiosity to most visitors now that the most conspicuous thing about the sign of the Green Man should be a black grinning head set up on the beam that spans the main street, as though it were being exhibited for some crime. This originally was the sign of another posting inn a bit farther up the main street, the business of which was taken over by the Green Man.

Ashbourne Church is called the Pride of the Peak, but it is large and has a rather vacant atmosphere. It is best from outside, having a fine spire ribbed with decorative moulding. At Ashbourne Hall Prince Charlie stayed a night on his march to Derby and King James was proclaimed in the market place. But as I have said, Ashbourne today reminds me more of quiet than of turbulent times. Perhaps it is not so with everybody, for the town has inspired at least one rather wild romance—*Young Leslie*, written by R. J. White. He opens his tale with a scare and shooting at the Green Man. There is a Sir Brook Boothby in it, presumably from Ashbourne Hall, the old home of the Boothby family, and there are adventures in Dove Dale, and finally there is the Jacobite march of 1745.

All roads from Ashbourne pass through good country, but the roads to Wirksworth and to Buxton I like best. Somewhere off the Wirksworth route, I fancy, is the dale which Romer Wilson (wife of Edward O'Brien, compiler of *Best Short Story* books) chose for her novel *Greenlow* and called Greenlow Dale. Romer Wilson died very young, or possibly we should have had many more good books from her about this district. However, the country on either side of the Ashbourne–Buxton road is that most generally thought of when Ashbourne is mentioned. Thorpe, Tissington, Alsop-en-le-Dale, Hartington—those are the places. The single-line railway which links Ashbourne with Buxton, wandering as near to each of the villages in between as it can get, is one of the loneliest lines in England, and has the longest high length of any. Don't expect to catch many trains on it! Buses have, in fact, practically taken all the passenger traffic that it used to carry. But I still like to come on the line, perhaps in a narrow cutting near some hill brow where I little expect to find such a thing. Then it reminds me of the wild line through Galloway to Stranraer, or of a line in the remote Scottish Highlands.

Between Parsley Hay and Hindlow, where it climbs to 1,254 feet above the sea, this Ashbourne–Buxton line follows the route of the old Cromford and High Peak Railway, engineered by Joseph Jessop, which was one of the first and most remarkable lines in the country, being operated, for part of its length at least, before 1830. Within living memory Parsley Hay Station was known as Parsley Hay Wharf, because the original line was "the missing link" between the Cromford Canal and the High Peak Canal at Whaley Bridge. If there had been any water on this high ground Cromford and Whaley Bridge would have been connected by canal, and the railway had to be used as a substitute, but they called all the stations wharves, anyway. Some of the gradients were extraordinary: 1 in 8¼ up the Sheep-pasture incline, 1 in 8½ up the Middleton incline, and 1 in 7 at Bunsall. These could not be worked by ordinary locomotives, and the goods trucks were uncoupled and wound up first by chain and later by wire rope by stationary steam-engines. Originally passengers as well as goods were carried, but after a bad accident passengers were stopped. Edward Bradbury, who was privileged (?) to take a trip on the line about 1880, has left an amusing description. The engine "spits its way along spitefully,

269

and starts with a jerk, and stops with a jump, and goes with an irregular lurch throughout that is trying to one who has not acquired his 'sea-legs'. The waggons . . . batter away at each other as if each individual truck had quarrelled with its partner, and was settling its grievances in blows."

The truth is that the engines had to do very hard service. I recently talked with a man who twenty years ago worked under very similar conditions on the narrow-gauge line in Eskdale, and what he told me gave me a good idea of what must have happened on the old High Peak line. The chief art was to know the capabilities of the particular engine which one happened to be driving and to have a thorough knowledge of the line. It was then mainly a matter of correct stoking. At a certain tree or rock, coal must be put on generously, so that when the next gradient was reached there would be enough steam for the engine to charge it, the only way it could ever get to the top. And it was no use beginning to stoke at the top again ready for the next gradient, because the down-run draught would use up coal and water far too generously. Yes, even with the railway water was a problem, and at Hurdlow it had to be brought in large tanks from Ladmanlow.

The line was thirty-two miles long, and at least five changes of engine were required on each trip. The fastest trains did the journey in just over five hours, according to a guide published in "December 1876, and until further notice", though the wonder is not that they took so long, but that such a line was made and worked successfully at such an early date. Certainly in this bleak West Derbyshire it is much more in keeping to find the "Stonehenge of the Peak" than a railway.

Arbor Low, two and a half miles from Parsley Hay
Station, is one of the largest and best-preserved stone
circles in England. It is enclosed by a circular bank,
or vallum, about fifteen feet high, with a ditch, or
fosse, within, enclosing a little plateau on which the
stones lie like the hour marks on a clock face. Some
persons say that the stones once stood upright, others
that they have always been flat; some persons say that
it was a place used by the Druids, others that the
users were Neolithic men; some claim that the circle
is not more than 2,000 years old, others that it is
3,500 years old. Let the experts disagree; when I go
there I feel sure that it was a place of worship, and
that it was set there in very far back time, for the wide
views of desolate, rolling hills over which the circle
seems to preside bring on a religious mood, especially
when the sky is low and the world seems in danger of
being overwhelmed by the heavy drift of grey endless
cloud. There appears to be no escape; eternal doom is
at hand; and it is the time to pray, and to plead to God
for mercy. Surely the old priests realised this mood,
and so worked on the simple minds of their people
that they were ready to take greedily and thankfully
any religion that might be offered. Burial urns and
ashes have been found here, and in barrows in a
number of places round about, and that is in keeping,
for men have nearly always buried their dead in the
same place as they worshipped, for there the ground
was hallowed.

Arbor Low is one of the most impressive ancient
monuments of Derbyshire, if you go there in the right
mood, though I have heard of several Mothers' Meeting parties who have got here and sat down wearily
to cool on the stones, wondering why ever they had
struggled to such an outlandish place, and why it is

so famous. A plaster scale model of Arbor Low is kept in the British Museum. The local authorities about Arbor Low are Mr J. Clee Heathcote, of Birchover, and his son; it has now been taken over by H.M. Office of Works, the custodian living at Upper Old-hams Farm, on which land the circle lies. Out of the fields round about many flint arrow-heads have been ploughed up, some of the Neolithic leaf-shaped type, others barbed in the Bronze Age way. All about here, the days of prehistoric man seem much closer than it is ever possible to imagine them in genial, sheltered Ashbourne.

Let us go back there, but if it is Shrove Tuesday, beware of getting mixed in the annual football match. This has been played in Ashbourne "from time immemorial". The pitch is three miles long, as wide as anyone cares to go, and includes, or rather included, the whole town. Unfortunately so much damage was done to property that the police nowadays keep play out of the main streets. Everybody in the town is eligible to take part, those born above the centre of Ashbourne playing upwards to Sturston Mill, and those born below the town centre playing down to Clifton Mill, everybody trying to get the ball through their own goal, so to speak. The ball, though, hasn't to go through anywhere, but has to be carried up the mill-race and be struck against the mill wheel. The person who manages this keeps the ball and becomes a local hero till next Shrove Tuesday.

Because of the roughness of play the ball is made of cork covered with leather, but is about the size of an Association ball. The game starts in the Shawcroft with a throw-up, often done by the Duke of Devonshire, the Duke of Rutland, or Lord Hartington, and once—in 1928—by the Prince of Wales. Play ranges

272

"The Cathedral of the Peak", Tideswell

through woods, streets, fields, and often into Henmore
Brook where the players in overalls, working clothes,
or shorts and jerseys plunge, dive, and thrash about
as though mud and slime are nothing. When the ball
gets close to either mill play often becomes drastic, so
that fists, sticks, and stones are used, and, says an old
song,

> . . . as fierce as a bull-dog's is every man's face,
> Whilst kicking and shouting and howling they run,
> Until every stitch in the ball comes undone.

There used to be a free-for-all game of the same
kind in Derby every Shrovetide, but there it was
stopped. The people divided into two parties, All
Saints and St Peters, and the ball was thrown from
the Town Hall into the packed Market Place.

"I have seen this coarse sport carried to the barbarous height of an election-contest; nay, I have
known a football hero chaired through the streets
like a successful member," says W. Hutton. ". . .
Black eyes, bruised arms, and broken shins are
equally the marks of victory and defeat. . . . The
professors of this athletic art think themselves
bound to follow the ball wherever it flies; and, as
Derby is fenced in with rivers, it seldom flies far
without flying into water; and I have seen these
amphibious practitioners of football-kicking jump
into the river . . . when the ground was covered
with snow. Whether the benefits arising from
exercise pay for the bloody nose is doubtful; whether
this rough pastime improves the mind, I leave to
the decision of its votaries; and whether the wounds
in youth produce the pains in age, I leave to three-
score."

18*

The Hall Well, Tissington

CHAPTER XXV

AN "INGENIOUS" REPORT

IN November 1691 John Houghton, "citizen of London and Fellow of the Royal Society", sent out a proposal to a wide number of persons that he should supply them weekly with a letter or "gazett" giving produce prices "from most of the principal places of the kingdom", and "in short, all useful things fit for the understanding of a plain man". This "gazett" was to be "for the advantage of tenant, landlord, corn-merchant, meal-man, baker, brewer, feeder of cattle, farmer, malster, grazier, feller and buyer of coals, hop-merchant, soap-boyler, tallow-chandler, wool-merchant, their customers, etc". On March 30th, 1692, Houghton sent out the first number of what he now called *A Collection for improvement of Husbandry and Trade*. It was a small sheet, for which he charged twopence. Apparently this *Collection* was well received, for it went on until September 24th, 1703, ending with number 583, because Mr Houghton could not "without great inconvenience to my private affairs, which must not be neglected, spare time to carry on this history so well as I would do".

Mr Houghton started his *Collection* very thoroughly with the beginning of the world, went on to explain water, air, and fire, bubbles, vacuums, and other "chymical" mysteries, but by April 14th, 1693, we find him saying: "Next Friday expect some natural history of Derbyshire", and it seems among those correspondents that his *Collection* had attracted was "an ingenious man of Derby", and perhaps because he was somewhat at a loss how to keep his weekly "gazett" going, Mr Houghton proceeded to fill his next numbers with all that this man had written him. I have not seen any reference in any book on Derbyshire to these letters—they are not even mentioned in *Simpson's Collections for a History of Derby* which otherwise is so comprehensive—and I have accordingly thought them worth a chapter, preserving a picture of the county that we should not otherwise possess.

Under the date April 22nd, 1693, Houghton writes that he has it from his "ingenious friend" that in Derby "there is not one wholesale tradesman in the town, that lead costeth seven shillings the sother (?) carriage from the smelting mill to Derby, and half-a-crown more down to the ferry, from whence it is carried by water to Hull; also abundance of lead is carried over the country to Nottingham bridges from Critch and the mills about Wirksworth, where there is a Barmoot court to determine matters between miners, every Tuesday their market day. Abundance more lead is carried from Chesterfield, and all that side to Bawtree; from Sheffield and all those parts to Doncaster, and so to the German-Ocean.

"That hops grow not in those parts, but the country is chiefly furnished from Sturbridge Fair and Shrewsbury. That the chiefest coal-mines are at Smaly, four miles, at Heaner six miles, and at Denby five miles from Derby; through which abundance in summer are carried as far as Northamptonshire, from whence is brought back barley. Those coals at Smaly and Heaner are in the hands of one Mr Samual Richardson, who finding that Derby consumed annually about three thousand loads, besides what was fetched into Leicestershire and Northamptonshire, designed to sell his coal for threepence the hundred; and had got them to six shillings and sixpence the load; but the worshipful John Lowe of Denby Esq; after an expense of between nine hundred and one thousand pounds in perfecting a sough to lay his delf dry, the last spring accomplished the same, and has laid as many coal dry as will be got this forty years, and before the sale came he had got above one thousand loads upon the bank, any of which he upholds to be at least five and thirty hundred-weight, and sells them for five shillings six pence, so that this year we bought coals delivered for three pence half penny the hundred.

"These coals are drawn up by a horse as in a malt mill, where there is a barrel, on which a rope winds, so that while one end winds up, the other goes down through the pulleys, and so contrary, the particular description whereof I have, but tis not easy to those who are not artists therein without a cut (picture).

"At Smaly my friend went down the pit twenty fathom, by ladders of twelve staves each, set across the pit one by another: when he was so deep he went underground (he believes as far as from my house to St Paul's Church, which is well near half a mile) in a mine or vein which was about six foot, where were coals overhead and underfoot, the workmen knew not how thick; from this place he was led twenty yards through a narrow passage upon hands and feet, till he came to a large space, which was the head of a sough (a place to carry away water) which laid all the pits dry that were on that level, and presently he came to a pit twenty yards deeper than before, out of which they drew water brought from another pit twenty yards deeper, with two vessels, which would hold above sixty gallons each: they were hooped with iron and biggest in the midst: when one of these came to the top a boy with a hook drew them to him, and easily did throw the water down, which in that concave made a noise like thunder.

"There is in Derby a soap-boiler who drives a great trade, and his predecessor got out of it a good estate. And one Mr George Sorocold has set up a water-house to convey water-pipes to all the houses in the town that desire it, and 'tis likely it will be much used. Next Friday expect more from Derbyshire."

On April 20th Mr Houghton writes:

"My Derbyshire friend farther tells me that the river on which Derby is built has so small a beginning, that above Rowsley where the head of it is, it may be stopt with an oat-sheaf, at Rowsley bridge it is joyned by the Wee, whose head is above Buxton Bath, and may be covered by a man's foot: these two run together, till Critch and Windfield Park they are joyned by the Amber, which with other little rills run in one channel till they come to Duffield, where Ecclesburn falls into them, and at this town it's a fine river, and so continues till it loses itself and name in the Trent, at Wiln a little below the ferry, which is five miles from Derby, and to which place the river Trent is navigated. Great endeavours have been made to bring the navigation to Derby, and as far above as Darley in the peak. And whoever stood for parliament-man, and gave hopes for effecting of this, has commonly been chosen; although Nottingham for their own interest always opposes.

"Lately some few used to grind malt for the rest of the people, but now from Birmingham are brought steel mills at thirty or thirty-five shillings the piece, which with one hand will grind a quarter or more in an hour.

"I farther understand that Derby has five parishes,

277

viz. All Saints, in which are three hundred and seven-teen families, and twenty malt-houses; in St Peter's one hundred and twenty families, and eleven malt-houses; in St Warburgh's one hundred and four-teen families and thirty-three malt-houses; in St Akmund's ninety-four families and seven malt-houses; and in St Michael's forty-nine families and five malt-houses, in all six hundred ninety-four houses or families, and seventy-six malt-houses; in which is malted so much as supplies the town, and three hundred loads of six strikes (bushels) to a load, are carried weekly into Cheshire and Lancashire; and it is observed that at Maxfield or Manchester, and thereabouts, better ale can be made with a load of Derby malt than Derby can do with a quarter of the same, and limestone water, which is plentiful in Lancashire, is thought to cause the difference.

"The reason of Derby malt being so fine and sweet, my friend thinks is the drying it with cowkes, which is a sort of coal, (so called there) they having a very hard sort, that will not cowk, and are not of so shining a blewish colour as the soft, which are sometimes found to lye in a vein twenty yards or more, above the hard coal in the same pit, but most commonly in the delss by themselves: And they are cowked thus.

"The collier sets six or eight waggon loads of coal in a round heap upon the ends, and as pyramidal (large at bottom and small at top) as they will stand. If it be a wind he sets Fleaks to shelter from it, and then into a hole left in the middle to the top of the heap (or pit as they call it) he throws a shovel full or two of fire, which by spreading itself each way fires the pit round; this burns and blazes till the smoke and flame ceases, and it's all of a red fire, then he covers all the heap with dust, and that side first which by help of the wind burns most, or where the fire first breaks out, which immediately damps it, and makes them dead coals, which thus stands till next morning, or longer according to their occasion, and then with a rake like a gardiners with six or eight teeth, he pulls them down round the heap, and the dust falls to the bottom, which is thrown up on a heap to damp the next pit.

"'Tis observed that three hundred of coals make but one hundred of cowks, and the lighter they are the better; if they be curiously burnt they'll gingle like common cynders, and a sack of six bushels will weight about one hundredweight . . .

"He acknowledges other countries to have as good barley and maltsters; but for want of these coals 'tis dry'd with straw, stubble, etc. which quite alters the taste, and 'tis believed that London or places adjacent might have cowks from Derby at rates worth while, for they may be brought from thence cheaper than malt is, of which there comes a great deal: A sack of six bushels in summer may be delivered at the Trent-side for ten pence, and the water carriage may easily be calculated by those that bring lead thence; if this should take 'twould greatly improve navigation."

In his next issue of the *Collection* Mr Houghton gave his readers a little rest from Derbyshire, telling them the difference between avoirdupois and troy weights, but on May 12th he thought it good to pass on some more information about Derbyshire. First he gave a list of Derby tradesmen in addition to the seventy-six maltsters already mentioned. There were, he said:

"Ale-houses 120, Apothecaries 7, Baker 20, Butcher 18, Barbers 11, Braziers 2, Bodice-maker 1, Brickmakers 8, Cordwainers 25, Curriers 3, Clothworkers 25,

Coopers 5, Coller-makers 4, Dyers 3, Distillers 2, Felmongers 3, Felt-makers 5, Glovers 11, Ironmonger 7, Jersey-combers 3, Joyners 4, Mercers 13, Masons or Bricklayers 15, Nailor 1, Pewterers 4, Plaisterers 16, Soap-boyler 1, Silver-smith 1, Taylors 24, Tanners 3, Upholsterers 2, Weavers 6, Watch-makers 2, White-smiths 7, Black-smiths 8, Trunk-maker 1, Sadlers 5, Vintner 1, Haberdash. of Hats 1, Woollen-drapers 3, Tallow-chandlers 5, Booksellers 2.

"Besides these there are a recorder, four councellors, and three and twenty attorneys; there are also two physicians and one chirurgeon. They have two courts of trials in a year, which may be continued on by a fortnight court held on Tuesdays, where any action whatever may be tried; but if five pounds or upwards, there may be an appeal. The recorder, town clerk, and mayor are judges; they can hang and draw within themselves, but for many years it has been disused. The burgesses are exempted from toll every where in England except Winchester. They have eight fairs in a year, for horses and all sorts of cattel.

"They were formerly governed by two bailiffs, but since 1638 it has been turned into a mayoralty: they have ten aldermen (out of which Mr Mayor is chosen), fourteen brothers, and fourteen common-councilmen; and I am told by a gentleman, who should very well understand this town, that several of the burgesses are worth each ten thousand pounds or a better penny. They have a free-school, where the head master has forty, and the under master twenty pounds per annum, besides pay for foreigners and gratuities.

"They have many charities, but particularly a valuable one, given by Sir Thos. White, merchant-taylor, alderman and mayor of London, who has ordered once in four and twenty years, one hundred pounds to be lent to four young men of this town gratis, for ten years, and four pounds as a gift to the officers that manage. He has done the like to three and twenty other places, and good security is taken for the money, and where the will is not punctually performed, that town or city shall lose the benefit thereof for ever. This is received in Merchant-taylors-hall London and was first paid to York, 1577. And Derby had it, 1596, 1620, 1644, 1668, and, I presume, 1692.

"Tis rare at Derby if forty bushels of barley will make one and forty bushels of malt, sometimes they have not forty bushels again. Malt that is well made and dried, will weigh about forty pound the bushel, and good barley about forty-four, forty-six, or forty-seven pound. A bushel of wheat will weigh from fifty-three to fifty-six pound.

"Formerly a great deal of malt was carried to the Ferry by land, which is five miles; which costs as much as from the Ferry to Hull by water, which is sixty miles. Malt has been carried from Derby to London by land for 5s. 4d. and sometimes ten groats a hundred weight, and the cheaper according as he knew of carriage back; and there is not three bushels in a hundred weight, by which may be seen the difference of Derby malt betwixt London and Derby, and yet still my friend thinks that to bring cowkes would be the cheaper way."

In his next issue Mr Houghton gives a detailed description of brewing at Derby, and then more about Derbyshire coal. His friend has now told him that the soft coal previously spoken of "are far hotter fuel than the hard, but not so durable; the first being more sulphureous, and their ashes will be almost red, the other white. By lighting a pipe with the several coals a vast difference may be perceiv'd; that of soft coal giving a taste of the mineral, the other is pleasant as if lighted with paper.

"He thinks Derbyshire to make as good cheese as Cheshire or Europe."

In this same paper Mr Houghton gives some figures from his "ingenious" friend about the population and health of Derby. His friend believes "Derby to have six times the people it has families, and so 694 families makes 4,164 souls. . . . He observes that London is twenty-eight times bigger than Derby and has above 168 times as many people in it." Having looked up the All Saints parish register for the number of deaths he works it out "that Derby has not much more than one out of forty dies in a year. And if London has one in thirty, and Paris one in twenty-five . . . Derby is the healthfullest place of them three."

The next issue of the *Collection* in which Derbyshire is mentioned is dated June 2nd, 1693. I give this in full, for it is a comprehensive report.

"My friend goes on telling me," Mr Houghton writes, "that Derbyshire is bounded on the west by Staffordshire and Cheshire, and on the north by York-shire, on the east with Nottinghamshire, and on the south Leicestershire; it's in form of a goose wing, long and narrow, there being no place in the whole country more than six miles or thereabouts from a border. It's about thirty-four miles long by computation, and forty-six by the scale: it has six hundreds, viz. Morleston and Litchurch, Appletree, High-peake, Scarsdale, and Wirksworth. Two Wapentakes, Repton and Greaseley. It has also eight market towns, viz. Ashbourne, Alfre-ton, Bakewell, Chesterfield, Derby, Tideswell, Sawley and Wirksworth. It sends two knights of the shire, and two burgesses of Derby to parliament. It has always been famous for wool and lead; the southern parts are well stor'd with all sorts of grain, the northern with store of oats, of which is made oatmeal and oat-cakes, which is the bread they generally live upon. Sometimes there will be snow upon the corn in the peak, before it is got in, and yet it is well got in too. It's well stored with all sorts of gardenware, as cabbages, coleworts, asparagus, etc., he has seen a turnep as big as a peck, and right good to the heart; he has weighed a cabbage of thirty pound weight. The rivers are well stored with fish, as trouts, eels, barbels, pikes, etc. In Sir Francis Burdet's hall of Farmarke is the exact picture of a pike above a yard long, which was taken in a net just as she was gorging another about two foot long. It has abundance of deer, red and fallow, hares, rabbets, etc. and all sorts of fowls common to any other part of England; all sorts of fruits, both wood and wall: and great store of cyder is made, some years he has known apples at six pence the Bushel or under; in short, there are great plenty of useful things above ground, but the wealth below can no man fathom. There is one piece of ground near Chatsworth, the seat of the Right Honourable William Earl of Devonshire, called Haddon Pasture, so rich, that as many shillings has been offer'd, as lying flat would make a border round it, which was refused, unless they should have them edge-ways, and some think that would have been a good bargain; the pasture of this ground is extremely rich, and he has heard say that rich oar is in it within less than a yard of the surface. Here is also store of iron-oar, of which are made rods, nails, and other utensils; also rich quarries of mill-stones, and they serve most of the kingdom, and they are worth eight, nine or ten pounds the pair, and grind-stones of all sorts, from five or six foot diameter and under, and scythe-stones in abundance, which serve all parts of the kingdom. There are also quarries of free-stone, alabaster and marble; of which as curious works might be made, as the world affords. There is also abundance of brick and tobacco-pipe, and my friend never saw better brick made or burnt. There is also store of lime that makes as good mortar as can be used; and Critch-lime is carried up and down for whiting, being as pure as any chalk. There is also great store of plaster, which being burnt is thresh'd to powder, to which it turns with ease being new; this being well wrought with water, and spread on a floor, in a few days will be as hard as brick, and may be made as smooth as glass, but the floors are commonly made part of old, and part of new plaster, and the new alone is used for drawing a thin fine white coat over the gray (viz. old and new beaten together) and if this prove to be curiously burnt, neither too much, for then it will be more soft when the floor is cast, and will sweep up in a short time, unless extremely watered, which sometimes recovers it: nor too little, for then it cannot be threshed to any purpose, and so makes the floor all lumps, as if it was full of stones, which will also be the ruin of it. But if both these extremities be avoided, it will continue a firm floor for hundreds of years, tho' constantly trod upon, and will be safe from all danger of fire . . .

"I am farther told, that in the peak in Derbyshire when they have washed the lead oar in a great vat, they cast the refuse upon heaps, which of late years has been dug up again, and certain heavy lumps which was not lead oar, pick'd out: these at first were sold for half a crown the bushel, and now they are grown to double the price, and are put in casks and sent from the ferry to Hull, and thence to London, etc. out of which when refined very good copper is gotten, and a warehouse is in Derby to take it in.

"As for cowkes and coals, which appear to be cheaper than in any part of England, New-castle not excepted, there has been an account given before: he only adds that it is not above half a century of years, since they dried their malt with straw (as other places now do) before they used cowkes, which had made that alteration since, that all England admires."

This is as admirable a summary of Derbyshire as has ever been printed. As I copy from Mr Houghton's *Collection* in my upstairs workroom, my chair stands on a floor of the kind he describes, generally known now locally as "ashlar", and it must have been made ten years or so before he wrote, so that I can confirm that one floor at least has stood firm for more than two hundred years, as he stated. Two more notes seem worth transcribing.

"An inquisitive gentleman has given me what follows," says Mr Houghton. "The reason that Derby malt makes pale ale, and that the same quantity and quality of malt will not make the drink so strong as formerly, is, that when the barley is steept and other preparations accomplished, they lay it thin upon the floors to come (that is to be made malt) by which means a great deal of the barley is not malted, and the rest is but barley turn'd: now the barley in Hantshire (which is much smaller and thicker skin'd) is laid thicker on the floors, and consequently heats, and all becomes rich malt, and makes stronger drink with the same quantity.

"Memorandum. All Derby ale formerly was high coloured, by this means.

"I am told by a person of honour, that the plaster mentioned in my last, with which they make floors in Derbyshire, is plaster of paris."

On April 20th, 1692, Mr Houghton stated:

"From a very understanding man at Derby, I have this following account, which I put here for a piece of natural history. The letter is dated April 13th, 1692, and the account is as follows:

"Upon the second instant we had such a storm and so much snow, as was never known here in the memory of man; between here and Sheffield there was a snow a yard deep in some places, and one John Webster, of Hogneston in Derbyshire, and six horses, between Pike-Hall and Hurdlow, were starved to death; he would needs adventure from Pike-hall, where others stayed and were saved, & their packs and horses, as they came from Derby. And Hurdlow is not two miles further, where Webster was lost."

On June 9th Mr Houghton has again heard from his friend and says:

"He adds that a carrier and six horses on April 2nd was lost in the snow on Brassington Moor, as likewise one Thomas Moseley a carpenter lost his fingers and toes, but the particulars which are very remarkable I have given already of the first, and the other follows.

"The said Thomas Moseley of Derby, coming over Brassington moor, on the second of April, in the same storm, in company of others, had his hat blown off, which he following fell over head and ears in a snow drift, and was lost by his company; he recovered his legs, beat down the snow round about him, and made

286

himself a little room on each side; he remembered he had a fowl cap in his pocket, which he put on his head, and in that cold prison was detained all night; next morning he was help'd out, being within less than 100 yards of a house, and was brought to Derby on horseback, his legs being swollen extremely: he recovered of it, but lost all the nails both of fingers and toes."

I wish that Mr Houghton had recorded more about Derbyshire, but that is all. Although the *Collection* continued to be circulated until September 24th, 1703, the county is never mentioned again. Possibly readers elsewhere had written that they had had enough about Derbyshire.

Chapter XXVI

DERBY CHANGES

It is interesting in going about Derby to contrast it with John Houghton's day. The brewing industry has gone to Burton, and no longer is there any busy traffic to the ferry. Instead there are such industries as motor-car manufacturing, electric-cable making, engineering, and spinning of artificial silk. Although pottery is still made—with a good reputation too—it is no longer the old firm that won Crown Derby ware its name. Derby today, despite its great age and long history, is much more new than ancient.

"It would be difficult to find a town in the whole kingdom whose rulers have for a considerable period been so strictly utilitarian," says Dr Charles Cox.

This spirit has during and since the nineteenth century led to the clearing of practically all the ancient buildings. Typical of modern Derby is the scene from the Riverside Gardens flanked by the new brick municipal buildings, looking on the new bridge, and the great modern mills in the background. In the official guide of the "Come to Derbyshire" Association there is a bold prophecy that Derby will before long become bigger in area and population than Birmingham is now. I sincerely hope that the prophecy is wrong, for I like the market town atmosphere that Derby somehow still retains despite its modern industries, and I like to think of its past.

The Roman station of Derventio was at Little Chester, and does not seem to have been of great im-

Sheep pasture incline on the Cromford and High Peak Railway

portance except to guard Rycknield Street, which some think had been made on an older British road. The great days of Derby were in Danish times, when it was one of their five chief towns. When Edward the Confessor reigned there were fourteen mills and a thriving population, but when the Norman invasion came the people resisted and Derby suffered. For centuries afterwards it remained an agricultural county town, and when on September 13th, 1642, Charles I marched through on his way to Shrewsbury all that he asked of the town (and one supposes that he asked for all that he thought could be afforded) was £300 and as many small arms as were available. A hundred years later when Prince Charles marched in he demanded £3,000, which indicates the increased prosperity of the industries that John Houghton's "ingenious" friend told about.

The visit of Prince Charles with his Jacobite army in 1745 is the only bit of popular history for which Derby is well known. Already at Swarkeston Bridge (page 176) we have seen how far the venture got, but now in Derby again I like to go to All Saints Church and think of the Prince attending service there. It has been said that a Roman Catholic Mass was held, but it seems much more likely that it was an Anglican service taken by an Anglican chaplain, probably Thomas Coppock, son of a tailor, who had joined the Jacobites in Manchester. The organ was played by Thomas Chadwick, another Manchester recruit. One of the tunes was "The Twenty-ninth of May" or "The King Shall Enjoy His Own Again", which the packed congregation of Jacobites much enjoyed. But generally one imagines that it must have been a rather sober service, for it was known that there was an English army somewhere close by and an early battle must have

19   289

The lime tree avenue, Tissington

seemed very likely. All Saints Church was practically the same then as now, for the fine tower with its three stages and lofty pinnacles was finished in 1527 and the body of the church (so heavy and different from the tower) had been completed in 1727; therefore it is in order to picture in present surroundings the Prince in white bob-wig and his Highland officers in their tartans, and the rough-haired rank men clustered under oil-lamps. Some of them would stare at the great tomb of Bess of Hardwick and wonder who she was, for her notoriety would hardly have travelled to the Highlands.

Outside in the Market Place fires would be smouldering while men on duty guarded the "13 pieces of cannon", six of them made of brass with the French King's arms on them, and the "20 Covered Carts and a Great Number of Wagons and other Carriages" in which the army carried its baggage. There would be standards about, some quartered white and red, and some with the different commanders' arms on them, though it may be that most of these were set up outside the houses in which the various leaders stayed. The Prince lodged at Lord Exeter's house (demolished 1854) in Full Street, and there is an amusing story about the then Mayor of Derby, Robert Hague, who, although he ran away before the Jacobites arrived, came back before the retreat had been decided on. He was stopped by the sentry at Lord Exeter's house, but the sight of the man's arms must have upset him, for at the top of the stairs when asked his business he said he wanted an audience with "the Pretender"! The Highlander kicked him down the stairs, shouting, "Rascal, if you want to see a Pretender, you should go to St James's!" The unlucky mayor hobbled away as fast as he could and was never seen by the Jacobites again.

The retreat from Derby began hurriedly at seven o'clock on Friday, December 6th, and before full daylight all the strange army had gone with the exception of a small rearguard of Hussars, which remained till about eleven. Although he had marched in on foot, the Prince left on an excellent black horse which had belonged to Colonel Gardiner and been taken at Prestonpans. He went over the Market Place, up Rotten Row, and by Saddler's Gate, for Ashbourne, and so Derby was left with exciting memories and an assortment of swords, dirks, targes, and cockades, yet with no serious damage, for the Jacobites as a whole had acted very reasonably, whatever the mayor might have thought for a day or two.

As Prince Charlie chose the road through Derby as the best way to London, so eventually did the Midland Railway Company choose it for their main route from London. This was the beginning of the growth of modern Derby.

Those who have read *An Autobiography* by Herbert Spencer will remember the enthusiasm, a sort of railway fever instead of "gold fever", that infected great numbers of the population of Britain when the first trains began to run successfully. Derby must have had a lot of this railway fever when the Midland Company decided to extend their London–Leicester line to Derby, and then to make Derby their headquarters. William Adam, author of *The Gem of the Peak*, got the fever, and wrote this about Derby Station:

"This is the most complete and magnificent Station yet erected. It has a frontage of one thousand and fifty feet, and the whole interior, comprising sheds, workshops, engine-houses and offices, is on the same stupendous scale; perhaps no single station presents in so high a degree, a picture so striking of the vast extent and perfection of steam power on railroads as this! In fact, as the author saw it, shortly after the opening of the Great North Midland, it exhibited a scene of such unusual energy, activity, and grandeur, as could scarcely be equalled. . . .

"The passengers' shed extends the entire length of the walls and buildings, covered with an extremely light elegant iron roof, of forty-two feet span; the centre part of the passengers' shed, fifty-six feet span, and one bay more of forty-two feet, including under them nine lines of rails with requisite turntables. The whole length of this immense *central* portion, is four hundred and fifty feet, with a width of one hundred and forty, supported by sixty handsome iron columns, twenty-two feet high from the top of the rails. The parade or platform, which is formed of large Yorkshire stone landings of superior quality, has a width of thirty-one feet, and is furnished with four very large iron tables for the adjustment of passengers' luggage; this part is exclusively appropriated to the departing trains, while the platform at each extreme end, with a width of sixteen and a half feet, is devoted entirely to the incoming trains, so that in this noble station, there is every facility for receiving and despatching four large trains at the same moment, without any possible danger of collision or confusion."

An illustration to this laudation shows sightseers in crinolines and bonnets with men in top hats parading in front of the "noble" station on a wide, open square; the vicinity has sadly deteriorated since then. Another writer of the time declared that there was "sentiment in steam, romance in realism, poetry in points and crossings, sermons in sleepers, songs in steel rails, books in signal-boxes, tongues in trenails, and good in all railway things".

Herbert Spencer before he became a philosophical and scientific writer was an inventor and surveyor for railways. Having been born in Derby, at 27 Exeter Row (now Street), in 1820, he was just at an adventurous age when the boom began about 1844, when dividends on the London–Birmingham line had risen to 10 per cent and £100 shares stood at £234. But Spencer lived to the age of eighty, long enough to see Derby tremendously altered by the railways, and, I think, to regret many of the alterations, for did he not write: "Places where I gathered flowers and gazed with interest at the catkins of the hazel, have now become places covered with iron works, where steam hammers make their perpetual thuds, and through which railway-sidings everywhere ramify"?

There is a medallion of Spencer on the new bridge over the Derwent where as a youth he fished ardently, sometimes from four in the morning till dusk. At the age of nine or ten he was nearly drowned in a deep place. A youth, George Holme, dived in and lugged him out, otherwise there would have been no *First Principles* written, and a great champion of evolution would have been missed. Holme became some fifty years later mayor of Derby.

Another medallion on the new bridge shows Dr Erasmus Darwin, who was born at Elston Hall, coming to live in Derby in 1781. His poetry had a vogue, but nowadays his chief claim to note is as grandfather of Charles Darwin, "the greatest of our scientists".

A question that often puzzled me was: What connection have the Earls of Derby with Derby? I found the answer in W. Hutton's *The History of Derby* published in 1801, which quaintly says that the title of earl, "the only title left us by the Saxons", is now "only titular, a name without a substance, a winter's sun without power". Hutton goes on: "Derby in the compass of 650 years has given this title to four potent families: that of Ferrers, in which it continued eight descents; Plantagenet, one; another branch of Plantagenet, three; and Stanley, twelve. The first had prodigious power and property in the place united to the title; the second and third had less; and the fourth has none." The title Earl of Derby was created in 1138 for Robert, a grandson of Henry de Ferrers who came to England with William the Conqueror. This Robert with a strong force of Derbyshire men and with other northern chiefs defeated David King of Scots at Northallerton in Yorkshire while King Stephen was absent, and the earldom was his reward.

I cannot put Mr Hutton's book down without giving a further quotation which has nothing to do with titles and honours, but, whether true or untrue, gives an amusing picture of Derby in 1732:

"A small figure of a man, of the name of Cadman, seemingly composed of spirit and gristle, appeared in October, to entertain the town by sliding down a rope. One end of this was to be fixed at the top of All Saints steeple; and the other at the bottom of St Michael's; an horizontal distance of 80 yards, which formed an inclined plain extremely steep. A breast-plate of wood, with a groove to fit the rope, and his own equilibrium, were to be his security, while sliding down upon his belly, with his arms and legs extended. He could not be more than six or seven seconds in this airy journey, in which he fired a pistol and blew a trumpet. The velosity with which he flew, raised a fire by friction, and a bold stream of smoke followed him. He performed this wonderful exploit three successive days, in each of which he descended twice, and marched up once; the latter took him more than an hour, in which he exhibited many surprising achievements, as sitting unconcerned with his arms folded, lying across the rope upon his back, then his belly, his hams, blowing the trumpet, swinging round, hanging by the chin, the hand, the heels, the toe, etc. The rope being too long for art to tighten, he might be said to have danced upon the slack. Though he succeeded at Derby, yet, in exhibiting soon after at Shrewsbury, he fell and lost his life.

"Feats of activity are sure to catch the younger part of the world. No amusement was seen but the rope; walls, posts, trees and houses, were mounted for the pleasure of flying down; if a straggling scaffold pole could be found, it was reared for the convenience of the flying; nay, even cats and dogs, and things inanimate, were applied, in a double sense, to the rope.

"This flying rage was not cured till 1734, when another diminutive figure appeared, much older than the first: with a coat in dishabille; no waistcoat; shirt and shoes the worse for wear; a hat worth threepence, exclusive of the band, which was packthread bleached by the weather; and a black string supplying the place of buttons to this waistband. He wisely considered that if his performances did not exceed the other's, he might as well stay at home, if he had one. His rope, therefore, from the same steeple extended to the bottom of St Marygate, more than twice the former length. He was to draw a wheel-barrow after him, in which was a boy of thirteen. After this surprising performance, an ass was to fly down, armed as before, with a breast-plate, and at each foot a lump of lead, about half a hundredweight. The man, the barrow, and its contents, arrived safe at the end of their journey; when the vast multitude turned their eyes towards the ass, which had been braying several days at the top of the steeple for food; but, like many a lofty courtier for a place, brayed in vain. The slackness of the rope and the great weight of the animal and his apparatus, made it seem, at setting off, as if he was falling perpendicular. The appearance was tremendous! About twenty yards before he reached the gates of the county-hall, the rope broke: from the velosity acquired by the descent he bore down all before him. A whole multitude was overwhelmed; nothing was heard but dreadful cries; nor seen, but confusion. Legs and arms went to destruction. In this dire calamity, the ass, which maimed others, was unhurt himself, having a pavement of soft bodies to roll over. No lives were lost. As the rope broke near the top, it brought down both chimnies and people at the other end of the street. This dreadful catastrophe put a period to the art of flying. It prevented the operator from making the intended collection; and he sneaked out of Derby as poor as he sneaked in."

Not many towns are as fortunate in having such a historian as Mr Hutton!

CHAPTER XXVII

A NATURAL PLAYGROUND

ONE begins a book with enthusiasm and ends in dissatisfaction. It is always so, for a book is never what one had hoped: it cannot be, because the will-o'-the-wisp of perfection leads us on, yet always eludes us. I had hoped to give Derbyshire complete, and now when I read back, so much is missing! Of course, another truth is that the whole of a county can never be held in one book. Many books together will contain more than one; therefore, those who want to know more than I have told may care to have the titles of other books. Guides can be got in generous quantity, and it would be foolish to try to list them, but the books that hold the spirit of Derbyshire, which is after all the chief thing, are few, and more often than not are novels.

Many have already been mentioned, but for convenience some may be mentioned again. Among the "classics" there are Charlotte Brontë's *Jane Eyre*, which tells of Hathersage and the Derwent there; and George Eliot's *Adam Bede*, in which Derbyshire has the name "Stonyshire", Ashbourne is "Oakbourne", Wirksworth is "Snowfield", Dove Dale is "Eagledale", and Norbury is "Norbourne". Scott's *Peveril of the Peak* is untrue to local colour. Not so *The Manchester Man*, by Mrs Linnaeus Banks, which tells of Whaley Bridge, Carr Cottage, the White Hart Inn close to the bridge, and scenes by the Goyt that are nicely recognisable.

I regret never being able to get or read one of the

oldest novels of Derbyshire, *The King of the Peak*. Anyone who has a chance of reading this book should do so, for the author, William Bennett, although he was born in Liverpool, came to Chapel-en-le-Frith when he was twenty-one and was a lover and careful student of the district for sixty-one years till he died in 1883. The book came out in 1823, one year after Lee Gibbons had published a book also entitled *The King of the Peak*, which according to J. B. Firth was the first novel to give the Dorothy Vernon legend. This book seems to have been extremely tedious, and should not be confused with William Bennett's. Some persons, disagreeing with the man I met in the bus, say that the best version of the Haddon Hall story is Charles Major's *Dorothy Vernon of Haddon Hall*; there is also *Sweet Doll of Haddon Hall*, by J. E. Muddock, and I fancy that there are some others that I have not found; but three "authentic" accounts of the romance, all different, are enough for me.

For those who like Edale district there is Dr Mary Andrew's *Jack o' Winnats* published in 1925. It deals with 1745 and has an over-drawn love story, but there is interest in some of the local pictures. Thomas Moult's *Snow over Elden* also is over-sentimentalised, for he is more poet than novelist, and it was written in 1910, but it deserves a place on any county bookshelf.

In 1937 Miss Nora K. Smith, a Manchester schoolteacher, was awarded £1,000 in a competition open to teachers all over the country, for her novel, *A Stranger and a Sojourner*. This was written mostly at weekends on a farm at Chunal, between Glossop and Hayfield, and tells of hardships and struggle on a Peakland farm which might be anywhere round Rowarth, Hayfield, or Chinley. Two years later Miss C. F. Goddard published *Silver Woods*, ostensibly about a Yorkshire dale, but it reads rather like a Derybshire farm in the Chinley district, and Buxton, Manchester, and Sheffield are mentioned. Miss Goddard belongs to a Chinley farming family and must have been writing from her own experience.

Axe Edge, where rise the Dove, the Goyt, and the Wye, is in Derbyshire, but Flash, so well known for its Races, is just over the Staffordshire border. The novel of this district is *Flash*, a moorland mystery by Judge Ruegg. The author admits that he took liberties with local history, but he has made an exciting tale.

The best writer about mid-Derbyshire, the moors and the villagers, is R. Murray Gilchrist. Many of his short stories carry more real feeling for the district and the folk than other writers have got into long books. He was born on January 6th, 1867 and died on April 4th, 1917, having written much, although he was very little known. Eden Phillpotts, who often stayed with him at Eyam, says that his character "was so fine, his indifference to passing popularity so genuine, that he did not suffer under the slight. He held the work supreme, the reward of small account". As a result he left such tales as *The Strolling Player* and *The Gaffer's Masterpiece*. Gilchrist's novels are not generally of the same excellence, but are most of them about Derbyshire. I like *The First-born* and *Willowford Woods*, which contain pleasant fancies, though that is all.

After Gilchrist, Katharine Bruce Glasier's *Tales from the Derbyshire Hills* are poor stuff. Miss Glasier and her brother lived in Chapel-en-le-Frith for many years, and most of her characters are pictures of local "worthies", and many of her incidents are only slightly adapted.

No doubt there are other fictional books about

299

Derbyshire that I do not know, but it is a county without any dominating author. That is chance, and not the county's fault. Generally it has had to be content with single books, or with parts of books, as in *David Grieve*; and even with sensitive glimpses here and there, as in Patrick Carleton's *Desirable Young Men*. What a pity he didn't give us more; but now he is dead, a victim of pneumonia at Buxton in the early years of the late war.

There are two books that might be called guides, which I like because they are written freshly and are not copies of other books. The first is Patrick Monkhouse's *On Foot in the Peak*, the second, *The Peak: Some Places and People*, written by a Sheffield journalist, Miss Jean Thorburn, with drawings by a Sheffield art-teacher, Bernard Casson. This is very simple and restful. But however much one may read, no book and no number of them can speak of a county as well as it can for itself. If you do not know Derbyshire, come here; if you know the county, study it with friendliness, and it will repay.

I have a theory that Derbyshire is already the most loved county in England. Half the population of the British Isles lives within a sixty-miles radius, and into the county are drawn extraordinarily large numbers of persons, chiefly at that impressionable time when, like my younger self, they cannot afford to travel farther. Very often these young people are in love, even if it is only calf-love. They are ready to see beauty anywhere and everywhere. Therefore they remember, even when they may have travelled much and seen many more impressive, or more wonderful, scenes. In fact, if Derbyshire is not our most loved county because of these early and repeated associations, then I am very much mistaken after watching so many happy young persons swarming out on every Bank Holiday and on every suitable weekend (and on many unsuitable ones!). But however many lovers of its variety and beauty the county has, never can there be too many. The more there are, the stronger will be the outcry against any more spoiling by uncaring industrialisation. For a great part of Derbyshire is pre-eminently country which should be kept as a natural playground. It is "on the doorstep" for the thousands of grim Lancashire and Yorkshire towns who need change and new air. Let its beauties be safeguarded. No better area could have been chosen as the first National Park.

INDEX

INDEX

INDEX

INDEX